Dannii
My Story

Dannii

My Story

Dannii Minogue

**SIMON &
SCHUSTER**

London · New York · Sydney · Toronto

A CBS COMPANY

First published in Great Britain in 2010 by Simon & Schuster UK Ltd
A CBS COMPANY

Copyright © 2010 by KDB Artists Pty. Ltd.

3 5 7 9 10 8 6 4 2

Simon & Schuster UK Ltd
1st Floor
222 Gray's Inn Road
London
WC1X 8HB

www.simonandschuster.co.uk

Simon & Schuster Australia
Sydney

A CIP catalogue copy for this book is available
from the British Library.

ISBN: 978-0-85720-052-5 (Hardback)
ISBN: 978-0-85720-053-2 (Trade paperback)

Typeset by M Rules
Printed in the UK by CPI Mackays, Chatham ME5 8TD

Dannii

My Story

For my family who have always been there
with love and open arms

For Kris and Ethan Edward who are my world

In loving memory of my dear friend Laura

Contents

Prologue

This Isn't How It Was Supposed to Be

Having a baby: joyful, a quiet celebration with family. An intimate and magical moment of discovery shared with your partner. Hmmm . . . I wish!

Tuesday, 24 November 2009

The car is stuck in rainy London traffic and, as usual, I'm running on what some of my closer friends would call 'Minogue Time', which basically means I'm late. For most of the afternoon, I'd been hurtling around Somerset House on ice skates, filming a segment for *The X Factor* with one of my contestants, Stacey Solomon. It was all good fun, but now I'm tired, and I'm wilting into the soft leather back seat of a very slow moving Jaguar.

My friends, Sam and George, are due to arrive at my apartment in Battersea at any minute for supper and I'm not even close to home. What's worse is that I've recklessly opted to make my much-lauded veggie lasagne tonight, which, as the cooks among you know, takes some time to prepare and then an hour or so on top of that to bake, so I'll almost certainly have to rustle up a hearty salad as soon as I get in to keep us going in the meantime.

Damn! My BlackBerry is ringing again and it's a work call. I feel too tired to talk. I just want to get home and chop vegetables.

'Hello!'

At least the car is moving now.

'Hi, D.'

It's Nathan, who works for my management, and he's chuckling. 'You're gonna laugh at this,' he says, cautiously.

Something tells me I won't.

'Simon from our PR company has just called to say that a national newspaper is claiming that you're three months pregnant and that you went for a scan at the weekend. They're running it front page tomorrow and want us to comment – isn't that ridiculous?'

I don't answer. I'm numb and I feel slightly faint.

'Obviously, need to confirm with you that it's a load of rubbish before I get back to them,' Nathan says.

I still don't answer and now I can hear my own breath.

'D?'

'Er . . . can I call you when I'm out of the car?' I ask him flatly.

'Oh!'

When I usher Sam and George into my apartment, minutes after I get in myself, I settle them in the lounge and tell them I have to make a quick business call before I start dinner.

'Guys, pour yourselves a glass of wine,' I say. 'I won't have one. No, it's fine – really. I'm too tired. I need to be fresh for work tomorrow. I'll just pop some music on . . . Sorry about this . . . Won't be long.'

I wonder if I got away with that. Do they think it's odd I'm not having a glass of wine with them?

Now quite flustered, I dash into my bedroom, which is next to the lounge, and call Nathan and tell him the truth. He tries to calm me down, then puts me on to Simon, my publicist, who informs me that the newspaper is going to print with the pregnancy story. Front cover. In thirty minutes. It's literally sitting on the press waiting for the editor to give the go-ahead to run it.

'Simon,' I whisper urgently. 'You've got to help me. How can we stop them running this story? Yes, I'm pregnant, but only about six weeks. Kris knows, of course, but we haven't even told our parents yet. I want to tell my mum and dad face to face when I go back to Australia, not like this, not splashed across the papers . . . I can't breathe, hang on a sec . . .'

My face feels flushed and my palms are sweating and shaking – so much that I almost drop the phone. I pop my head around the bedroom door.

'Sorry, guys. Won't be long,' I call out to Sam and George. 'I'm doing a lasagne for dinner. Nice?'

Back to the call.

'Seriously, is there a way we can stop this?'

It turns out that the only way we can stop it is by admitting to the newspaper that I am, in fact, pregnant, but just six weeks. Simon informs me that it's an infringement of a woman's rights for any media to make a pregnancy public knowledge before the three-month scan. If the newspaper knows for sure I'm only six weeks pregnant, then they can't print the story.

'But I have to call Kris and ask him if it's OK first,' I say, now brimming over with tears. 'I'll try to get hold of him now and get back to you.'

'We have to do it soon, Dannii, or they'll run the story anyway,' Simon says, solemnly. 'Call me straight back.'

I try calling Kris, but it's 5:30a.m. in Australia and his phone is off. I text him and then try calling him again but still there's no answer. The clock is ticking. My blood is running hot and cold. What do I do?

I stick my head out of the bedroom again.

'Won't be long now, boys. Help yourselves to more wine. Chat among yourselves and all that!'

Right. I'm going to have to make this decision all on my own, aren't I? I've already had to tell my management and my PR company that I'm pregnant before I was ready to; now I'm going to have to tell a

national newspaper too, just in time to stop the whole world from finding out – even before Kris and I have had a chance to tell our families
and friends the happy news, and while cooking a veggie lasagne. This
isn't how it was supposed to be.

Dannii
My Story

Chapter 1

Gumboots and Tutus

My life hasn't always been quite this convoluted, of course. It's often at moments like this, when I feel slightly out of control or a little bit misplaced, that I try to remember a simpler and more tranquil past: times spent at home in our back garden in Wantirna, wearing a big toothy smile, head to toe in mud and ecstatic with my latest catch of frogs or blue-tongued lizards, with my brother, Brendan.

What? Dannii Minogue? Covered in mud and grappling with a big, fat scaly lizard? Can you imagine? Most of my friends now can't imagine, but it's true. It's where it all began.

We lived in what my dad called a 'battler's area', which was a suburb of Melbourne called Scoresby. It was full of struggling young families with new mortgages and very little money. There were no roads, no footpaths and, believe it or not, no sewage. Dad worked as an accountant at a place called Mackay's in Moorabbin, while Mum had a part-time job dishing out cups of tea at the local hospital. In comparison to now it was pretty much a 'no frills' way of life. We lived in Scoresby until I was about three.

My brother, sister and I had all come into the world while Mum and Dad were living at their previous house in South Oakleigh, Melbourne. I was born in Bethlehem – that's the hospital, not the holy city – on 20 October 1971: Danielle Jane Minogue, the third and last child of Ron and Carol Minogue. Apparently, I was very late – about two and a half weeks – and Mum always says that nothing much has changed since then.

My earliest memories are mostly of playing with my brother, Brendan; I guess because we were closest in age – only seventeen months apart. Brendan was the one I could attempt to keep up with because my sister, Kylie, who was a whopping three years older than me and therefore much more grown-up, would be off playing with the bigger girls and doing her own thing. The consequence of this was, of course, that I played the games and did all the stuff that my big brother wanted to play and do, so I became a complete and utter bloody tomboy.

To be honest, I remember having only one doll that I'd pestered Mum and Dad for at Christmastime. She was a Baby Alive doll: you could feed her, and she would pee and cry and do all the things real babies do. Apart from that I wasn't into girlie stuff and was just as content playing with the toy trucks and cars that Brendan left lying around. I did have a few homemade knitted teddies and a toy Snoopy dog, which I loved and still have now.

When Brendan was feeling mischievous and was well out of Mum's vigilant sightline, he'd kidnap Snoopy and peg him to the washing line by his ears so I couldn't reach him. He'd then test my mettle by drenching poor Snoopy with the garden hose, which distressed me no end, and I'd be screaming and beside myself until I got him back safely in my arms. I can't remember how many times my brother subjected Snoopy – or any of my other poor down-at-heel knitted teddies – to this terrible torture, but it's a very vivid memory.

Kylie and her cooler, older girlfriends would often play a game called elastics, which some people called French skipping. This involved two girls standing a couple of metres apart with a bit of elastic tied in one big circular loop around their ankles. Then a third girl in the middle had to do a sequence of jumps in, on and around the stretched elastic. The elastic got hiked upwards as the game progressed: first to the knees, then bums, waists and up around the two girls' necks, so the one in the middle had to jump higher and higher until it became impossible. It was brilliant, uncomplicated fun and a cheap game to get together. I often wonder why you don't see girls playing it these days. Anyway, *sometimes*, and only sometimes, I'd be allowed to have a go at elastics with Kylie and her friends. For the most part, though, it was a game for the bigger girls, so, more often than not, I'd end up back in the mud with Brendan.

I didn't care. I loved being outside more than anything, and my brother and I were happiest when we were covered in dirt or drenched with water from the garden sprinkler. We also loved to find and collect frogs and lizards, particularly blue-tongued lizards, often spotted in the suburban garden areas around Melbourne. These lizards are big, thick and fat – about the size of a hot dog – and great fun to catch.

I was such a tomboy, in fact, that even my name, Danielle, started to annoy the hell out of me as I got a bit older. There was a very famous Aussie-rules football star and journalist called Dan Minogue, who was no relation to us, but we'd often hear people asking Dad: 'So are you related to Dan Minogue, the footy player, then?' I couldn't for the life of me understand why my parents hadn't named *me* Dan or Danny. To my mind, you didn't have to have a girl's name or a boy's name – they were all just names.

'I want to be called Danny!' I'd tell anyone who'd listen.

Our house in Deauville Court, Wantirna, is the first house I really remember – we moved there in 1974 and stayed for about five years. It's completely suburban now, but then beautiful apple orchards sur-rounded us. I remember feeling very free there, and safe. The house was on a corner looking into a court and there were always loads of other kids to play with, tearing around and riding our bikes in the street all day until our mums came out and called us for tea – so very differ-ent to today.

There was much more of a community vibe then. There had to be – nobody could afford nannies or babysitters or anything like that. You relied on your extended family and the people who lived around you. Someone might pop a head around your back door and yell, 'I need you to mind my kids for an hour and then I'll be back.' And the next week she'd do the same for you. You lived very much within the community of your particular street, and all the people on it were a big part of your world. In fact, with hindsight, it was a lot like Ramsey Street in *Neighbours*.

Our next-door neighbours at that time were Frank and Dawn, who were a mixed race South African couple – quite unusual for Melbourne in those days – and they were kind and gracious friends. They were fabulous cooks and loved their food. They were both rather large; our family seemed tiny in comparison. Sometimes Dawn would pop by with delicious and exotic spicy foods for us to try. Once I picked and ate what I thought was a red capsicum from their garden, only to have my whole mouth ablaze moments later. I'd bitten into a hot chilli pepper, and it sent me running in to Mum, screaming blue murder.

Another time I remember a huge commotion and dreadful shouting coming from Frank and Dawn's house – screaming like you couldn't imagine. Dad was convinced they were trying to kill one another but, as it turned out, they'd just been trying to wallpaper a very small toilet together, which, Dad said, barely one of them could fit into, let alone both of them.

We still weren't all that well off then but we never wanted for anything – even a swimming pool wasn't out of the question. Dad set up an above-ground pool in our back garden; we adored it, and played and played in it for hours under the scorching sun. There would always be at least ten kids from the neighbourhood in that pool at any given time. Dad says it was probably full of snot, pee and God knows what, and you could probably walk Jesus-like across the water, but we didn't mind. We all jumped in and out of it and nobody ever got sick. Dad would just chuck some chlorine in it every few days. We loved it!

One memorable Christmas, I got my very first bicycle, and I was terribly excited. It wasn't exactly a new bike – in fact, it was my brother's old one that Dad had lovingly refurbished and repainted. We had a grand ceremonial unveiling in Dad's garage, and I couldn't have been happier. I didn't know, or even care, that it wasn't brand new. As far as I was concerned, it was a bike, and it had streamers, which Dad had attached to the handlebars, and training wheels and a basket with a flower on it. I was over the moon.

Of course, Brendan saw my pretty 'new' bike as an opportunity for him to test my skills as a daredevil stuntwoman – something he was very fond of doing when we were growing up. One bright afternoon, we were both at the top of a steep hill when Brendan said, 'Hey, Danielle! Let's see how fast you can go down.' That's what boys do, right? They dare one another to do dangerous stuff. With me often being the only one around, and being a bit of a tomboy, all the dangerous stuff seemed to come my way. That particular day I found myself hurtling down the hill, unable to stop, not knowing how to control the bike or use the brakes, or anything. At some point during this terrifying ride, the pedal of my new bike came off, and to this day I have a very visible scar on my leg where the exposed metal of the broken pedal jammed into my skin.

This was only one of the many times Brendan encouraged me to stare death in the face as a child. As an adult I've got my motorbike licence, jumped out of planes and swum with sharks – and I've loved the experiences. I truly believe that if it hadn't been for my brother and his perilous dares, I would almost certainly not have had the strong lust for adventure that I have.

As a little girl, I loved hearing the story about how Mum and Dad met at a barn dance at a place called The Powerhouse in 1964, when Mum was a ballerina. There she was, blonde and beautiful in a gorgeous black cowl-neck dress, cut low at the back, while Dad was on the other side of the room wearing stovepipe jeans and too much California poppy oil in his hair. He was not, however, wearing his customary Clark Kent-style glasses, which he always took off to impress the girls. Dad had spotted Mum earlier in the evening and thought, 'That's the girl for me.' He decided to ask her out as soon as he got to dance with her. By the time they were finally partnered up for a do-se-do, he couldn't tell, without his glasses, if she was the girl he was dancing with. He went ahead and asked her out anyway; as it turned out, it was indeed Mum. They got married in October 1965.

Both of them were always very loving and fair in the way they brought us up. Mum was definitely the one with the softer touch, while Dad enforced the rules, which I think was the norm for most of the families I knew back then. Mum and Dad have always been quite traditional in their marriage: Dad runs the house and finances, and Mum runs everything else.

Dad gave us a small amount of pocket money each week, which was just enough to buy some sweets. I didn't like sweets much, so while Brendan and Kylie would dash to the shops for a Golden Gaytime (I kid you not) or a Drumstick, which were both types of ice cream, my favourite thing to buy from the newsagents was swap cards, which had pictures of animals or football players or cars on them. Kids would collect, swap and attach them to the spokes of their bikes to make an exciting clackety-clack sound as they zoomed around.

I adored anything to do with fashion and dressing up. When I was still little, with white-blonde hair, my absolute favourite thing was to team a tutu and gumboots (or wellingtons, as the Brits call them) as one magnificent outfit. The tutu, I reckon, came from a fixation I had with pictures of my mother as a ballerina when she was younger, and wanting to emulate her poise and femininity. Perhaps the gumboots, which were bright yellow and had 'stop' and 'go' written on either foot, were there to reaffirm my status as a little tomboy . . . as Danny.

Our grandparents were a very big and important part of our young lives. So much of what I learned from them has helped fashion the woman I am today. They were always around when we were kids, and would sometimes babysit us so Mum and Dad could have a bit of well deserved time off. My dad's mum has always been 'Nana', and her husband, my step-grandfather, we call 'Grand-pop' because he's American. Nana always had beautiful cutlery and serving dishes, and she would teach Kylie, Brendan and me how to lay the table and how to make and serve tea in a proper teapot. After we'd eaten at Nana's, the three of us kids would be expected to help clean up, as there weren't dishwashers then. One of us would wash up, one would dry and the other would put away, and we'd take each chore in turn whenever we were there. Nana showed us how to do these little tasks correctly. That's something that I really want to do with my kids too – teach them all those good old-fashioned ways of doing things.

We know my mum's mother as 'Nain' and her dad was 'Taid' as they are Welsh. Nain, who is now ninety and still going strong, migrated to Australia from a place called Maesteg in South Wales with Taid and their four children in 1955 – Mum would have been about ten. The journey took a gruelling six weeks, most of which Nain says she spent sick in bed. The ship they travelled on was named *The New Australia*; ironically, it was on its final voyage before being sold to Japan for scrap. In those days, you had to be nominated by a relative to come and live in Australia, and Nain had an aunt who lived on a sugar cane farm near Townsville, Queensland, so that's where they settled. Nain instantly fell in love with the place, and with seeing the sun every day. Once settled in the tropics, she and Taid added two more kids to their brood.

Whenever we were with Nain, she was either sewing or cooking. We'd be in the kitchen, and Nain would whip up scones, or cookies, or cakes. She'd wield a rolling pin, and there would be clouds of white flour filling the kitchen and dusting the bench. She used to make clothes for us all, as did Mum, so there was always a Singer or a Janome sewing machine around, and the house would quite regularly be covered in all types of fabrics and cottons, plus beads, buttons and sequins and pins all over the floor. Nain had brought up six children with very little money, so rather than buying new clothes when they were needed, she had to make them, and then I guess she just carried on making them for her grandkids.

I was completely fascinated with clothes and fashion from a very young age. While I wasn't particularly eager to use the sewing machine myself, I was totally spellbound by all the fabrics and the patterns and what we could make with them, and, as I got older, how we might change the pattern to make something completely unique – something only I would wear. Kylie was always a whizz on the sewing machine, and loved making things herself, but I wanted to create a design in my head and then get someone else to do the hard work for me. To tell you the truth, it's pretty much the same now: I'm really good at coming up with unique ideas and designs for clothes, but I can't draw them very well, and I don't have the skills to sew and make them myself either. From my very first fashion statement with the gumboots and tutu, however, I was hooked.

My memories of the house in Deauville Court, Wantirna, are incredibly happy on the whole. We weren't wealthy, no, but we were loved and looked after, and I learned so much from my grandmas, and from my parents too. I think many kids did then. They learned how to cook and how to make things and mend things, and I loved that about being a kid. I wish the world were a bit more like that now.

Chapter 2

That's Not My Canary

Mum and Dad moved from house to house every few years after we were born, renovating as they went. Each house they bought was a bit of a dump at first, but then Mum and Dad would gradually spruce it up and sell it on, each time moving to a nicer area and into a bigger house that needed even more TLC. Dad would always say, 'Buy the worst house in the best street and then do it up!'

Today, I can appreciate what they were doing, but as kids, of course, we didn't understand this strange and, as we saw it, daft philosophy. We got our houses all pretty and just the way we wanted them, then we'd move to yet another dump and live in an even bigger mess. 'What's the point of that?' we'd all demand to know, petulantly.

Anyway, we moved to a new place in St John's Avenue in Camberwell, Melbourne in 1979, when I was around seven or eight. The house had the most hideous, garish tiles and patterned lino throughout, and, like a lot of houses in the seventies, bright flocked wallpaper on every single wall. The whole place needed a lot of work – in fact, at one point half the floor was missing – but for the first time I had my own bedroom, which was tremendously exciting.

In the house in Wantirna, I'd had to share a room with big sister Kylie. Although we usually got on pretty well, like all siblings we did sometimes get into fights. It was never anything major, but she was someone I very much looked up to, so I'd always ask to borrow things, or want to know exactly what she was doing every minute of the day. After one quarrel, when I was six or seven, I remember her sticking a line of thick black tape right down the middle of the room – a dark, forbidding border dividing the territories.

'That's your side,' Kylie informed me firmly, 'and this is my side!'

I eagerly nodded in agreement, looking towards the door, which was on my side of the room.

I guess it must have been hard for her being the older girl and having a little sister hanging around all the time. We were both overjoyed when we each finally had our own space.

The house in St John's Avenue, Camberwell, had another big plus to it, which we all adored, and that was the rumpus room. This fun-packed area was right at the back of the house, past the lounge and all the bedrooms, and was the thoroughfare to the back garden. The rumpus room was all things to all people. It had a pool table that turned into a ping-pong table, which was used non-stop, especially by Brendan and all his mates; a piano, which Kylie was learning to play; and, right in the corner, a birdcage where my beloved canary, Bluey, lived.

This lovely little bird would sing beautifully for me every morning, and I'd feed him little bits of apple, or put cuttlefish in his cage for him to peck at, and sometimes I'd let him out to fly around the room – always making sure the back door was tightly shut, of course. I absolutely loved him and I promised Mum faithfully when I got him that I'd look after him myself.

'Don't worry, Mum,' I said. 'I'll clean out his cage and feed him. I'll be the one looking after him.'

But, of course, half the time Mum would end up doing it herself, as I'd be off playing somewhere and forget all about it.

The sun-filled rumpus room was without a doubt where all the action was. Kylie would be hammering away at her piano and my canary would be singing, while Brendan and his mates would endeavour to drown them out by turning up their KISS or AC/DC records on the stereo while they were playing pool. The house was a noisy and happy if slightly insane place to be, and I have exceptionally fond memories of it.

For our first holidays when I was little, we'd go to Phillip Island, which is a popular family holiday destination about 140 kilometres from Melbourne. Back then, holidays smelled of fish and chips, vinegar, ice cream, the beach and suntan lotion, and they were magical. We would stay in a caravan by the water, and we'd spend most of the time running around in the sand or sun-baking in our bathers.

On one scorching Australian summer day, Dad fell fast asleep in the sun, and the three of us kids drew a smiley face on his stomach in thick sunblock. He was there for ages while we played. When he finally woke up, he was bright red from head to foot except for two white eyes and a grinning mouth across his belly. These days, with all the things we now know about the dangers of getting sunburned, you'd never leave someone asleep cooking on the beach for that long. It seems horrific now, but at the time we all thought it was hilarious – except Dad, of course.

The whole family would gather on a picnic blanket and watch Phillip Island's famous fairy penguins come up out of the water each evening just as the sun was going down. These tiny penguins would, as a rule, return to their colonies in groups at this time to feed their chicks, and we'd all be enchanted, letting our eyes adjust to the dim light of dusk as we watched their little parade. There's a whole viewing area there these days, with concrete stands and lights and scores of people coming to watch the fairy penguins every night, but I remember when it was just me, Kylie and Brendan with Mum and Dad, watching from a little plaid blanket by the water.

As we got older and outgrew the caravan, we'd drive up to Surfers Paradise in Queensland, which was something like a twenty-hour drive in those days. We loved it there as teenagers: a beach resort chock-a-block with fast-food joints and theme parks galore – what wasn't to love? Mum and Dad hated it, and I guess it's not the first place I'd pick for a vacation these days either.

Back at home in Camberwell, Mum and Dad loved to entertain, and had lots of dinner parties. They didn't have much money to go out, and Mum says there weren't all that many places to go then even if they had, so their friends would come over for a regular get-together at the house. Mum would serve up sliced salami with cubed cheese and cock-tail onions on sticks, and follow it with a spaghetti bolognese or the occasional fondue. For an added touch of class, there were after-dinner mints at the end of the meal, and we kids would always hope to find some left in the box the next morning.

Once again, on those nights, the rumpus room would come into its own. We'd all end up playing records there and dancing around like mad after dinner. Mum and Dad always had great taste in music. The two albums I remember over the years were Stevie Wonder's *Songs In The Key of Life* and Roberta Flack's *Killing Me Softly*; I still love both artists and albums today.

I was becoming as wildly obsessed with music as I was with fash-ion. When the movie *Grease* came out, a year or so before we moved to Camberwell, I remember Kylie and I going completely nuts over Olivia Newton-John and the movie's soundtrack. We gyrated on top of our imaginary cars in the lounge and did the dance routine to 'Greased Lightning' over and over again. Kylie wanted to be Sandy, but I always secretly wanted to be Rizzo, the bad girl.

The other group I was completely obsessed with back then was ABBA. I was under the spell not only of the music, but also of Agnetha and Frida's fabulous costumes: silver platform boots and blue pan-taloons, corresponding satin catsuits and the obligatory understated glittery cape. They were super-successful in Australia, and there had been something akin to Beatlemania when they came over for a con-cert tour in 1977.

In Camberwell, we lived next door to a bloke called Harry, who had always lived with his mother. While my mum and dad were making our house in St John's Avenue more and more lovely as time went on, Harry and Mrs Jenkins lived in very poor circumstances. The house was quite dishevelled, and they never had anything electrical. In fact, all they had to heat the house with was an old-fashioned brickette heater that used pressed coal and turned all their walls dark; they never put it on until after six o'clock even when it was very cold.

Harry was a slightly odd chap. A war veteran who proudly went to the Anzac parade in all his medals, he lacked confidence after years of very serious alcoholism, and therefore couldn't work. By the time we knew him, though, he was completely on the wagon. Harry often spent his days wandering around Camberwell with his head down, eyes to the ground, hoping to find coins or, if his luck was in, the odd note along the pavement.

Mum used to drive Mrs Jenkins to the doctor when she needed to go, and I remember Mum and Dad once taking them both for a big day out at the races. In turn, Harry would always keep an eye out for us kids, and I recall having a particularly special friendship and connection with him. Harry would teach me all sorts of useful stuff that he'd learned in wartime that I'd never have got from school: how to keep warm if you had no heat by lining things with newspaper and, believe it or not, how to cook and eat a lobster.

After finding some money on the street one day, Harry headed straight to the food market – not to buy meat and three veg but a fresh, live lobster. Of course, this was a luxury item and not something he'd be able to get his hands on very often, but Harry took great delight in sharing his lobster with me, and he taught me exactly how to prepare and enjoy it at its best.

'Never smother it with sauce and stuff,' he said. 'Just squeeze some fresh lemon on it and add some salt and pepper to bring out the flavour. Enjoy it as it is.'

Then he taught me to crack it and eat it properly, and exactly where all the best bits of meat were hidden. I've sometimes stopped and smiled when I've found myself in magnificent restaurants around the world, from Hôtel Costes in Paris to Claridge's in London. I might be much more worldly these days, but it's ironic to think that I can order a lobster with confidence, and know exactly what I'm doing with it, because of the nice old war veteran who lived next door to us all those years ago.

*

My school, Camberwell Primary, was right around the corner from the house. It was a gorgeous old red-brick building with old-fashioned wooden desks and chairs, and it stood in a charming little playground. In the blazing heat of summer the teachers would open all the windows, and I'd lie slumped over my desk, trying to concentrate, while listening to the high chirruping choir of cicadas in the trees outside the classroom.

My best friend there was Jacqui, a wonderful girl with long strawberry-blonde hair, freckles and cute round glasses. Jacqui was very studious – much more so than I was; in fact, she was a complete bookworm, and I really looked up to her. We both regularly got good grades, but I remember that we would laugh and laugh so much in class that we often had to be separated to save the sanity of the teacher. I was never one to have tons and tons of friends. Jacqui and I spent all our time together and never cared whether or not we were in the cool group or the not-so-cool group – it was just the two of us.

There was, I recall, one boy at Camberwell Primary who made it clear to everyone that he didn't like me at all – Fat Billy. I remember Fat Billy very clearly because he seemed to have a twisted fascination with me. He picked on me and teased me relentlessly in an attempt to get my attention, and I hated him. However, this was where having an older brother came in handy. If things got sticky, I would call on Brendan and his mate Frenchy to come and keep Billy in line. Still, whenever he got the opportunity, Fat Billy made my life hell, tripping me up in the playground, throwing things at me and generally being a bully. To be honest, I can't imagine what became of him. He was always so busy getting involved in other people's business and trying to ruin things for them that he was never particularly proactive in his own affairs, and never achieved good grades or had many real friends.

On 16 February 1983, a blistering hot, dry day towards the end of my time at Camberwell Primary, we tore out of the classrooms to look at the skies, which had turned an eerie black. It looked just like one of those 'end of the world' movies, and for a while we had absolutely no idea what it was. The ominous cloud turned out to be ash that had risen in the heat from the horrific bushfires raging out of control in the Dandenong Ranges that day. The whole of Melbourne was literally surrounded by fire. As we stood transfixed in the playground, a huge, dark blanket covered the entire city. This terrible event became known as Ash Wednesday and saw the worst bushfires in Australian history until the fires of 2009. More than seventy people died, as well as a countless number of livestock and native animals, and thousands of people lost their homes. Seeing the black skies above our school that day is something I'll never forget.

One afternoon I came home from school and dashed straight to the rumpus room to see my beloved Bluey. It didn't take me long to figure out that something wasn't quite right, and eventually I went to find and confront Mum on the matter.

'Mum, that's not my canary,' I said, hands on hips. 'I don't know who that is, but it's definitely not my canary.'

Then Mum 'fessed up. She'd been cleaning out Bluey's cage and he'd somehow got out while the back door was open and flown away. I was horrified. Mum assured me that she had looked and looked but was unable to find him, and, in the end, had conceded defeat. She'd been so afraid of telling me the horrendous truth about my fugitive bird, knowing I'd be completely broken-hearted, that she'd gone straight to the pet shop and bought another yellow canary that she thought looked similar enough for me not to notice. Of course, there was no fooling me, and I was inconsolable, leaving Mum feeling awful. No, I didn't want the new canary, however pretty he was, I wanted Bluey and that was that.

Suddenly, amid my seemingly interminable anguish, there was a knock at the front door. When we opened it, there stood my friend, Harry, the old soldier from next door, and nestled delicately in his cupped hands was Bluey. Harry had spotted him in the tree in his garden during Mum's desperate search earlier in the afternoon but hadn't been able to catch him. Eventually, though, Harry, just like the hero I knew he was, had rescued Bluey, knowing how much I loved him, and was now delivering him safely back to me. I was overjoyed.

'That's my canary!' I smiled.

Thanks, Harry.

Chapter 3

Just Like Olivia

I wanted to perform before I really knew what being a performer meant. I didn't know, or understand, that it was a profession or a job that you could actually get paid for. All I knew was that people who sang and danced were on TV and in the movies, all looking like they were having a great time, and I wanted to do it too.

As we got a bit older, Brendan, Kylie and I were each allowed to participate in one weekly after-school activity that Mum and Dad would pay for and ferry us back and forth to. Kylie loved her piano lessons. I'd also had a shot at the piano but wasn't too fussed about continuing. I thought that I'd like to try singing, but I wasn't sure it was quite enough.

'I want to learn how to sing *and* dance,' I announced to Mum. 'Like Olivia Newton-John does in *Grease*. She sings *and* she dances. I want to be just like Olivia.'

Mum and Dad didn't know where to start, not having been brought up in performing or show-business families, so Dad opened the *Yellow Pages* and began searching for a talent school, or club, that was both close by and reputable, where I might be able to give my burgeoning theatrical itch a bit of a scratch.

'What about this place?' Dad suggested.

He was pointing at the biggest ad in the section, which was for the Johnny Young Talent School – that was a name we all knew! Much like *The X Factor* is in the UK today, *Young Talent Time* was a hugely popular prime-time Saturday-night TV show in Australia, and had been since before I was born. We never missed it in our house. It was a bit like *The Mickey Mouse Club* in America, with a regular core team of youngsters performing glitzy, fun musical numbers and pop hits of the day, plus a junior talent contest each week. Johnny Young was the well-known, enigmatic creator and presenter of the programme; he'd been a pop star in Australia in the sixties. His warm demeanour, flashy clothes and wonderfully corny delivery had made him and the programme a massive hit with both old and young, and some of the team members from the TV show had come from his talent school. Yes, this was definitely the place for me!

Mum wasn't especially keen on me singing and dancing, as she'd been a dancer when she was young and knew how tough it could be, but Dad phoned the school and said that he would take me if I really wanted to go, so it was settled. At the grand old age of seven, I was going to the Johnny Young Talent School to learn to be a singer and dancer, and I was thrilled to bits. My first experience there, however, came as quite a shock.

Television House was a lovely old white-stone building in Richmond, an inner-city suburb of Melbourne, and that was where the classes took place. It was also where the production offices for the TV show were and where the rehearsals for the show were held, so everything was under one roof. At the back of the building there were two very large rooms: one for singing, and the other, which had a ballet barre and mirrors all along one wall, for dancing. The kids would go from one room to the other for their various lessons. All the action happened within these two rooms. Students would be dancing around, practising their demi-pliés or their tap steps, while their over-enthusiastic mothers sat at the tables, furiously sewing sequins onto elaborate stage outfits or fussing with ridiculous hairdos – it was quite an eye-opener.

Being new, I obviously wasn't expecting to be the best dancer or singer, but the first class I attended was full of kids my own age, about seven or eight, who already had what I thought was a wealth of experience. Some of them had old-fashioned stage mothers who really pushed them, painting make-up on them and constantly yelling at them to smile; then there were others who had already taken part in competitive shows and performed professionally and knew exactly what it meant to be a professional performer. I didn't know a thing! Still, I threw myself into it as best I knew how. After only a few weeks of classes, I was invited, along with my parents, to go and meet the famous Mr Johnny Young himself. We were asked if I'd like to appear on the show as one of the 'Tiny Tots'.

The Tiny Tots were a group of younger kids who featured principally as extras in big Christmas scenes, circus and fairground scenes, street scenes or whenever they needed to pad out the cast a bit. Apparently, my singing teacher at the school, Liana Scali, had singled me out to Johnny and the producers as someone to keep an eye on, but at seven I was much too young to be one of the full-time team members. Putting me in the Tiny Tots would give them a chance to find out how I came across on camera, how I coped in the studio and whether or not I had that special something they were always on the lookout for. Of course, at the time, I didn't know any of this – I was just excited to be going on the show, and maybe a little bit surprised. I knew I wasn't the best singer or the best dancer in my class by a long shot, but, as I found out later, being the prettiest or the most accomplished wasn't what *Young Talent Time* was about. Johnny wanted to find young performers with a certain kind of charisma who really connected with the show's wide-ranging television audience: kids who had qualities that other kids would love, and whom the mums and dads and grandmas would love too. Mum says she was always surprised they'd picked me as she didn't think I could sing.

'I guess you must have had something, though,' she muses now. 'The X factor, I suppose.'

Cheers, Mum!

*

Once I'd joined the Tiny Tots, there was absolutely no stopping me, and when Mum's sister mentioned that she knew of a female casting agent who was looking for kids to appear in various television shows, I begged Mum to take me along to meet her. Mum said, 'No!' She was dead against me going for auditions and castings when I was so young, and didn't want her children going into the entertainment business at all if she could possibly help it. Eventually, though, I wore her down with sweetness and good behaviour, and she agreed to take me to meet the casting agent on the condition that Brendan and Kylie came along to meet her too, just to make it fair.

It was an exciting day out for us kids. While we were at the offices, we answered questions, listed hobbies and had Polaroids taken while Mum filled out forms, and that was about all there was to it. I don't think Mum thought anything would come of it, to be honest. Then, Kylie got picked for the part of a little Dutch girl in *The Sullivans*, which was a popular period drama of the time. Soon after that, I was cast too, with a featured role in a show called *Skyways*, which was a Channel 7 soap opera set in an airport. I played a little girl who was smuggling her pet mouse aboard a plane to London, and I loved it. Then, like Kylie, I also got a small part in *The Sullivans*, which was exciting as it was such a big show back then. Kylie and I were both extremely happy that we'd been to see the casting agent that day. Mum still wasn't convinced, however.

On my eighth birthday, 20 October 1979, I appeared on *Young Talent Time* as one of the three contestants in the talent-quest section of the show. I sang 'On The Good Ship Lollipop' in a rather fetching sailor hat and nautical top that Nain had lovingly made for me, with my long brown hair tied in bunches. One of the judges, Evie Hayes, a respected grande dame of the theatre, proclaimed to the audience, 'Danielle is a darling little girl, who, with proper coaching and tuition, could have a very fine future.'

Well, I smiled vacantly and looked as cute as I possibly could, but I didn't really understand what she was saying, and I didn't win. Still, having experienced a brief moment under the glare of the studio

spotlight, I now had the bug to perform and a determination that surprised everyone, including Mum and Dad. I wasn't thinking about
being super-famous or being the all-out star of the show, I just wanted
to be the absolute best that I could possibly be beneath those glorious
lights. And yes, maybe I'd have to work harder than some of the other
kids with their fancy costumes and their pushy stage-mums, but I'd get
there in the end.

Back at the Minogue family home in Camberwell, things were as loud
and hectic as they'd ever been. As we were growing up, Kylie, Brendan
and I were all developing our own individual styles and tastes. Though
we were never bad kids, I'm sure Mum and Dad must have had their
hands full, given some of our antics. Brendan was into his rock music,
and his room was a no-go area for us girls – a real boy's room, with
posters of cars and his favourite band, KISS, all over the wall. He was
still a daredevil too: now re-christened by Dad 'the Evel Knievel of
Camberwell', a whole catalogue of bone fractures, bruises and other
minor injuries befell my brother during our time at St John's Avenue.
He'd gone over the handlebars of his bike more than once, and when
he broke his arm in two different places, poor squeamish Mum almost
fainted at the doctor's surgery and had to be helped onto the exami-
nation bed instead of her injured son. Then, one afternoon, Brendan
came into the house screaming at the top of his lungs after crashing
through a plate glass window while playing next door: he had glass
embedded in his eyeballs! How Mum coped with all the constant
blood and guts I'll never know. I'm not sure how I'll manage with one
single drop of blood on my kid.

Kylie gave Mum the odd bit of trouble, too, as she blossomed into
a teenager. One night, when Mum and Dad believed us all to be tucked
up in bed, Kylie was, in fact, all done up in her spray-on skinny jeans
and bright blue eyeliner, clambering out of the front window en route
to the Golden Bowl for a secret liaison with her boyfriend. The Golden
Bowl was a ten-pin bowling alley around the corner from us, and it was
the cool place for teenagers to meet their friends, play pinball and
smoke or 'pash', and do all those things young teenagers like to do but

aren't supposed to. Now, this was a frightful dilemma for me, because I'd witnessed Kylie disappearing out of the window, and for that reason I knew I'd have to face the wrath of either Kylie or my mother. If I didn't spill my guts to Mum about her renegade eldest daughter, then I'd be in deep trouble once it came out that I'd known. However, if I did blab, I'd have to face an angry big sister and be labelled a tattle-tale. In the end, though, I was so terrified that something might happen to my big sister out on her own at night that I confessed to Mum what I knew and, of course, she was furious. It makes me laugh now when Mum tells the story of how she dashed straight over to the Golden Bowl and appeared at the top of the stairs, looming over poor Kylie like a big ogre and yelling, 'What the hell do you think you're doing? Get home this minute! OUT!'

A few days later while she was driving around the neighbourhood, Mum says she caught Kylie and her girlfriend Georgie wandering the local streets during school hours.

'We're on our way to the library!' Kylie had offered, meekly.

Mum was having none of it, though, and swung open the car door angrily.

'Get in the car right now, the pair of you! And Georgie, I'm ringing your mother!'

To this day, poor Kylie swears that she and Georgie were on their way to the library.

I, meanwhile, was getting a bit too old to be my brother's stunt double, but was still too young to be thinking about boys, so I concentrated on my singing and dancing, and gaining as much experience as I could from the talent school. I'd really enjoyed doing the little bit of acting that I'd done, but I was absolutely mad about music. I wasn't keen, though, on all the rock music that was blaring out of Brendan's room back then. By the time I was ten, I had my own favourite bands: I adored Culture Club and Wham!.

Every week, I would record all the songs that I loved from the chart countdown on my cassette recorder, obsessively making sure that I hit the pause button whenever the annoying ads came on; then I'd go back in my room, and play the recorded songs over and over again until I'd learned every single lyric and knew them all sideways and backwards. Every spare moment I had, in fact, was spent listening to pop music, practising my singing and dancing, or dressing up and performing for everyone in the lounge at our house in St John's Avenue.

Finally, all my hard work paid off, and in June 1982, on *Young Talent Time*'s special eleventh-birthday edition, I became a full-time team member, performing my first song, 'Who Wants To Be A Millionaire?'. Johnny Young, surrounded by the rest of the team, and as suave as ever in a tuxedo jacket and dickie bow, delivered a rousing build-up as he introduced a tiny, ten-year-old Danielle Minogue, dressed in a sweet blue-and-white frock. I sang the song alongside fellow newbie team member Mark McCormack. Now I really *was* on my way, regularly singing and dancing in the homes of millions of TV viewers . . . just like Olivia!

Chapter 4

Goodnight, Australia!

Being a regular team member on *Young Talent Time* was heaps of fun and a dream come true, but it was also incredibly hard work. It demanded a lot of commitment not just from me, but also from my whole family. Rehearsals for the show would be after school most days, and could finish any time from six in the evening until as late as ten at night. In those days, I didn't have my own driver ferrying me backwards and forwards to rehearsals; Mum or Dad had to take me there from school and then come and collect me again.

This often meant that family life at home could get a bit topsy-turvy, with dinner being delayed or poor Brendan and Kylie missing out on someone to help with their homework. For me, it meant hours and hours of extra work. All the kids on the show, like me, went to regular schools – there was no special tuition – so all week we had to find enough spare time to get all our homework assignments done, while attending every single rehearsal and learning all the songs and dance numbers for the live TV show on Saturday night.

It makes me smile now when I think about all the regulations there are for kids under seventeen working on TV shows like *The X Factor* and *Australia's Got Talent*. These days, there are quite rightly very strict rules about how many hours young people are allowed to work outside school, and if they *are* out of school for any amount of time, there are tutors and chaperones galore on hand to make sure they get their studying done. We had none of that back then; we finished at whatever hour we finished, and that was that.

The schedule went something like this: Monday, after school, we recorded all the vocals for the show. On Tuesday, again after school, I would squeeze in an extra singing lesson off my own back (I was well aware that I needed that little bit of extra tuition). Wednesday night we might have off, if there wasn't a photo shoot or something extra to do, and that's when I'd cram in most of my homework. Then on Thursday and Friday we'd dash straight from school to dance rehearsals at Television House. On Saturday – show day – we'd have twelve to thirteen hours of camera rehearsals for the actual show, which went live to air on a Saturday night.

The live show was, of course, the best part of the week and always a big thrill. At the top of the show, the entire team would come out to perform the big opening number, and I loved to hear the cheers and applause from the studio audience. Then, throughout the show, we'd all have our different solo spots or maybe a duet or two, and then we'd have the talent-quest section of the programme with Judges Ronnie Burns and Honor Walters. This was always fun, and saw kids with stars in their eyes from all over the country competing to be the best singer that week, with the added allure of a possible slot on a future show.

At the end of *Young Talent Time* each and every week, Johnny Young would come on and sing the Beatles' classic, 'All My Loving', in a lullaby style. All of us kids on the team would line up and sing along with him, swaying from side to side, while the studio audience swayed from side to side, and all the kids at home watching on television swayed from side to side. Then, as each team member in turn was captured on camera in a big, cheery close-up, Johnny Young would say with a smile, 'Goodnight, Katie . . . Goodnight, Vince . . . Goodnight, Karen . . . Goodnight, Danny . . .' and so on. (I was now known as Danny, with a 'y'.) At the close of every show, while the kids on the team grinned and waved to the viewers at home, Johnny would say, 'Goodnight, Australia!'

It sounds so cheesy now, but at the time the kids at home lapped it up. Hard work though it was, we knew how lucky we were. We somehow managed to get through each week, having a brilliant time along the way.

Working most days on a TV show like *Young Talent Time* was a bit like having another, rather extended family, and because I was at work so much, I probably saw them more than I did my real family. Johnny Young was very much the head of the clan. He was round faced and dark haired, and generally warm and smiley; his bright jackets and huge, wing-collared shirts from those days are legendary. We'd usually see Johnny only on Saturday afternoons, a few hours before the show went live, when he would breeze in and cast an eye over everything to ensure he was satisfied and make changes where he felt they were needed – very much like Simon Cowell might do on one of his shows now.

Being a staunch supporter of Essendon – an Aussie-rules football team nicknamed 'The Bombers' – Johnny would often be at one of their games before the Saturday show, sometimes taking a helicopter back from wherever they were playing to make it back in time. On those days, everybody in the studio, cast and crew alike, would be keeping a keen eye on the scores of the game, knowing full well that if his team lost, Johnny's usual bright mood would sour and it would be best to keep out of his way. Elements of the show that might not have bothered him at all on another day would suddenly become a huge problem on a day that 'The Bombers' had failed to make the grade – this musical number would be all wrong, or that scenery wouldn't be right. Of course, if they won, Johnny would be all sweetness and light and buzzing like mad when he walked into the studio ready for the evening's live broadcast.

I always found him very approachable. Being a reasonably confident girl, I was never put off by the fact that he was my boss and I was just a kid; I'd go straight to him with my own ideas for my numbers or out-fits for the show. Of course, with my fervent eye for fashion I was quite vocal about what sort of styles I liked and, indeed, what songs I wanted to perform.

I knew exactly how I wanted to present myself as I entered my teenage years. This is the time when children really start to get a sense of who they are, and I was doing it in front of a million people every week. It had to be just right! Whereas some of the kids would rock up and put on the costumes they were given and do everything they were told, I remember having my 'producer's cap' on from a very young age, and would always be fussing around in the wardrobe room or stalking the studio floor, making all kinds of suggestions and probably getting on everybody's nerves.

'Why can't I wear something like this?' I'd say, holding a picture of Boy George or a young Madonna aloft. 'And I've seen this really cool camera angle in a pop video. Do you think we can copy it?'

Johnny Young reminds me now that I was always very determined and strong-minded, but I never thought about it back then. As far as I was concerned, I was a young girl with lots of wonderful ideas, and I wanted to get them out to whomever would listen.

Some of the ideas and 'looks' during my time on the show, however, are now grisly testament for all to behold: a canary-yellow-and-lime all-in-one bathing suit to perform the ELO song 'I'm Alive', with the *Young Talent Time* team and entire studio audience doing an aerobics routine all around me; a cerise pencil skirt and matching bat-winged top with white stilettos, topped with a fright-wig of frizzy, crimped hair to perform Diana Ross's 'Chain Reaction'; and a dress that made me look a bit like a Catholic monk in heels, which I tore off halfway through the second chorus of Madonna's 'Open Your Heart' to reveal a rather fetching tangerine mini-dress underneath. Adding insult to injury, this particular fabulous ensemble was complemented by a heav-ily lacquered quiff which probably helped start the hole in the O zone layer. Gorgeous!

At the time, I loved the dressing-up aspect of the show, and would always strive to avoid the customary sparkly camp clothes and go for the coolest or most way-out image I could concoct. Wild hairdos, bubble skirts and seasonal scenes painted on long fingernails at Christmas were the norm for me, and I'd proudly catwalk model each new get-up for my good friend Barbara, who ran the *Young Talent Time* wardrobe. She always encouraged me to be bold with my clothes, and couldn't wait to see what I'd come up with next.

We filmed most of the *Young Talent Time* programmes at the studios of ATV-10 in Nunawading, Melbourne. We were in studio A but, of course, there were other studios within the complex, and one of them, right down the corridor, was the home of the hit TV show *Prisoner*, known in the UK and America as *Prisoner Cell Block H*. Back then, *Prisoner* was a gritty drama series set in a tough women's prison; it has since become a campy, cult hit that spawned a stage musical. At one stage, our cast was sharing a green room with the ladies from *Prisoner* and we would all, at some point, pass through or hang out there while we were en route to the studio floor. There wasn't much in the green room, just a couple of couches down either side, but we'd often end up in there together: the ladies from the fictitious Wentworth Detention Centre in their austere blue prison attire and the kids from *Young Talent Time* in their sparkly, sequinned gowns and ridiculous costumes. One of the actresses from *Prisoner* would be sitting, studiously learning her lines, while next to her there was a giant lobster on one side and on the other a kid dressed up as a pineapple. The ladies were very courteous in front of us and there wasn't as much colourful language from them as there was from us kids. They did seem to like the booze and fags, though, and a few of the ladies kept bottles of gin stashed in their lockers in case of emergency.

One of the actresses was named Sheila Florence and she played a good-natured old jailbird called Lizzie in the series. Sheila was a lovely, gentle lady in her seventies who always sat in the same spot in the green room, and it seemed to me that she was the real matriarch of the cast. I never once saw Sheila without a lit cigarette. Quite a lot of the *Prisoner* women smoked but she really went for it, lighting one ciggie off the other; consequently, she had one of the most gravelly voices you're ever likely to hear. These days you can't smoke in any public buildings, yet there she was then puffing away like mad around a gaggle of young kids in highly flammable outfits. It's odd to think of it now.

As well as Barbara in wardrobe, who is still a close family friend today, there were plenty of other adults from the team whom I became close to back then: Maggie, the choreographer, and her husband, Ronnie, who was one of the judges; Greg, who became the show's musical director; and Bill, who did the make-up. Bill was wonderfully flamboyant, and he was great with all the kids. Although he let us muck around a bit, he didn't take any backchat, and he was always there when someone needed a shoulder to cry on or to pour out their heart. Let's face it, with a crowd of hormonal teenagers working the long hours we did, there was bound to be, and often were, a few tantrums and tears, and Bill would always be the best person to unburden yourself to. Although I'd heard people talking about the fact that Bill was gay, I didn't know what that meant when I was seven. All I knew was that Bill was funny and kind and that was enough for me. We spent hours cooped up in the make-up room with him over the years, and he always made it a fun place to be, coming up with the most ingenious ways of keeping everyone in line and all egos in check.

As well as a heart of gold, Bill had a whiplash tongue, and he had crafted a way to mince across a room like I've never seen since. He also, while entertaining everyone with his latest outlandish stories, managed to gesticulate while cocking an eyebrow and peering at you over the top of his glasses all at the same time – I thought this was utterly fabulous.

As time went on, I began taking an interest in something other than singing, dancing and fashion – boys! True, some of those who worked on the show could be quite annoying, especially when clambering out of their dressing room through the roof to catch a peek at us girls in our undies through a gap in the ceiling, but I started to pay a bit more attention to the opposite sex when I was about twelve or thirteen.

My first, and very innocent, crush was a boy called Vince Del Tito, who was a handsome, dark-haired boy almost exactly one year older than me. Like me, Vince had attended the Johnny Young Talent School and then graduated to the TV show, so we were already friends. During the run of one series, however, this friendship graduated to hand-holding in the studio, and on the tour bus whenever we performed around the country, and then to a kiss on the lips – my very first!

I didn't fare quite so well with some of the other boys. There was one called Bevan Addinsall who was utterly out of control and hyperactive; certain things he ate and drank sent him completely over the edge. Bevan was a good-looking boy with a fantastic voice. He got his spot on the *Young Talent Time* team after seeing an ad in the newspaper and auditioning against 5,000 other applicants, so was clearly very talented. If he managed to get his hands on any of the sugary goodies that triggered his over-energetic madness, however, there would be absolutely no calming him down.

He lived fairly close to me, so my parents and his would take it in turns to drive us both to and from the studios or rehearsals. That was anything up to six nights a week, so Bevan and I spent a lot of time together – perhaps a little too much. Being an only child, and having just moved to Melbourne from out in the sticks, the excitement of being around loads of other kids and a TV studio was often too much for Bevan. He could never concentrate for more than about five minutes. He would tear around everywhere, disappearing and running amok unless his feet were virtually nailed to the floor. This used to drive everyone up the wall, of course, especially me, as I prided myself on being very focused and always strove to concentrate on the job at hand. Whenever the rest of us were trying to get on with something important, at some point there would invariably be the cry of 'Where's Bevan?' and we'd have to wait until he'd been duly located and dragged back to wherever he was supposed to be.

One afternoon during dance rehearsals at Television House, Bevan finally crossed the line with me. He'd been taunting and annoying me all day while I was trying to practise a routine, forcing me to issue him with a stern threat.

'Bevan, I've had enough. If you don't go away and leave me alone, you're gonna get it!'

To be honest, I had absolutely no idea what I was going to do if he ignored me and carried on – I guess I thought the threat would be enough. But, of course, it wasn't enough, and back he came to taunt me again and again while I was trying to concentrate. I don't really know what happened next. Somewhere from within my little frame, this ball of energy and fury fused together and my arm left the side of my body, fist tightly clenched, and connected with Bevan's face – hard. I'd never thrown a punch before, and didn't think I even knew how, but poor Bevan fell like a tree in front of all the other astonished kids, who looked on, completely agog. I was in shock too, but knew that some-how I'd have to follow through with my bolt-from-the-blue tough-guy act, so I puffed my chest out, dusted my hands together and said, with as much bravado as I could muster, 'Right, that'll be the last time you do that, then, Bevan!' and walked off.

This event transformed my previously rocky relationship with Bevan. Eventually, believe it or not, he became like another brother to me. We've stayed friends to this day, and I occasionally visit him and his wife and two children in Queensland. He's still a singer and performer too, and by family request sang at my grandmother's ninetieth birth-day in 2009.

When I was about fifteen and becoming a young woman, one of my other male friends from the show, Joey Perrone, brought his pal from Sydney along to the studio. The friend's name was Gary. He was a striking blond Italian boy with full lips and a strong Roman nose, and I was quite taken with him . . . OK, he was hot! Some of us from the team would socialise outside work, and one sunny afternoon, a whole gang of us, including Joey and his gorgeous friend Gary, went horse riding in the country. As usual, we all had a great time together, and as the day wore on it became more and more obvious that Gary was just as smitten with me as I was with him. We laughed and talked as we drifted leisurely through the beautiful open countryside on our horses, both realising that this was most definitely the start of something.

The only problem was geography. Once we were going steady, Gary would drive all the way down to Melbourne from Sydney to spend time with me whenever he could, and I'd visit him and his wonderful

Italian family in his home town, where he'd take me waterskiing and on romantic dates by the sea. We both had our own lives and work to get on with in different cities, and it was hard being apart for as much time as we were. This wasn't the innocent, holding-hands type of romance I'd had with Vince – Gary was my first real boyfriend. I'd fallen in love for the first time, which can be pretty intense when you're fifteen, and talking on the phone just wasn't the same. I missed him terribly when he wasn't around.

The long-distance relationship has been a recurring theme in my love life. There was Julian in New York, Steve in LA and Kris in Manchester, and me in a different city – or country. I'll save all that for later, but suffice it to say that in those circumstances both parties have to be really strong if they want to keep the flame alight. Sadly, as in the case of gorgeous Gary and me, it often just flickers out.

Sometimes, the team members' families would feature in skits or 'up close and personal' sections of the show. I once had the whole camera crew round at our place in St John's Avenue, giving the TV audience a guided tour of the Minogue household and everyone who lived there – even our dog, Gabby, appeared on *Young Talent Time*.

It suddenly dawned on me that I was now quite famous. At my school, Camberwell High, I would notice some of the other kids whispering or making the odd remark about me as they passed me in the corridor. I'd ignore them most of the time and hang out with my best friend, Alethia. Of course, having big brother Brendan and his mates at the same school and looking out for me was always a great deterrent for any potential tormentor.

When *Young Talent Time* toured the country, playing shopping malls and arenas across Australia, it really hit home how famous we were. Thousands of kids from every area would turn up to see the live shows and they'd go nuts. There was one horrible incident in a Sydney shopping centre, which turned into a virtual riot, with something like 17,000 fans all surging forward to get a bit closer to their favourite team member. It was terrifying for us, and a few of the audience there that day were injured.

In 1985, Johnny Young introduced my sister, Kylie, on the live show. She was starring in a brand-new Aussie show called *The Henderson Kids* and becoming quite the actress – I was very proud. A year later, she was back on the show performing a duet with me, which was amazing for us after all those years of performing together for Mum and Dad in the lounge at home. It was a big moment in *Young Talent Time* history too. Kylie had just landed the television role that would change her life: playing the part of feisty car mechanic Charlene Robinson in *Neighbours*. We strutted out on stage in matching silver dresses with tons of eighties poodle hair and performed a cover of the song 'Sisters Are Doing It For Themselves'. There was no doubt about it – we absolutely were!

In April 1998, when I finally bowed out of *Young Talent Time* at the age of sixteen, there were lots of tears. Vince Del Tito helped me choose my final song, which was 'How Do You Keep The Music Playing?' by the composer Michel Legrand. My mum and Kylie were in the studio audience, along with hundreds of tearful fans holding up posters of me. In fact, by the time I'd got halfway through the song, all the team, girls and boys, were in absolute floods and I could barely make it to the end. I was wearing a bottle-green silk, strapless gown and my hair was swept up in a demure, Audrey Hepburn-style beehive. As I sang, a waterfall of silver confetti fell around me – very dramatic stuff! When I finished the song, I broke down completely, with Johnny and all the team lovingly surrounding me. In the dying seconds of my final *Young Talent Time*, I got to say the famous closing line of the show: 'Goodnight, Australia!'

It was then that a message flashed across the screens of TV sets all over the country. It said: 'Goodbye and good luck . . . DANNII.'

Chapter 5

A Knack for Negotiating

I am absolutely shocking at ball sports and always have been. I cannot throw or catch a ball. In fact, if any terrifying, fast-moving spherical object comes my way even now, I'll wave my hands in the air and scream like a banshee rather than attempt to catch it. This had ruled out most of the PE curriculum at Camberwell High apart from swimming, which is the one sport I loved, especially as it gave me the opportunity for a bit of sun-baking around the wonderful outdoor Olympic-sized pool adjacent to the school. Anyway, with all the work I had on with the TV show, plus all the homework being piled on us by the teachers every week, something had to give – and I had a plan.

Mr Anderson was the games teacher, and he was a good guy with a great sense of humour. The kids liked him because he didn't talk down to them, and they respected him because he was firm but fair. One morning, when I was about fourteen years old, I strode up to Mr Anderson in my little green-and-white-checked school uniform and announced: 'Sir, I'd really like to discuss something with you if that's OK. Can we set up a meeting?'

I can see myself standing there in the school corridor, shoulder-length brown hair with blonde highlights and a spiky fringe, with sparkly blue eyes – by this time I'd even grown into my teeth. Mr Anderson nodded, slightly bewildered, and when we finally sat down, I put my case forward.

'You and I both know that I can't do ball sports,' I said. 'It's not me, Mr Anderson. It is never gonna happen. You also know that I have a full-time job after school, which is five or six days a week, so it's very difficult to find the time to do homework.'

Mr Anderson nodded again, still bemused. I went on.

'You've seen my report card, and how studious I am: all of my other subjects are either 'A' or 'A-plus', but I'll be lucky if I get a 'D' in PE the way I'm going this year, right?'

More nodding.

'So here's the deal I'm proposing: I get lots of exercise with all the dancing I do, and I'm happy to stick with the swimming, but other than that, if your lessons are going to involve me running in the opposite direction whenever a scary ball comes at me, then I'd be better off in the library working hard on all my other subjects to keep those grades as good as they are now, don't you think? Fail me now at PE, and let's just call it a day. I'll have more time to get all my other homework done, and you won't have to hear me screaming every time there's a netball game on – everybody wins!'

Well, as I said, Mr Anderson was firm but always very fair, and I never played another ball game at school. Job done!

Towards the end of my run on *Young Talent Time*, I'd had a lot of fan mail about the wild and wonderful stage clothes and costumes I'd worn on the show, and Kmart, the department-store chain, approached me about the idea of coming up with my own fashion range for young people. I was over the moon, as fashion design was something I was really keen to try. I knew I'd have a real blast working with professional designers to come up with some fresh, new ideas for kids' clothes.

By this time in Australia I was well known as 'Dannii'– finally having settled on the double 'N' and double 'I' simply because nobody else spelled it that way, and I decided that was what I wanted to call my clothing range too. I was very eager to get started with the designs. I knew the clothes had to be practical, not too elaborate and, of course, nothing like some of the stagy get-ups I'd worn on *Young Talent Time*. I felt I had an instinct about what kids my age would or wouldn't like, so I kept that in mind all the time I was working with the designers. Luckily, my instincts were right: when the first Dannii fashion range sold out in a record ten days in the spring of 1988, I was ecstatic.

While all this was going on, Dad suggested I might need a manager to look after me. Kylie had taken on a manager from Melbourne called Terry Blamey, and her career was exploding. She'd been a big hit in *Neighbours*, and her pop career was taking off too. She'd signed a deal with Mushroom Records in Australia and had a huge hit with a cover of 'The Loco-Motion'. Her next single was 'I Should Be So Lucky' which was, of course, absolutely massive all over Europe. The rest is pop history!

Dad thought it would be a good idea if I met with Terry, with a view to him managing my career, even though I wasn't sure exactly what that was going to be. Yes, I was still passionate about music, but I wanted to finish my studies and then perhaps go to a technical college or film school so I could learn how to be a director. I'd spent so much of my youth in television studios and was fascinated by what went on behind the scenes, it seemed a sensible progression to me. Few *Young Talent Time* team members had gone on to have professional singing careers after they'd left the show – why should I be the exception?

Over the years, people have always said to me things like: 'Dannii, you must have been so ambitious as a child,' or 'I guess you were driven to be successful because your sister was.' The idea that I'm very competitive and ambitious is one of the biggest misconceptions about me and it makes me smile when I think of it now. The truth of the matter was I had no vision, no target and absolutely no game plan. Ever since I was little I'd loved performing and I'd been lucky to grow up doing just that on TV.

After a couple of meetings with Terry Blamey, both Dad and I decided that he was the right man for the job. He was taking Kylie's career from strength to strength and was obviously well connected in the entertainment industry. He played a big part in setting up the Dannii clothing range deal with Kmart, and suggested that he had big musical plans for me too. I had no idea what other sorts of opportunities were going to arise and, to tell you the truth, I was just going with the flow.

Terry was a smart cookie, though, and had the idea of taking me to meet Michael Gudinski, who ran Mushroom Records and had originally signed Kylie after hearing her sing at a benefit concert with some of the other *Neighbours* cast members a couple of years earlier. Terry's thinking was that I was already famous and popular all over Australia as a singer on TV, so why not make a pop record? If people were snatching the Dannii clothing range off the shelves as fast as they were, why wouldn't they do the same with a Dannii album? Gudinski wasn't really a 'pop' man back then, and definitely favoured rock music, but he and his right-hand man, Gary Ashley, agreed with Terry. In January 1989, I was offered, against all my expectations, my very first recording contract. Everyone around me was very excited, but no one was more surprised than I was.

Whenever Kylie was home, it was thrilling to hear about all the exotic places she'd been. Dad had taken us all on a wonderful trip to Europe, Canada and California a few years earlier, but Kylie had been to Tokyo and New York, and places that I dreamed of going one day. Every time she unpacked her suitcases, I'd peer over the edge, wide-eyed at some of the weird and fabulous gadgets and trinkets she'd brought from places like Japan, never really believing that I'd eventually go there too.

Mum and Dad were always so happy when she was home too. Being the parents they are, and the family we are, nothing important ever changed. Although they now had a world-famous daughter, they took it in their stride and tried to keep our family life as happy and as natural as it had always been. They'd been exactly the same when I was on *Young Talent Time*: yes, I was dressed up in a posh frock, singing and dancing on TV sets all over the country every Saturday night, but once

I was back home, I was just Ron and Carol's little girl, Danielle. This, during some of the events that were to come in later years, is what kept us grounded.

Imagine Mum and Dad's surprise, though, a few months later when I told them that my A&R man at Mushroom Records had decided that my debut album would be recorded in . . . New York City!

When Gary Ashley met with Terry Blamey and me to discuss the album, he told us that if we were going to do this, it had to be right.

'Dannii needs her own sound,' he said. 'I've met these great pop writer-producers in New York who would be perfect. Dannii should go and record the record there.'

Mum, once again, was the voice of reason.

'But I thought you wanted to carry on with your studies,' she said as I sat down with her and Dad to discuss this awesome proposition.

'Well, why don't I give it a year?' I suggested. 'If it doesn't work out, then I'll go back to studying. I'm not expecting anything big to come of it anyway, but I'd be mad not to give it a go now it's been offered. Even if I do just one album, it'll be a great experience.'

Poor Mum – she hadn't wanted me or Kylie to go into the entertainment business when we were young, and now she had one daughter who'd spent the last six years on the country's top variety show, and another who was a famous pop star travelling all over the world and hardly ever home. My brother Brendan, at least, had decided on a career behind the camera, not in front of it, but even he ended up travelling around the world for months on end as an award-winning news cameraman for Channel 9 in Australia. Still, after much enthusiastic urging from me, both Mum and Dad finally agreed to it.

'Your grades at school were always good,' Mum said, 'so I guess I can't really argue with you trying this out for a year.'

My dazzling negotiating skills had been put to good use once more. I was off to the Big Apple, baby . . .

Chapter 6

Strewth! Where the Bloody Hell Are We?

When the yellow taxi turned the corner, the whole of Manhattan rose up before me under a bright blue sky. It was an incredible moment. New York City has been such an iconic setting for so many movies, TV shows and photographs, you almost feel like you know it before you get there. My eyes were everywhere as the cab snaked along the streets. As I was only seventeen, my A&R man, Gary Ashley, had come along on the trip to look after me and make sure the recording sessions went smoothly, and also to set me up in an apartment. My own apartment in Manhattan – wooooooooooooow!

It was the summer of 1989, and Soul II Soul's 'Keep On Movin" seemed to be pumping out of every car stereo. I was captivated by New York from the moment I arrived. There was an energy and buzz about the place that was completely contagious. The myriad different faces, the clothes, the noise and the smells – even the steam rising up out of the manhole covers and drains – were mesmerising to me. It was a whole world away from the calm quiet of the Melbourne suburbs I'd left behind. When we reached the huge building that housed my apartment in the heart of Midtown, I was again knocked for six. 'It's the Trump Tower!'

When I walked through the doors and clapped eyes on the ostentatious pink marble and gold and mirrored walls of the lobby, I could hardly believe my eyes. There was even a waterfall that cascaded down a wall of mosaic marble bricks into a pool below. What's more, I was escorted upstairs and shown into a massive, beautiful two-bedroom apartment. I couldn't get my head around the fact that for the next month or so I was going to be recording my own album with a New York production team and living in my very own apartment in the Trump Tower.

I got used to the city very quickly. People had said to me that you either love it or hate it when you first arrive – I was in love with it. I'd walk out of my apartment each bright morning and watch the horses and carriages ferrying tourists around Central Park, where people were doing all those very American things that I'd always imagined they would be: catching Frisbees, playing baseball and buying oversized pretzels and Dr Pepper from the carts of various vendors. I'd walk past the Plaza Hotel, which I'd seen in a ton of famous movies, and, of course, Tiffany's is right next door to the Trump Tower.

My producers were Alvin Moody and Vinnie Bell, who had worked with artists such as Whitney Houston and Neneh Cherry. Our first meeting with them was going to be at Alvin's studio in the Bronx. Gary and I got ourselves ready, then hailed a cab outside the building, but the driver who stopped wouldn't take us. We tried another cab with the same result, and then another. None of the yellow taxis would take us to our meeting in that part of the Bronx. That didn't sound so good to me.

'Ah! No, it's fine – perfectly safe!' Alvin assured the two of us anxious Aussies when we called him. So Gary and I took a private-hire car with a driver out to the Bronx, exchanging nervous glances as we went. Our driver explained that some of the taxi drivers were feeling a bit apprehensive about that area of the Bronx at the moment. Apparently, a couple of cab drivers had recently been shot and killed very near the address that we needed to get to; even if we'd found a taxi to take us there, we'd never have found one to bring us back. When we arrived at what we thought was our destination, Gary and I got out of the car. 'Strewth! Where the bloody hell are we?'

We weren't quite where we needed to be. The two of us fretfully headed up the few blocks towards Alvin's place, sticking out like a sore thumb in that neighbourhood. We were two fresh-off-the-boat Aussies with broad accents trying to navigate our way around the big bad Bronx. Now it seems hysterically funny, but at the time I was petrified.

Alvin and Vinnie were great, though, and I clicked with them right away. We'd already heard a demo song that they'd written before we left Australia: it was called 'Love And Kisses' and I thought it was perfect. They had some other songs that I was excited about, too, like 'Work' and 'Call To Your Heart' – great pop dance songs that I could see myself performing. I would get the chance to co-write some lyrics myself as the sessions progressed.

We were recording at the Greene Street Studio in the heart of SoHo in Manhattan. Once Gary had settled me in and gone back to Melbourne, I'd walk there alone from the apartment every day, which was quite a trot. I felt comfortable, almost at home, and even though I was still a wide-eyed Aussie girl in the fast-moving metropolis, it certainly wasn't the scary place that I thought it might be. I wanted to soak up the whole vibe of the city while I was there and take in as much as I could; plus, with all the amazing food I was enjoying, I needed the exercise!

One day while on a wander, I discovered the fabulous boutique owned by Patricia Field, who is now famous for her work as a costume designer on *Sex and the City* and *The Devil Wears Prada*, and I bought myself the coolest cropped black leather jacket with 'tattoo-painted' sleeves, and a gold crucifix necklace, both of which I ended up wearing in my very first video for the single 'Love And Kisses'.

Once at the studio, Alvin, Vinnie and I had many laughs: they were both hilariously funny guys and so enthusiastic. Sure, it was hard work, because we had to get as much done on the album as we could in only a few weeks, but they were both easy to work with, which was quite a relief as the studio sessions were often long ones. We'd end up having almost all our meals – lunch and dinner on most days – ordered in from the great array of diners and restaurants around SoHo. It suited me: at seventeen I was still four years below the legal drinking age in America, so I couldn't go out partying anyway. You couldn't get into most clubs and bars without ID, let alone drink. My tipples were Snapple iced tea, and cinnamon coffee from the coffee shop down the block – divine!

So Alvin, Vinnie and I were pretty much in a world of our own, jamming in the studio and making music. The best part of it was that they didn't know me from a bar of soap. I had none of the 'child star from *Young Talent Time*' baggage when I walked into their world every day; I was just a fresh new potential pop star straight out of the box. I felt completely free. The recording sessions went brilliantly, and it was decided at the end of the trip that I would come back again to record more, once Alvin and Vinnie had written the songs for me.

The following month back home in Melbourne felt desperately quiet by comparison. I missed the constant buzz of Manhattan terribly, but I knew that the work I'd done with the boys so far was great, and I couldn't wait to hear the finished mixes. They were going for a real American pop dance feel, which I was into at the time. I had the rest of the album and my first video to look forward to as well.

There was something more immediate on the horizon, however. Some time before the New York trip, I'd been asked to audition for a part in the Australian soap *Home and Away*. The show was becoming more and more popular, and, like *Neighbours*, was also doing well in the UK. At that point, I wasn't going to pass up any opportunity that came my way: the more auditions I did, the more experience I'd be gaining as an actress. When I read for the part of the character Marilyn, though, I remember thinking that the role wasn't right for me, and sure enough I didn't get it. After meeting me that day, however, the producers approached Terry Blamey with the idea of writing a part in the show especially for me.

What they came up with was a character called Emma Jackson, a rude, rebellious, troubled teen with an almost punk image – the absolute opposite of my quirky but wholesome *Young Talent Time* persona. Of course, I loved it right away. There were just a couple of problems to overcome: for one thing, I was still in the middle of recording an album and at some point would have to fly back to New York; and secondly – and this was the thing that scared me – it meant moving to Sydney, which was the setting and backdrop for the fictional town of Summer Bay, for a year.

No, I couldn't possibly do that. I'd committed to recording my album and I was going to see it through. Terry came up with the idea that I should do a short run on the show to see how it went – thirteen weeks to be exact – with an option to extend if all went well. That way I could go back and get the album done when I'd finished filming, and not miss out on what could be a great opportunity as an actress.

Leaving my family and moving all the way to Sydney to work on a soap opera and then flying back and forth to America to finish my album – could I possibly do it all? It seemed completely inconceivable. For a start, I'd have to get my driver's licence – *Home and Away* was shot in two completely separate locations that were quite far apart. I'd also have to find somewhere to live, as I certainly didn't want to be stuck in a hotel for all that time. My life would be turned upside down. Since leaving *Young Talent Time* and not having a clue what I was going to do next, suddenly – and this has been a recurring theme in my professional life – there was a lot going on.

Chapter 7

It's Always Summer in Summer Bay

Everything seemed to be one big crazy rush once I'd agreed to take the part of Emma Jackson in *Home and Away*, as filming was starting in a matter of weeks. Mum and Dad seemed happy enough about me dashing off to Sydney – after all, it was just for thirteen weeks, right? Wrong. When my character, Emma, proved a big hit with audiences across Australia, I ended up staying for the full year that the producers had originally offered.

Terry Blamey's brother, Ted, solved the problem of where I was going to live. He had a friend called Marissa who rented a house in Neutral Bay, which is over the Sydney Bridge on the North Shore. Palm Beach, where the location shots for the programme were filmed, was up the coast further north, and Epping, where the studio shoots were done, was inland, so there was a fair distance between them. Neutral Bay seemed a good spot for me, and I certainly didn't feel ready to live on my own in a strange city.

Mum and Dad, too, were anxious about my living arrangements. 'We'd like to meet Marissa before you move in with her, of course,' Dad told me.

I think it was to make sure she wasn't a wild party girl, to be honest, but Marissa was a mature young woman in her mid-twenties who took the ferry across the harbour every day to a respectable banking job in the city, and was a terrific girl. She wore smart suits, stockings and pearls to work, and she was very responsible, so when Mum and Dad went up to visit her, they came away happy.

It was fortunate for me, too, that I didn't end up rooming with another seventeen-year-old like me. Never having had to look after myself, I had absolutely no idea what to do when all these cryptic letters addressed to me started to arrive through the post.

'Marissa, what on earth is this?' I remember saying to her, waving the bizarre document under her nose.

'It's a telephone bill, Dannii!' she'd explain.

Having already been married and divorced, Marissa was worldly like that.

When I got to the Channel 7 studios to prepare for the part of Emma, I was happy to discover that the producers wanted me to go for it. The interesting thing about having Dannii Minogue on the show, as far as they were concerned, was to take the character as far away as possible from the all-singing, all-dancing, sweet, smiling girl that people knew from *Young Talent Time*. And that's what made it interesting and worthwhile for me: I was thrilled with the leather jacket and the full-on make-up because it was so different to anything I'd done before.

The surly, dark, punk Emma Jackson was the first impression that the British public had of me: I was known as a tough, cool, rebellious teen, full of angst. In Australia, they could still remember me dressed as a pineapple. The role was also a complete contrast to Kylie's portrayal of bubbly Charlene in *Neighbours*, and that's what Channel 7 also wanted – an explosive character that *Home and Away* hadn't seen before.

For the first couple of weeks working on set, I have to admit I felt very homesick, and I missed my family and friends terribly. Sydney is a great city but it has a very different vibe to Melbourne. At first, I found it hard going, despite the fact that I'd felt at home on the other side of the world in New York. There were a lot of other *Home and Away* cast members around the same age as me. When I first got there, they knew exactly who I was but I didn't know any of them, so I didn't feel part of the gang. I felt they saw me as the girl from *Young Talent Time* who'd had a role created especially for her and was sure to get special treatment. After all, I hadn't rocked up to a cattle-call audition and won the role; it had been handed to me on a plate.

This uneasiness was compounded by the fact that because I still couldn't drive when I first arrived, I had cars provided to shuttle me back and forth between locations and to and from home, while everyone else was expected to get around under their own steam. Even at weekends, when some of the other cast members would hang out together, I'd travel all the way back to Melbourne to be with my family because I was so homesick. To be honest, none of the other teenage cast members was ever mean to me, and things got better as time went on and I became more established, but I felt there were a few sideways glances and an air of 'who does she think *she* is' in the early days.

Two people I did click with right away, and consequently adored, were Judy Nunn and Ray Meagher, who played Ailsa and Alf Stewart. They were two of the older members of the cast and were just gorgeous to me on set during the first couple of weeks of filming when I was more than a little nervous. After all, this was the biggest acting job I'd had and I didn't want to disappoint. The filming of the scenes seemed to move very quickly, and everyone knew exactly what they were doing except me. It took me a while to get the hang of hitting marks on certain words to get the desired camera shot exactly right, with no shadow from the lights. Judy and Ray, though, were eager for me to feel comfortable and settled in those first weeks, so they would engage me in chitchat between takes to keep me relaxed. I expect they could see the fear in my eyes.

Ray is a sweet, gentle man who was loved by everyone working on the show. His character, Alf, would make me chuckle with lines such as 'Stone the crows' or 'Ya flaming Galah' (this is Aussie slang for idiot, and comes from the native Australian bird of the same name). Judy, meanwhile, is an accomplished author as well as an actress, and I remember her working on her books between takes. She kept all her notes and manuscripts stashed behind the bar at the Summer Bay diner.

Unlike the teenagers in the show, who were understandably excited about being newly famous and on the cover of this teen magazine or that, Ray and Judy were seasoned actors, and I suppose I related to them more because I'd already been through all the excitement of being on television every week. At the tender age of seventeen I was, absurdly, already an old hand, despite my initial jitters.

I also grew fond of little Katie Ritchie, who played Sally, and of Craig McLaughlin, who played the part of schoolteacher Grant 'Mitch' Mitchell. He had previously played Kylie's brother in *Neighbours*, and he had the most evil and contagious sense of humour on set, which often got me into trouble. If I was doing a close-up shot and Craig was off camera but in my sightline, he would pull a ridiculous face or do something infantile to get me to crack up laughing and ruin the shot. Of course, I would be the one in hot water with the director.

None of the crew wanted to have to shoot scenes over and over again. Still, Craig would get you every time, even if everyone was tired and wanted to go home. He did it all in such good spirits, simply wanting to keep people smiling, that even when everyone was pissed off, they'd still end up falling about laughing at his antics. He was absolutely brilliant to work with.

Work days were long and hard on *Home and Away*, and often utter madness. I'd find myself dashing from the location site to film one scene in a bikini, then back to the studio to film another scene in my school uniform. Palm Beach, where all the main location stuff was filmed, is a gorgeous beachside suburb about 40 kilometres north of Sydney. With its golden sands and beautiful azure water, it's always been a Mecca for surfers and sailors. It was a fabulous drive up the coast from where I lived in Neutral Bay. On days when I was filming there, I'd often arrive before sunrise, desperate to get to the catering van with all its steaming hot drinks and tasty breakfasts, especially in the winter months. Then I'd stand and watch the sun drift up over the wild surf, clutching a much needed cup of coffee and think: 'This is the best job in the world!'

This early-morning euphoria wore thin after eight hours of standing in the drizzling rain in a minuscule swimsuit and thongs (flip flops). The rain had to be really heavy for filming to be halted, and if you had to walk along the beach in a light downpour, so be it! One of the crew would hurtle alongside you with a screen to make sure your face didn't get too wet and show the rain on camera.

We'd all spot lines in the script, such as 'Let's go for a swim', which, in the winter months, filled us with utter dread. On one particularly arctic morning, I approached one of the producers with what I felt was a practical initiative, given the unmistakable drop in temperature.

'I know I'm supposed to be in a bikini today,' I said, breezily, 'and that's fine, but could I maybe pop a little shirt or a cardigan over the top of it?'

He looked at me as if I might have lost my mind.

'No, Dannii,' he said. 'It's always summer in Summer Bay.'

They knew their market well. *Home and Away* was now huge in the UK, and one of its major selling points was that it was chock-o-block with gorgeous, sun-kissed Aussie teenagers tearing around a beautiful beach in a state of semi-undress. I had no idea how popular the show had become in Britain. The public there were enjoying soaking up a bit of what us Aussies took for granted, and it was bringing in the big bucks.

Despite the show's popularity, Channel 7 seemed to be feeling the pinch of recession, and every week there seemed to be another few cutbacks made, and fewer crew members to say 'G'day' to. All the crew, in fact, were constantly making jokes about the very real possibility of getting fired from their jobs at the channel, as times were so tough. One such gag was cheekily circulated on *Home and Away*-headed notepaper, with the production-office details in the top right-hand corner. I discovered it stuck to the front of my script folder:

As you know, we had planned to have our previously cancelled

Xmas party under the Wisteria arbour in The Eastwood Hall. This was replaced by our subsequently cancelled Xmas party, which was to have taken place next to the ladies' dressing room – by the pile of empty 'spring water' bottles. However, due to a managerial oversight and a small financial glitch, all of the above are now replaced by a free pizza of your own choice (small) or two spring rolls per artist, available only from studio '0' on 31 December at 4a.m. . . . . B.Y.O.

There was also a note stuck up on our green-room noticeboard. It was again written on Channel 7-headed paper, and had a gold dagger attached to it with a Channel 7 logo on it. The note read: *'Available now! The hand-finished Channel 7 dagger. To be worn between the shoulder blades (or bum cheeks.)'*

I guess the tight budget explained why the sets looked like cardboard when you got up close to them – they were all propped up with sandbags and stands at the back.

There was one person in the cast of *Home and Away* who would one day change my life but, of course, I couldn't have known it then. His name was Julian McMahon. Julian was the six-foot-two, brown-haired, blue-eyed son of the former Australian Prime Minister, William McMahon, but he'd also been a model in a Levi's jeans TV advertisement, which was much more of a big deal to me at the time. He was charismatic and funny and seemed to get on well with most of the other cast members and, I have to admit, I was somewhat bowled over when I met him.

Julian knew how to work a room: if he was around, you always knew it, and not in an annoying, showy way either. He was charming and witty, and loved nothing more than to entertain people and make them happy. As far as I was concerned, that was a nice sort of person to be around. Sometimes, Julian would be quite flirty with me but, to be perfectly honest, he flirted with absolutely everyone, so I didn't think it was any big deal and played along innocently, with nothing ever coming of it – at least not then anyway. I liked the fact that, much like Craig McLaughlin, he wanted to make people laugh, which, of course, meant he was usually the centre of attention – a typical Leo. Although we didn't have any storylines or scenes together on the show, Julian McMahon was definitely on my radar.

Thinking back on some of the storylines and scenes – especially the more meaty ones – I *did* have on *Home and Away*, though, makes me smile. My character, Emma Jackson, a wayward teen taken in by Ray and Judy's characters, Alf and Ailsa, could be a real tough bitch, and was great to play – she was always the bad girl. My arch-nemesis in the show was a character called Vicky Baxter, played by Nana Coburn. Vicky was also not a very nice young lady, and I had some great scenes with her, including the classic cat-fight at the bus stop after school, with tons of arm twisting and hair pulling; I even got to dump a milkshake over her head in the diner, though I can't for the life of me remember what flavour it was.

Emma ruined the Summer Bay beauty contest by parading up and down in vile clothes with hideous make-up. She had decided that beauty pageants were sexist and degrading to women, and said as much to the assembled crowd. The contest was won by the character Marilyn, who was the Summer Bay bimbo, and the part I'd originally read for but didn't get. I guess it was pretty obvious that I'd ended up with the right role for me: the feisty tomboy was always going to be so much more fun to play than the dizzy blonde!

Things started to go well for me once my character was established in *Home and Away*. In September 1989, the second Dannii clothing range sold out in record time again, and at the end of the year everyone at Channel 7 was over the moon when an Australian magazine called *TV Hits* voted me 'New Star of 1989'. I was an excited teenager! Then, early in 1990, things started to rev up even more. Mushroom Records decided to release my debut single in Australia before the album was finished. After all, I was appearing on television every night as a popular character in one of the country's hottest shows – I guess it would have been mad for them not to take advantage of that.

'Love And Kisses' was released in February, and climbed the charts to number four. I was overjoyed. My song was in the top five – it was almost too much to take in. Suddenly, I was flying all over the place to do radio and TV promotion for a hit single while still working on *Home and Away*. Though I loved every minute of it, it was exhausting; I wasn't getting nearly enough sleep.

I'd taken time off from the show to do a video clip for the song, and as usual wanted to be involved in absolutely every aspect of the process. I worked with the directors, Paul Goldman and Craig Griffin, on the storyboard, had a hand in auditioning the dancers and even chose my own clothes – including the fabulous leather jacket and gold cross I'd bought at Patricia Field in New York. It was the era of white faces and bright red lips, so I remember caking on the pale foundation to cover up my beautiful, bronze tan to get the desired look for the shoot.

The whole thing felt great – it felt like *me*! I was finally stepping into my own skin. The thrill of meeting so many new and talented people was electric. Whether they were producers, dancers, stylists or make-up people, I learned so much from them all and soaked up every new experience like a sponge. When I look back on that time now, I see one big explosion of fun, colour and vibrancy.

After the success of 'Love And Kisses', I had to take a short sabbatical from *Home and Away* to go back to New York and finish the album. It was wonderful to be back in my favourite city with Alvin and Vinnie, making music again. With the chart success of my single, I felt relaxed and confident that we'd laid the foundations of something great. While we were beavering away one day, I got a call from Australia: it was my A&R man, Gary Ashley.

'You've gone gold,' he said with excitement. '"Love And Kisses" has gone gold!'

My first single had sold over 35,000 copies in Australia and everyone at the studio was ecstatic. This fabulous news inspired Alvin and me to write the song 'Success', which eventually became my second single.

By then, I knew for sure that it was time for me to leave *Home and Away* and concentrate on the upcoming release of my album. True, I'd be leaving a stable job with good money, and I'd certainly miss some of the friends I'd made, but the days had started to feel so repetitive in comparison to all the different experiences I was having with music, and I hated being away from my friends and family in Melbourne. It seemed like there was nothing left for me to learn on the show, so I made a decision to say goodbye before I started hating it. I left Summer Bay how I'd like to remember it – always summer.

Chapter 8

Fish and Chips and Lori Lipkies

Lori Lipkies was about the most glamorous thing I'd ever seen: tall, with long, wild curly hair and always, *always*, fire-engine red lipstick, coupled with long, perfectly manicured matching red nails. She would wear the finest clothes from Europe, and she seemed to have a glamorous lifestyle like nobody else I knew – with gorgeous dinners here, fabulous parties there, amazing overseas trips with her parents and everything in between. The first time I walked past her in the corridors of Television House, in about 1984, I was in the middle of a *Young Talent Time* rehearsal, so I was wearing something very comfortable but wholly unglamorous. Lori, who looked like she might have been there for a *Vogue* cover shoot, gave me the once over, which meant staring down at the top of my head as I walked past her. I thought to myself: 'She looks like a model; I look really short next to her. I bet she's really stuck-up.'

She was at the studio visiting her friend Joey Perrone, who was one of the other *Young Talent Time* team members, and the guy who later introduced me to my first boyfriend, Gary. On that first encounter, Lori and I didn't give one another the time of day. It was only down the line, when I was dating Gary, that the two of us spoke. Being mutual friends of Joey, Gary and Lori knew one another fairly well, and Gary would always be chirping on about her.

'You have to meet Lori, Dannii. She's so cool, you'll love her. You *have* to meet her.'

I wasn't that bothered, as she'd seemed rather icy to me when we'd crossed paths at Television House, but I agreed to go to lunch with Gary and her. Three hours after taking our seats in the restaurant, the two of us hadn't stopped talking for a single second.

'Here's my number, Dannii,' Lori smiled, as we went our separate ways that afternoon. She handed me a pink silk card, which had her name and number on it embossed in gold. 'Give me a call some time.'

So I did.

I found Lori as fascinating and inspiring a person as she appeared to find me, although she was a year or so older than me and we came from different backgrounds. After that fateful lunch, we started hanging out together regularly, becoming inseparable as each week went by. Eventually, I ended up spending half my life at her parents' place, almost becoming a member of the family. In fact, when Lori's big sister moved out of the family home, her old room became known as Dannii's room, and I got my own key to the front door.

Lori came from quite a wealthy Jewish family. Not having been brought up with any kind of religion, I found the Friday-night Shabbat suppers and the customs the family observed quite intriguing, and, of course, the food was always spectacular. It was an unwritten rule that the whole family had to be there on a Friday evening for Shabbat supper, and to me that was great: everyone talking and catching up on what everyone else in the family was up to over food once a week – what could be better? My favourite meal, though, was the big Sunday brunch that Lori's mum, Ruth, would make, with homemade pumpkin soup, bagels and lox with cream cheese, and chopped herring salad.

When I heard about a job going in my manager Terry Blamey's office, I knew Lori would be perfect for it, and got on the phone to her.

'Terry's looking for someone to help him out,' I told her. 'Things are so full on with Kylie and now it's getting really busy for me, too. Terry needs a right-hand woman, and I think you should go for it.'

'Really?' Lori said. 'I'm not sure, Dan.'

Even after Terry himself had agreed that she would be perfect for the position, Lori wasn't convinced, as she had just started her second year at university, majoring in political science and psychology.

'I guess I could juggle my studies and do it part time,' she finally suggested.

That's what happened, for a while at least. Then Terry needed Lori to travel with me to Japan, and then London, so her academic career eventually went out of the window.

It was February 1991, and Mushroom had licensed my album overseas to various different territories. I'd had three singles out in Australia, and the album, simply called *Dannii*, had sold well. My new European record label, MCA, were confident that it was going to be an absolute smash in the UK, because *Home and Away* was such a huge TV show there and my character, Emma, was so popular. They were also happy that I'd been voted 'Best Female Star' in *TV Hits!* in Britain, and was still on TV every weeknight there, too, because the broadcasts of *Home and Away* in the UK were so far behind Australia. It was the perfect time for me to travel to London – in time for the release of the single 'Love And Kisses'. My best friend, Lori, was coming with me.

When we arrived in London for what was to be a three-week promotional trip, it was wet and freezing cold. Having come from a blistering Aussie summer, it was quite a shock. We'd come via Japan, where I'd been doing radio promotion for the release of 'Love And Kisses', and that had been a shock too – a wonderful culture shock.

Japan was like nowhere else I'd ever been, and everyone we met seemed so very joyous and excited about us being there. The delicacy and politeness of the people was a world away from the boisterous, straight-talking Aussie way I was used to, and nobody spoke English, so we had interpreters everywhere we went. The whole promotional set-up was very efficiently structured. Whenever we had time off, the people at the Japanese record label organised the most amazing sight-seeing trips and nights out for Lori and me. At first, our eager-to-please hosts seemed to take us only to restaurants with Western cuisine, thinking we'd want a steak for dinner every night, but after a couple of days of insisting that we wanted to try real Japanese fare, our wish was granted. My long love affair with Japanese food started on that trip.

We visited the beautiful temples in Kyoto, and a wonderful onsen (a hot spring that you can bathe in) in a small village in the far north of the country. Of course, Lori and I stood out like freaks in a village that wasn't used to Westerners: Lori was a complete 'Glamazon', with her scarlet lips and fabulous clothes, and me standing next to her, much shorter and with long, dyed jet-black hair and bright blue eyes. We found it terribly amusing when a busload of Japanese schoolgirls arrived at one of the temples that Lori and I were being shown around by our interpreter: the giggling teenagers were far more excited about taking pictures of the strange and outlandish Western ladies than the beautiful building they'd come to visit.

London was another experience altogether, and I wasn't quite ready for it when we touched down. Although people had told me many times how popular Aussie TV shows like *Neighbours* and *Home and Away* were in the UK, I wasn't prepared for all the press attention I was about to get.

During the first few weeks, I was sucked into a tornado of television, radio and press interviews, with everyone eager to find out who Dannii was. Kylie was a huge pop star by then, and now here was her little sister . . . While Kylie was seen as the blonde, wholesome pop princess, I seemed to be a mysterious, dark punk version of my older sister: the raven hair, the black leather jacket, the bitchy, tough kid I played on *Home and Away* – it was all there, and that's the way the press were going to play it. This had its advantages at first, to be honest, as it gave me more street cred.

Kylie was often away in Europe or America when I first arrived in London, so Lori and I got to crash at her apartment in Chelsea. It was comfy and central and had pictures of the family all around, so it felt like a little home away from home. Terry would often be away with Kylie, too, so I pretty much had to rely on Lori to organise my life and everything I had to do day-to-day. There was a host of record-company meetings, TV shows and press and radio interviews to coordinate, and Lori did it all – working twenty-five hours a day, eight days a week.

I, meanwhile, felt like I had to be switched on to my 'pop star' setting every time I stepped out of the door, with not a hair out of place and perfect make-up the whole time. This was often a hard enough job in itself and I started to realise what it must have been like when Kylie had first arrived during the frenzy of *Neighbours* publicity. One day, when Lori and I were leaving a TV studio, we got followed down the street by a gaggle of fans who were waving excitedly and screaming at me, 'Emma, Emma!'

'Why are they calling out Emma?' I asked Lori. 'I'm not Emma Jackson any more; I'm Dannii.'

My episodes of *Home and Away* were still showing every teatime in the UK, so as far as they were concerned I was still Emma. I've sometimes thought over the years that Britain's first image of me as cold and tough may have resonated for a lot longer than it should have done.

Pretty soon, my three-week promotional trip was being extended, first to a month and then to three. 'Love And Kisses' had hit the UK Top 10. There was no point in me going back home to Australia, as the second single, 'Success', was hot on its heels. A month after 'Success' charted, and after a bit of remixing and updating under the guidance of my UK A&R manager, Adrian Sykes, my album was released across Europe and Asia. Instead of being called *Dannii*, it was called *Love and Kisses*, like the debut single.

Once Kylie returned from her travels, there wasn't enough room at her place for Lori and me and our huge collection of luggage, so we moved into a hotel in Notting Hill called the Pembridge Court. It was a gorgeous nineteenth-century townhouse near the famous Portobello Road market. Lori and I knew it was the place for us almost as soon as we saw it: each room was lovingly and individually styled and furnished with exquisite antiques, and the place was full of quaint little touches, like framed Victorian gloves and fans. It was divine. It was known as a music-industry favourite, and the staff there couldn't have been more charming. Within weeks, we were on first-name terms with everyone who worked there, and I started to feel right at home. This was fairly fortuitous, as it turned out, because I would live there for the next two years.

Back then, when a record started to climb the charts in the UK, every new artist's dream was to perform on *Top of the Pops*. Coming from Australia, I didn't, at the time, realise the cachet this show had and I knew very little about its long history. Now, having appeared on it so many times over the years, I feel very privileged to have been a part of this British institution while it was still on the air.

There was such a buzz around the show back then, the whole day was an adventure. We normally had to arrive at the BBC first thing in the morning for stuff like camera rehearsals and interviews with *Top of the Pops* magazine. After that, Lori would help me to choose clothes and get my hair and make-up done, so I'd be ready for the noisy and exuberant audience to arrive in the early evening.

When I first went on the show I didn't recognise the importance of it, and consequently wasn't that nervous – after all, I was just singing and dancing on another live TV show, something I'd done all my life. When my single 'Love And Kisses' jumped from number thirty-three in the Top 40 to number fifteen after my debut appearance, I began to realise just how important a spot on *Top of the Pops* could be for an artist – even if said artist was dressed in a silver bra and leather cap.

Yes, once again and this time in Europe, I was becoming known as the girl in the outrageous outfits. I intended to live up to the title with a never-ending parade of crazy gear that I snatched off the rack myself when the stylist wasn't around, and, I reckon, would probably have given Lady Gaga a run for her money. Of course, not all of it was loved or applauded, and I did end up on some of the 'What on earth was she thinking?' pages of various publications.

By the time my single 'Baby Love' was released in the autumn of 1991, I'd had four singles out in less than seven months and was a regular on the iconic *Top of the Pops*. After two months in the Top 40, my album went gold.

I was living out my young girl's dream of being a pop star. *Smash Hits* magazine had voted me Best New Artist of 1991. It was almost impossible to pick up any of the teen publications without finding a 'Dannii' interview or feature inside. Are you scared of spiders, Dannii? What do you think of your sister's new haircut, Dannii? Dannii, do you like English fish and chips? I was suddenly the girl people wanted to know all about, but there was something missing . . .

Although I loved my job, and had Lori with me through all my London adventures, I started to feel something that I'd never really felt before: loneliness. The novelty of living in a hotel, however cosy and friendly it was, was starting to wear thin. With poor Lori stuck in her room surrounded by a mountain of faxes and phones, I began to feel slightly empty whenever I didn't have something to occupy me. The other thing about living at the Pembridge Court was that if we had to go away for more than two or three days at a time on a promotional trip, the record company would insist that we pack up our suitcases, check out of the hotel and then check back in when we came back and start all over again, sometimes in a different room.

I started to miss the simple stuff, like being able to brew my own coffee and make my own meals, and all the fundamental things you do when you have a home of your own. The furniture wasn't my furniture, the walls weren't my walls, and I gave up adorning the hotel rooms with the framed family pictures I'd brought with me from home because I was fed up with packing and unpacking them every time we had to check out. I desperately missed having a group of friends I could hang out with and talk to about something other than whether I liked fish and chips or not. Even having Kylie close at hand in Chelsea wasn't a big help, as we were both always so busy; the chances of us having the same day off were almost zero.

I tried telling myself that I was being ungrateful, that I should be on top of the world. After all, according to *Smash Hits*, I was very nearly the world's sexiest female – second only to Madonna – so I had lots to be thankful for, right? Shouldn't I be happy? Maybe.

But what had started as a fun, three-week promotional trip had morphed into what seemed like an eternity. I was losing touch with all the people I loved back home, and it scared me.

When Lori and I let off steam, though, we'd really let off steam. We'd go to the fabulous Kinky Gerlinky parties in London, and dance the night away with fabulous freaks and glamorous drag queens. Lori would spur me on to have fun and be a little wild.

We were obsessed with buying wigs at that time, and our collection was growing fast. I'd often throw one on to go out clubbing, so I could enjoy myself incognito, without worrying about getting photographed doing something outrageous. When we were out of the country, we'd take our wig-wearing fetish a stage further and have some fun. Whenever we had to do promotion in Europe, we'd pack all the wigs we'd bought in Hyper Hyper, which was a super-trendy mall in London's Kensington High Street, and head for the airport.

I can remember us both once wearing PVC hot pants with matching thigh boots, while hanging out at a very cool club called La Bandouche in Paris. Lori was in a poker-straight black bob wig and false eyelashes, and I was wearing a long red wig that was something like Farrah Fawcett, *circa Charlie's Angels* 1977. We had a blast during those trips, and I'd let loose and feel utterly free. Those were the times I was happy and could banish all the loneliness I'd felt while staring at the four walls in my hotel room. Lori never once asked me if I was scared of spiders or whether or not I liked fish and chips. Thank God for Lori Lipkies!

Chapter 9

Cristal by the Bucketload

One of the most unforgettable trips Lori and I took was in November 1991, when Mushroom Records licensed my album to a small record company in New York. My first release there was a cover of the Stacy Lattisaw disco hit 'Jump To The Beat', which had already been a top-ten single for me in Britain. To mark the occasion of its release in the US, a grand reception was being thrown in my honour. I was very excited to be going back to America to launch the single, particularly as the small label I was signed to had lined up some club gigs for me after the Christmas holidays. As much as I loved London, this trip would be a much needed change and might well blow away a few cobwebs.

Once we were in New York, everything seemed so exciting. The party that the label laid on was a blast and the bubbly flowed like waterfalls. One of the invited guests was none other than Mike Tyson, then at the height of his boxing career. I remember that he spoke very quietly, almost in a whisper, but also that his giant hands almost crushed mine when he greeted me with a rather firm handshake. There were lots of cool people there, and I was very impressed when I met the production team C+C Music Factory, who were absolutely huge at the time.

As Lori and I were taken round and introduced to some of the many 'old school' music-biz types that seemed be on the small label's payroll, Lori recognised a couple of the names from a book she'd been reading called *Hit Men*, which was about corruption in the music industry and the old 'payola' system in America, whereby record companies would illegally make under-the-table payments to radio stations so that the stations would play their records – something that had been rife in the fifties and sixties. Lori had quite a giggle about the fact that there were so many of these old timers working for such a small set-up. Some of these guys had apparently been real high-flyers in the music industry twenty or thirty years before, but now here they all were with various jobs in this tiny, family-owned record label. The record-company offices, however, were very ostentatious, with gold ashtrays and marble all over the place, so we thought, 'Great! They must have had a ton of money to throw at us for promotion.' That didn't turn out to be the case at all.

In February 1992, as we made our way across America on an extensive radio and club promotion tour – mostly on buses and trains – the organisation and, indeed, the conditions seemed to get worse and worse. We were left to our own devices most of the time, even though there was a little old guy with a bad attitude who billed himself as 'tour manager' tagging along. Lori and I would constantly be frustrated when he'd disappear at a moment's notice, leaving us to try to figure out what the hell we were supposed to be doing next. Indeed, each hotel we stayed in was worse than the last. Of course, in small towns we didn't expect to be staying at the Four Seasons, but we couldn't understand why we were being put up in such grizzly places when the record company seemed to have so much money. We'd already been told the clubs would not be paying us a fee for playing: any shows we did should be seen as promotion for my record and I should be grateful.

'It's what Madonna did,' the label manager told us. 'It's what everyone does here with pop dance music. You come up through the clubs and let the cool kids discover you.'

Of course, we didn't know any better, and just got on with it, trying at all costs to remain professional. Every morning, Lori would get up to call our 'tour manager' to find out which radio station we were scheduled to be at in which town, or what time the sound check was for the evening's club date, but he couldn't have cared less. There was never an itinerary, and no rehearsals and little advertising for the shows I was playing – and usually no sound check either. In fact, a lot of the time the gigs were me with a backing track at the town disco. Although the record company did organise a couple of 'showcase' gigs on the tour – where people from the music industry were invited to come and see me perform songs from my album – I had to face the fact that I was essentially doing a karaoke tour of the Midwest.

After one gig in Chicago, halfway through the tour, I came off stage and Lori grabbed me and pulled me into the grim, microscopic dressing room. 'There's something not kosher here,' she said to me, with an anxious frown. 'I've just seen the club owner giving our so-called tour manager a big fucking lump of cash. We may not be getting paid for all the work we're doing, Dannii, but somebody sure as hell is.'

'I think we should call Terry,' I said, solemnly.

Lori and I were both still so young and inexperienced. We weren't used to having to deal with this kind of thing and we were completely on our own.

'You're right. I'll do it now,' Lori agreed.

Terry told Lori that this had to be an 'on-the-road' decision, and she'd have to trust her own instincts. After all, he was thousands of miles away. Although he could deal with the record company in New York by phone, only we could decide whether it was worth carrying on with the scheduled promo.

'If Dannii wants to pull the plug on it, then do it,' he said.

Against my better judgement, I decided to carry on.

When we returned to New York for some radio and club promotion there, I hoped things might be better. After all, this was the Big Apple and the clubs were all fabulous. At least the record company might wine and dine us a little after our gruelling schlep across the country. However, when we arrived back in the city – on the train, of course –

nobody was there to meet us, except our less than friendly tour manager, who just handed us the address of the hotel that had been
booked for us.

'It's over that way,' he said to Lori with a vague hand gesture before
he jumped in a cab and went home.

When we finally found the hotel, our hearts sank. We would gladly
have traded it for the very worst of the dumps we'd stayed in on the
road.

'This is the bloody Roach Motel, doll!' Lori said.

I nodded. It really was.

Once inside my room, nauseous from the musty smell, I surveyed
the grubby, worn curtains, tatty wooden furniture and smoke-stained
wallpaper – it was a miserable landscape. 'No,' I said to myself. 'Fuck
this! I may be an unknown artist trying to crack America, but that's no
reason for me to be staying in a room I wouldn't let a donkey sleep in.'
I grabbed the phone and called Lori's room, which was on the floor
below. After quite a few rings, she finally answered, but her voice
sounded far away.

'Hello?'

'It's Dannii. Are you OK? You sound funny.'

'Yes, I'm fine, but I was too scared to touch the phone because it's
so filthy, and I'm certainly not putting it anywhere near my mouth.'

'Gotcha!'

'Are you OK, Dannii? Do you want something?'

'No. Just get me out of here.'

And she did. Right then and there Lori called Gary Ashley, my A&R
man from Mushroom Records, who was in Chicago at the time.

'Gary, we've done the whole tour in shit conditions, but this is the
worst – it's positively infested. We've had it.'

Mercifully, Gary spoke to someone at the label who very quickly
found us somewhere much nicer to stay. Once we'd freshened up, we
headed out to dinner with the head of the record label and some of his
associates at a very swanky bar/restaurant downtown, feeling quite a
lot brighter. As was the norm at any of these dinners, there were at least
forty people coming and going, dining and drinking champagne, all at

the expense of a record label who hadn't booked us on planes from one city to another or put us in half-decent hotels. It wasn't cheap fizz everyone was quaffing either – it was Cristal.

This went on night after night while we were in New York. Lori and I couldn't work out what on earth the deal was with these people: the large flashy dinners with expensive champagne, the opulent offices, the dozens of so-called 'employees' who didn't ever seem to do anything and, best of all, my hard-earned club performance fees going straight into the pocket of that miserable human being who called himself a tour manager.

'It's gotta be a scam,' Lori whispered to me on our last night there.

I had no idea, but by now I just wanted to get back to London and the comfort of the Pembridge Court. Later that night, a few of us were at Nell's club on 14th Street, and still nobody was sipping water. It was Cristal and Cristal and Cristal and then more Cristal. It was Cristal by the bucketload, in fact. There weren't that many of us as it was late: the owner of the label and his main sidekick, and a couple of other people, including the then hotshot record producer Al B. Sure! Lori decided in her wisdom, and possibly slightly inebriated state, that perhaps, as it was our last night, we should order and pay for at least one bottle of champers as we hadn't paid for a single drink all week.

'It's the polite, sophisticated thing to do,' she said with an air of self-assurance.

'Absolutely,' I agreed.

After all, the owner of the label had always been very kind and generous to us personally, despite our misgivings about the label's strange set-up, and the appalling way my so-called tour had been run.

While the others were all dancing, Lori called the waitress over.

'Another bottle of the same,' she said.

Presently, the smiling waitress brought over the open bottle in a silver ice bucket, and handed Lori the check.

'It's totally cool, doll,' Lori said, turning to me while grabbing the bill from the waitress, 'I've got six hundred in cash to cover it, so . . . Oh!'

'What?'

Lori's face was ashen.

'Er . . . that bottle was thirteen hundred and fifty dollars.'

That capped the trip off nicely.

'But there have been forty or fifty people out with us every night, all drinking the stuff non-stop,' Lori said, disbelieving, in the taxi as we headed back to our hotel with seriously damaged credit cards.

'Where the hell does all the money come from?'

'I dunno!' I said.

The next day we returned to the UK none the wiser.

Chapter 10

Brand-New Things

Throughout 1991, I travelled so much I'd started to forget what it was like to have a home or family life. I'd travelled to New Zealand for a while in June to film an independent Aussie movie called *Secrets*, in which I played an introverted Beatles fanatic called Didi. I also went across Southeast Asia to promote the *Love and Kisses* album, and got to see some wonderfully exotic places: Indonesia, Taipei and the Philippines to name a few, but there never seemed to be much opportunity to get back home to see my family in Australia.

London was my main base. Though my manager, Terry Blamey, was now there most of the time, and I still had Lori with me, I felt desperately lonely. All too often, while lying in my pretty four-poster bed at the Pembridge Court Hotel, I'd cry myself to sleep.

Apart from not having made any real friends in London, I wasn't dating either. What was wrong with me? It wasn't like I was a shrinking violet, and I certainly met enough people through work – though I'm not sure how many of the dancers and drag queens Lori and I partied with at Kinky Gerlinky would have fitted the bill. But really! Wasn't I 'Woman of the Year' as far as *Number One* magazine was concerned?

The world's best female pop star according to *Big* magazine? *And*, lest we forget, the world's sexiest female after Madge? Still, dates were very rare, and though I didn't have an awful lot of spare time, a little bit of romance certainly wouldn't have gone amiss.

After one kind thought from someone at my record label, though, things suddenly seemed a little brighter. Penny Feuer was my press officer at MCA Records, and I spent quite a lot of time with her at magazine interviews and photo shoots. I guess she must have sensed that I was having a bit of a hard time. When the managing director of MCA, Tony Powell, threw a lunchtime cocktail party for all the staff and recording artists on the label, Penny suggested I mingle a bit and try to get to know some of my musical stablemates. I remember meeting Kim Wilde, and Wendy James from the band Transvision Vamp, but then Penny ushered me over to meet an artist named Terry Ronald, who was laughing and chatting with my A&R manager, Adrian Sykes.

'Terry's big in Spain,' Penny said with a wry smile and a wink.

Terry laughed and threw back a comically evil stare. 'Bitch!' he said.

Penny was also Terry's press officer at the label and the two of them had become good friends. He was older than me – in his mid-twenties – but he was confident and a lot friendlier than some of the other people I'd been introduced to.

'I know exactly who you are,' he said, and we shook hands.

It was a few weeks later, in late September 1991, when Terry Ronald and I met again. I had to fly out to Spain on a promotional trip, and I was disappointed because Lori was in America and was unable to come with me. I'd been invited to a swanky music-business awards dinner on my last night there. As I walked into the plush lobby of the gorgeous hotel in Madrid with some of my European promotional team, I was happy to see a familiar face coming towards me.

'Hey, remember me?' Terry said, smiling. 'Well, I've just been forcibly ejected from the fucking hotel bar for wearing shorts. Literally snatched my martini out of my hand and marched me out. I said to them, "Are you insane? These shorts are linen from Paul Smith, and

Danielle just six weeks old, Melbourne, Australia

With Brendan and Kylie at the beach

With Brendan in
Scoresby

Enjoying summer and
Christmas in Australia

With Kylie in Nain's
kitchen, Ferntree Gully

Me at *Young Talent Time* rehearsals, already loving the make-up!

With Brendan and Kylie at Surfer's Paradise, Queensland

Performing 'Chain Reaction' at a *Young Talent Time* concert in one of my own creations

My final performance on *Young Talent Time*

Performing with Vince on *Young Talent Time*

Goofing around with Craig McLachlan on the set of *Home & Away*

With Gary on a romantic date

A record company press shoot

New York, New York!

Learning my way around Manhattan,
Yellow Taxis beat walking when
wearing heels!

Kirsten, Kylie, Ron, me, Julian, Carol, Lori, Brin, Lauren, Tiffany
and Elisha – the big day!

1991 and 1995: the stress of my marriage break up was clearly taking its toll

Chilling on set – the *Playboy* shoot in the Nevada Desert

With my friend and confidant, Terry Ronald in Paris

'Rusty' and friends join me and my red 'Farrah Flick' hairdo for the Studio 54 birthday party in London

With 'the girls' at Mardi Gras: (Left to Right) Verushka Darling, Farren Heit, Victoria Barracks, Atlanta Georgia, Claire de Lune and (on ground) Vicky Vegas.

the loafers are Gucci. What kind of a place is this, anyway?" I bet they wouldn't have chucked Madonna out for wearing linen shorts.'

That night, when he performed a set of his songs on stage at the awards dinner – in trousers – I was somewhat gobsmacked.

'He sounds just like a black girl,' I said to one of the women from the record label. I fell in love with his voice, and the next day told him so as we were leaving the hotel.

'I'd love you to meet my friend, Lori,' I said, knowing full well that the two of them would hit it off. 'I'm having a birthday party in London in a couple of weeks. It would be great if you could come – 20 October.'

Terry grinned.

'That's actually my birthday, too,' he said. 'Can I bring my boyfriend? He's a marine.'

'Of course,' I laughed.

After that trip to Spain, Terry Ronald became my first real friend in London, and over the next year or so we got to know one another well. It was wonderful to have found a brand-new friend who was in the same business as I was, who understood the ups and downs of it, yet always managed to keep a smile. Through him, I met a whole bunch of other people, who all shared the same great sense of humour, and eventually I started to feel more confident about making new friends myself. These days I have the most fantastic London family and the city is my second home.

1992 was as busy a year as its predecessor, what with the aforementioned crazy trip across America, two new singles and a remixed version of the *Love and Kisses* album with some new songs added. In October of that year, just after my twenty-first birthday, Lori and I went back to Australia for the premiere of the movie I'd made, *Secrets*, which told the story of five Australian teenagers who became stuck in the basement of a hotel in an attempt to see the Beatles. It was great to be back home in time for Christmas with the family, and to soak up some of that wonderful Aussie sunshine. Little did I know it but there was a surprise waiting around the corner for me in the shape of a former work colleague.

On 1 November, at the People's Choice Awards, I bumped into Julian McMahon, the handsome ex-Levis model who had been in the cast of *Home and Away* at the same time as me. Obviously, I looked quite different to the way I had when he used to walk past me every day in my girlish, Emma Jackson school-uniform costume or leather jacket. I now had long, tumbling dark curls with a trendy blonde streak at the front, and rather more demure make-up. It was great fun catching up with Julian again and, as when I'd met him before, I was rather taken with him. Yep, he was still hot. He was also just as charming as I remembered. As the evening progressed, the sparks were flying between us – in a very good way.

After the awards ceremony, I invited Julian and some of his friends to a small soirée I was throwing in my hotel suite. We all ended up sitting around, telling jokes, playing games and having a great time. We partied on fairly late into the night, but just as I was about ready for sleep, one of my guests announced that he'd locked his keys and passport in my hotel safe and neither of us could remember the combination. It was 7a.m. before an engineer came to get the damn thing open, but Julian waited up with me until the sun came up and it was then that we kissed. It was divine!

Before he left that morning, we exchanged numbers and planned a date for the following week. And after that date we had another . . . and then another . . . and then . . . Finally, the romantic drought had come to an end. The more I saw of Julian, the more I fell. He had such a sense of fun, and was so incredibly handsome and romantic. After so many months of feeling lonely and withdrawn, I felt I could finally let my hair down.

Before I was due to fly back to London, Julian took me to a beautiful little hotel on the beach in Sydney, which is where he lived. We spent several blissful days together, just the two of us, holed up there having wonderful private dinners and talking about anything and everything, plus, of course, doing all the things that two people who are falling in love do. It was amazing. Suddenly there was a whole other dimension to my life and it dawned on me what I'd been missing all this time. I'd only been in love once before – with Gary – but I'd been so much younger then; what I felt for Julian was a whole new ball game. After years when work was the centre of my existence, now there was something or, more to the point, *someone* else.

There was an ominous cloud on my starry-eyed horizon though, as I knew I had to get back to London. There was a new album to record, and a brand-new job too. I'd been asked to co-present Channel 4's *The Big Breakfast*, which was a popular, zany alternative to the rather more conservative morning shows on BBC1 and ITV. The show's main host, Chris Evans, needed someone to fill a spot while his co-presenter Gaby Roslin was away on holiday and I jumped at the chance: after all, it was another string to my bow, and, though I didn't know it then, the experience of presenting a live TV show would stand me in very good stead in years to come.

Of course, being on a breakfast show meant very early mornings – up at 4a.m. for a 5a.m. script meeting – and a lot to learn in a very short space of time. Chris Evans was very specific about the way he wanted things done, but he was very generous and helpful to me. I learned a lot from him during my time on the show, including how to work under pressure on a live show where the information and direction was changing every five minutes. On this show, if you didn't have someone screaming in your earpiece every five seconds, you didn't know you were alive. On my first day, I was absolutely dreadful and quite deflated, but Chris came and gave me some valuable advice.

'You will make mistakes,' he said, 'but if you fuck up, the audience will always forgive you if you laugh at yourself. So don't get frustrated if something goes wrong, just put your hands up in the air and say, "Welcome to *The Big Breakfast* – I have no idea what's going on!" Then look at your notes, take a deep breath and move on.'

It was a fantastic piece of advice, and one I have always carried with me. On *The X Factor* or *Australia's Got Talent* now, if things ever go tits up in a live situation, I always try to remember it.

Paula Yates had a fun section on the show in which she interviewed people in bed, and she used to bring her now famous kids, who were still very young at the time, to the set. There was a rumour among the crew that Paula used to walk off with some of the competition prizes that were meant to go to lucky members of the public. Prizes would go missing and some of the crew would say that Paula had been spotted with boxes under her arm as she left for home. Whenever questioned about it, she would shrug her shoulders and play dumb about the whole thing. I don't know if it's true or not, but it certainly made me smile. Paula was definitely the most colourful host on *The Big Breakfast*.

My short spell on the show led to a whole new career in television presenting over the next couple of years, including further stints on *The Big Breakfast*. This aspect of my work has been important ever since.

By the start of 1993, I'd given up believing that my short promotional trip to London was going to end. After two years of living out of boxes and suitcases in hotels, I waved goodbye to the wonderful Pembridge Court, bit the bullet and rented an apartment. I didn't want to live on my own though. Lori was back in Australia permanently – with Terry Blamey looking after both Kylie and me in London full time – so I moved in with a girl called Laura Harding who worked at MCA Records and was good mates with Penny Feuer and Terry Ronald. It was an added bonus that she made me laugh.

Laura found us a small two-bedroom apartment in Fulham, which was nothing fancy but very nice, and at least I could call somewhere home at last. I could also entertain: suddenly I had friends dropping by for drinks, dinner and video nights and crashing on the couch, like a normal person. When Julian decided to come and stay with me in London for a while, the picture was complete. My life was now so much brighter than before: I had new friends, a new apartment, new career opportunities and, most importantly, a brand-new love in my life. I had a feeling that 1993 was shaping up to be a great year.

Chapter 11

'This Is It' and
That Was That

When Julian guest starred in the video for my next single, 'This Is It', in June 1993, we looked happy and we were – very happy. The whole idea for the clip was a fun, summer beach scene with loads of colour and lots of dancing. I'll admit, looking back at it now, it was pretty damned cheesy, but it suited the buoyant, disco feel of the song, and also, I suppose, my mood at that time. Having Julian on the video was a bonus, too, and we got the chance to cavort passionately in the surf under the warm Los Angeles sun. Julian and I were in love, and it showed.

Now why, you may ask, did we end up going all the way to LA to shoot a video? Well, I had been spending quite a bit of time in America during the previous couple of months, as Julian had got a part in the US daytime soap opera *Another World*. Although the show was shot in New York, it was easy enough to hop on a plane and head for the sun to get the right look and feel for the video. *My* look in the clip was quite a departure from my past video incarnations, when I'd be swathed in dark, moody clothes, often with lots of heavy make-up. Here, I was on a beach, jumping up and down on a trampoline in a puff-sleeved, multi-coloured bra top with a flower in my hair – and I relished every second of it!

'This Is It' was to be the third single from my new album, which I'd been busy recording in both England and America. For this particular song, I'd asked my good friend Terry Ronald to come into the studio and produce the vocals for me. There were a few reasons for this: for a start, the original of 'This Is It' by Melba Moore had a real soul feel to it, and I wanted to capture some of that on my version. Terry, with his soulful, androgynous tone would be the perfect person to help extract those qualities from me in the studio. Terry had been dropped by our label, MCA, and had told my roommate, Laura, that he felt a bit lost and didn't know what to do next. Knowing that feeling all too well, I called Terry right away and told him that I needed him to come and work on my album.

'I want to get more out of my vocals. You can do that, right?' I said to him.

'Well, we'll have a go, Babe,' Terry said. 'I certainly know one end of a disco record from the other, and I can replicate practically every vocal ad lib that Donna Summer ever sang.'

There was one other reason I wanted someone supportive by my side in the studio, and it was the most essential one.

I'd recently travelled to Chicago to record some tracks with a very big record producer of the day, at the very start of the recording sessions for the album. I didn't know the city very well, but my A&R man, Adrian, came over with me to get me settled in. Once he'd left, though, I was on my own, and I didn't feel the affinity with Chicago that I had with New York. I didn't walk to the studio, and couldn't get the hang of the surrounding neighbourhood. But I was there to work, and I was excited about the upcoming studio sessions with such a hot producer, so I was sure it would all be OK. I was wrong.

One of the songs that I'd been given by this particular producer and his team was much too high for me.

'I'm not sure I can sing like that, guys,' I told them. 'It's all a bit screechy. Can we take it down a bit?'

That didn't go down at all well. They insisted it was the right key and that I might as well try it, as they didn't have the track in any other key. I'd been used to easygoing Alvin and Vinnie, who did my first album in New York, where there was an atmosphere of give and take and trying stuff out to see if it worked; this was an altogether different proposition.

'Well, any of the other girls we work with would be able to do it in that key,' my producer insisted. 'What's the big deal? If you wanna have a big hit, you're gonna have to do it like we say.'

By this time, I was feeling uncomfortable, and didn't feel like singing anything, let alone a song that was completely out of my range, but I walked into the vocal booth and gave it a go. After all, if it didn't work, it didn't work. What did I have to lose?

My voice – that's what! After an hour or so of trying to achieve some of the vocal acrobatics that surely only dogs could hear, I was hoarse and tired. It wasn't even that I couldn't reach the notes; it was more that they were so high that I couldn't get a sound within my voice that was halfway pleasant to the ear. Yes, it probably would have sounded amazing with a fantastic soulful diva on it, but the little Aussie white girl wasn't cutting it. Rather than being helpful and supportive, the three guys in the studio thought I was crap and let me know it in no uncertain terms.

'I just can't do this,' I said, now slightly shaky. 'I'm trying my hardest but it's not working.'

'You have to keep going,' the producer said. 'This is the way we always work. We do it until it's right! Do it again.'

I started to feel boxed in inside the vocal booth and I wanted to run right out of the studio – but where to? I didn't know what part of town I was in, and I'd have to wait for the guys to call a car for me if they did let me leave. I had no mobile phone then, either. I felt trapped. I was in a city I didn't know, with people I didn't know, singing a song I didn't like. The vocal booth seemed to be closing in on me.

'Let's go *again*, Dannii,' the demanding voice suddenly barked in my headphones. 'Let's go!'

I tried to sing the song again, but, halfway through, and unable to control my now very tired voice, I began to cry, the song's relentless backing track still blaring in my ears. I was done. I'm not entirely sure how I managed to negotiate my way out of that vocal booth, or, indeed, that recording session, but the song never did end up on my album.

As a consequence of this experience, I told my manager that I wanted someone to come with me to all of my sessions to produce my vocals on the album – someone who knew my voice and knew exactly what I could and couldn't do, someone who would push me to achieve more without scaring the shit out of me. Ever since that session in Chicago, I haven't liked being in a vocal booth, and as much as possible like to record my vocals in the control room with the producers.

The recording session for 'This Is It' couldn't have been more different. The track was produced in a lovely town in Buckinghamshire called Beaconsfield by a production team called One World – Tim Lever and Mike Percy – who were so sweet. They'd both been members of the band Dead or Alive in the eighties and had had a massive number one hit with 'You Spin Me Round (Like A Record)'. I was a huge fan of their work.

Terry Ronald came down to the session. He had a different, if slightly unorthodox, way of getting me to achieve the right sound vocally.

'Right' – he'd always prefix his directives with 'right' – 'if we're gonna get that really lovely, gritty soul sound on these ad libs at the end of the song, we need to have a cigarette.'

'What?'

'Break out the Silk Cut, love. We'll have a couple of fags and a glass of red wine, and then crack on. Trust me, you'll loosen up and we'll get that fabulous soul rasp.'

Well, I looked like Olivia Newton-John in the scene from *Grease* when she tries her first cigarette, with a cough and a splutter at each puff, but I was prepared to give it a go: drag, splutter, drag, splutter! We worked out all sorts of great vocal riffs and ad libs for the end. When we heard the finished vocal back, we were completely over the moon. Once that was done, Terry worked out the harmonies and we did the backing vocals together, which was something I'd never done before.

I was having a great time. It obviously shone through: when MCA released 'This Is It', they put an a cappella mix (vocals only) on the CD single, as they thought it was the best I'd ever sounded. That, coupled with the joyful, romantic video clip I'd shot with Julian, sent the record shooting into the Top 10. Terry Ronald has produced the vocals on virtually every record I've made since. Minus the Silk Cuts.

One evening, while 'This Is It' was riding high in the charts, Julian took me to the beautiful Blakes hotel in Kensington and booked an overnight room. This was rather extravagant, as I had an apartment in London, but never one to shy away from a good old-fashioned romantic gesture, I went along with it anyway. We ate a wonderful dinner at the restaurant and then went back to our room. Once there, Julian completely knocked me for six as he dropped down on one knee. He looked me in the eye, took my hand and asked the simple but potentially life-altering question: 'Dannii, will you marry me?' He held out a gorgeous, classic diamond engagement ring set in white gold.

Oh my God! Was this actually happening? So many things went through my mind in those few seconds. True, our love affair had been a whirlwind and we'd been together only a few months, but every moment we'd been together had been such fun and I so wanted that to continue. True, Julian's work was in New York and I spent most of my time in London, but surely being married would bring us closer together even when we were apart physically. And, yes, I was still only twenty-one years old, but I felt like I'd already crammed in more than some people do in a whole lifetime: I'd travelled the world, I had a career, I had money in the bank. Most people might think that twenty-one was far too tender an age to consider marriage, but I knew what I wanted, and that was to be with Julian.

'I've called Australia and asked your dad already.' Julian smiled, waiting for my answer, which was a resounding 'YES!'

At first, I wasn't sure how Mum and Dad really felt about our engagement. Although Dad had obviously given Julian his blessing over the phone, I thought I might have caught an air of concern when I spoke to him on the phone. I guess I was still his little girl, despite having lived the last few years on the other side of the world, and I brushed the thought aside as nothing more than that. Mum seemed happy for me, and sounded excited at the thought of planning a wedding. If she did have any concerns about me rushing into marriage at such a young age, she kept them to herself. Julian's family, however, was a different kettle of fish.

He came from a real Australian blue-blooded dynasty, which was totally at odds with the working-class roots of my family. From everything he'd told me, it was clear *his* family had never been an especially happy one. His father, an ex-Australian prime minister, had died when Julian was about twenty – five years earlier – and since then his relationship with his mother, Sonia, had become steadily worse. There seemed to be a terrible amount of sadness and discontent within his family. Lady Sonia McMahon didn't approve of her son becoming an actor or, in truth, anything else he had done with his life. Having grown up in such a wonderful home environment myself, this upset me terribly. I kept thinking how tragic it was that Julian was unable to share all the good things in his life with his mother and sisters – including me.

I was never once allowed to visit the McMahon family house when we were in Sydney and I remember very clearly having to sit in the car and wait for Julian while he visited his mother. It was made very clear to Julian that I was *persona non grata* as far as any family events were concerned. Lady Sonia McMahon wanted nothing to do with me and she made no bones about it. In fact, my engagement to her son was the worst piece of news Sonia could possibly have had – I simply wasn't good enough. While Mum, Dad, Kylie and Brendan welcomed Julian into our family with open arms, the door to the McMahon mansion was slammed firmly in my face.

I told myself, however, that this would change in time, and that surely once we were married, Lady McMahon would come around. To be honest, I had too much to organise to dwell on it for very long. The first thing on my agenda was for us to find somewhere to live in New York. I had to keep the flat in London, of course, as I needed somewhere to stay when I was there, but as much as I could, I would be in New York with Julian while he was working on *Another World*. The apartment we found and rented in Manhattan was fantastic – on

48th Street between 8th Avenue and Broadway, which was on the edge of the up-and-coming and very trendy area of Hell's Kitchen. It had magnificent views of both rivers, right down to the Statue of Liberty. While Julian was out working, I'd be cooking up a storm or out buying things for the apartment and generally setting up a home for us. To be honest, I was more than happy to be throwing myself wholly into a whirl of domestic bliss, because at about that time, my busy and up until then glittering career hit a rather huge and unpleasant bump in the road.

Although 'This Is It' had gone gold in Australia and been a Top 10 hit in the UK, the two previous singles hadn't done so well, and the single that followed it, 'This Is The Way', performed poorly everywhere. Music seemed to be changing. Although I didn't understand why, I had to face it: there just wasn't much interest in a new Dannii record. In fact, there was no real positive vibe around me at all.

I found myself facing a barrage of unflattering press coverage, bad record sales and, most hurtful of all, mean, unfavourable comparisons to Kylie. Only a year or so before, I'd been voted the world's best female pop star in one magazine, and now, in *Smash Hits*, the readers had voted me worst female artist of the year. After the disappointing chart position of 'This Is The Way', MCA decided that they no longer wanted me on their roster. Although I still had Mushroom Records in Australia behind me, I'd lost my record deal in the UK and Europe, and that was that.

Chapter 12

A Lady in Name Only

Losing a major record contract was quite a blow to someone who'd had the run of success that I'd had since the age of seven. I think if it had happened at any other time, I'd have been much more devastated than I was. I was so blissfully happy and in love with Julian that I quite enjoyed having a bit of time off work and, indeed, playing at being a doting 'wife' before we were married. No, I wasn't running away by going to New York, I told myself. I was getting on with the next chapter of my life, and concentrating on all that was good about it rather than focusing on the negative.

Our social life in Manhattan was fairly hectic and I still absolutely loved New York. Julian and I had an eclectic group of mutual friends that was growing by the week, and I loved the fact that most of them weren't in the music or entertainment business. Every week there would be a Thursday-night dinner and then a big brunch on Sunday, and whichever friends, or friends of friends, were in town that week would come along, with one of us always making sure there was a large table booked at one of our favourite haunts, like Coffee Shop on Union Square, or Time Café, downtown on Great Jones Street.

I loved that about living in New York, and I miss it now. In London, everyone is so far apart because it's so big. In Manhattan back then it seemed like no one was more than a few blocks away from one another, and you were always ten minutes away from everywhere in a yellow taxi. The fact is that if you have a spare room in New York City, it's never empty for very long, and because of that, Julian and I were always meeting new and interesting people who were coming into town to hang out with our ever-expanding group.

One of the people I got very close to while we were living in Manhattan was a rather dynamic lady called Kathy Dolgin, who was known to almost everyone as 'High Voltage'. I'd first met her while I was performing some club dates in New York a year or so before. After the haphazard nature of my first promotional tour, the record label had brought her in to work on club promotion and, essentially, to look after me all the time I was there. Voltage knew everyone on the party scene back then; she was very much in tune with what was going on in the downtown clubs and knew exactly what the kids were into. She had wide eyes, a huge smile and a fantastic figure, and she was definitely a woman who'd 'been there and done that' as far as I was concerned – I warmed to her immediately.

She was very protective of me, and somewhat maternal, and I loved having her with me while I was working, as she always seemed to have such incredible energy. This energy was something she'd put to good use by the time I came to live in New York. By then, she'd set herself up as a fitness instructor on a mission to educate people not only about the physical aspects of health and fitness, but also about the importance and power of positive thinking. She certainly inspired me, and we trained hard together almost every day. Within a couple of months, I was in the best shape I'd ever been in. Voltage taught me so much about physical conditioning, health and nutrition. I've always tried to live by her manifesto of keeping a healthy mind as well as a healthy body.

There was only one slight blot on the otherwise beautiful Manhattan skyline and that was cash flow. Although Julian came from a wealthy family, he had very little money of his own and was only just starting to build up his savings while working on *Another World*. I, on the other hand, had been earning and saving money since the age of seven. With Dad being an accountant, I'd been taught to be sensible with my cash from a very young age. At this point, though, I was paying all the rent on our New York apartment and completely bankrolling our life together, plus paying the rent and bills on the London flat. Still, I told myself, it was all for the greater good. I was convinced that Julian was going to make it big, and I was happy to support him until he did – after all, he was getting no support from his family. Having lost my record deal, though, I was now dipping into my savings to keep us both afloat, and that's something I'd never had to do before.

There was also, of course, a wedding to organise, and after we'd set a date – the first Sunday of 1994 – there was a lot for a girl to do. I asked Kylie and Lori if they would be my bridesmaids, along with my friend Kirsten, who was Terry Blamey's girlfriend, and one of Julian's sisters, Deborah, which I thought might be a nice gesture. My young cousins, Tiffany, Lauren, Elisha and Brin, would be flower girls and pageboy. Then I had the dress to think about, which I went shopping for in New York. I'd love to have had Kylie or Mum with me on what should have been a fun shopping expedition, but, of course, they were both thousands of miles away, and I felt a little sad as I perused the wedding gowns all on my own.

Meanwhile, back in Australia, Mum and Dad were sorting out the venue and sending out the invitations, which had proved an interesting task when dealing with Lady McMahon. Mum had called her to arrange a get-together of the two families to discuss plans for the wedding.

'Ron and I could come up to Sydney to meet you,' Mum suggested to Sonia over the phone.

'Don't bother,' was the reply.

It was clear then that Julian's mum wasn't going to thaw, even with her son's impending wedding. As time went on there still was no RSVP from her, so we didn't know if she was going to turn up to the ceremony. Then, about a week before the wedding, Julian's sister told him that she wasn't going to be my bridesmaid – she couldn't do it. Of course I was sad, but I never held it against Deb, as I was pretty sure that her mother had had a hand in it, and there was nothing we could say that was going to change the way she felt about me.

The stress of the situation was more emotionally crippling for Julian, and I felt terrible for him. Coming from the loving, supportive background that I did, it was hard for me to accept that a family could behave this way, and I certainly couldn't comprehend why a mother would treat her son like she had. On several occasions, I hid in the bathroom to cry so Julian wouldn't see me. I wanted to be brave for him, and for him to believe things would be all right in the end.

When Julian and I flew into Melbourne from New York on Christmas Eve, 1993, the press and general excitement about the wedding had reached fever pitch. Of course, everybody wanted to know about the rumoured bitter feud between Lady McMahon and me. Everywhere I turned, people were asking me why she loathed me, and what I could possibly have done to deserve it. Everyone had got wind of Sonia's disdain at our engagement, but when people asked me if there was a problem, I always answered no.

'Not as far as I'm concerned,' I'd say.

It was true. I had no idea why it was that Lady McMahon was so against my relationship with Julian, and I never did find out. Some people who knew her said that she felt the marriage was a publicity stunt; others that she felt I wasn't the right sort of wife for her blue-blooded son. I felt the best way to deal with it was to be as dignified and quiet about the whole affair as I possibly could. After all, blowing it up into an even bigger furore would hurt only one person – Julian – and I didn't want that. He was already terribly upset about the state of affairs with his mum, and I hated seeing him like that. Julian's nature is to be cheeky and optimistic; he's a carefree spirit. I was quite prepared to put up and shut up in the hope that Sonia would resolve things with her son and make him happy.

Christmas that year was wonderful. It was the first time in ages that the family was all together, and everyone was so excited about the wedding. Mum and Dad had invited most of the extended family over: Nain was there, and Nana and Grand-pop, Mum's brothers and their kids. It was wonderful for me to spend time with Kylie and Brendan too.

Christmas Day itself was beautifully sunny. Mum and Dad now lived in a gorgeous house in Canterbury, and that day we all sat by the pool while the kids swam, and my uncle barbecued shrimp and chicken for our Christmas lunch. My friends from England, Terry Ronald and Laura Harding, had travelled out for the wedding, so I was happy that they spent Christmas day with us too. For a while, at least, I forgot about all the sadness surrounding the still unanswered RSVP from Julian's family. I guess I just had to accept that they wouldn't be there, especially now that his sister wasn't going to be a bridesmaid.

'Look, there's nothing we can do,' Dad had said to an anxious Julian and me on our arrival in Melbourne, 'so we'll just leave everything as it is. Their hotel suite is booked, and there will be a table set for them at the reception. If they come, they come; if they don't, they don't.' Dad's is quite often the voice of reason in times of madness, and this was one of those times.

A few nights before the big day, Kylie threw me a fabulously girly sleep-over-style hen party. She hired a hotel suite and all the girls wore pyjamas. We drank champagne and ate ice cream and popcorn and watched *An Affair to Remember* with Cary Grant and Deborah Kerr on video. It was simple and unfussy, and the perfect way to draw the curtains on my days as a single girl.

The wedding itself caused a complete media frenzy. A former child star turned pop star marrying the son of a former prime minister with a 'wicked mother-in-law' thrown in for good measure – it was the perfect front-page story. Held at the Grand Hyatt Hotel in Melbourne, the event had snowballed into the Aussie version of a royal wedding and all the TV news shows and magazines wanted an exclusive. Terry Blamey suggested we offer two magazines the rights to our wedding-day story: *Hello!* magazine in Europe, and *Woman's Day* in Australia. That way, all the press coverage at the event would be under our tight control, and the fees would help cover the cost of things like the extra security we needed to enjoy some privacy at the wedding and stop the rest of the paparazzi from having a field day.

On the morning of the wedding, I was buzzing with excitement from the moment I woke up. Like every girl on her wedding day, a big part of the thrill of it for me was getting my hair and make-up done and getting frocked-up – my tomboy days were a distant memory. The dress was pure ivory silk and decorated with elegantly embroidered roses, and my veil was held by a diamond-and-pearl tiara, which was shaped into interlocking hearts. In keeping with tradition, my tiara was new, and I'd borrowed a piece of blue ribbon from Lori, which I pinned to my dress. For something old, I wore an antique lace garter that Mum gave me.

When I walked into the beautifully decorated room filled with two hundred or so people – including Lady McMahon and Julian's two sisters – my whole body was tingling. Dad was gently holding my arm, and as we walked, slowly, down the red carpet, I caught Brendan's eye, which was filled with tears. As I got nearer to Julian, I could see that his face was lit up in a smile, and I suddenly realised that none of the bad stuff mattered. This was about Julian and me, and right then, in that Cinderella moment, nothing could touch us.

At the reception in the Savoy Ballroom, Kylie sang with the dance band for my bridal waltz, 'Fly Me To The Moon', and, after we'd cut the cake, she sang 'Celebration' with Terry Ronald. Eventually, I was up on stage too, still with my bridal gown on, singing 'We Are Family' as a special request from Brendan. Even my old *Young Talent Time* friend, Ronnie Burns, got up and did a few numbers. It was such a joyful party and I was so happy to look across the room and see Julian dancing with his mother. Maybe this would be a turning point for them after all.

The day after the high of the wedding, though, we all came back down to earth with a bump. First off, I got a call from my manager, Terry Blamey.

'One of the official wedding pictures has been stolen and sold to a rival magazine – *New Idea* has printed it on their front cover before it has been officially released!'

Great! *Woman's Day* were now going to be furious with us for letting their biggest rival get hold of one of their supposedly exclusive wedding photos. But how did they get it? Who the hell had stolen it? It was a complete nightmare and one I could well have done without. And yes, *Woman's Day* demanded to know why we'd promised them an exclusive on the wedding and then gone behind their backs to the competition. They thought I'd done the dirty on them with my own wedding pictures, and I had no idea how to convince them otherwise. When, on my wedding night, would I have had the time or the inclination?

The whole point of giving the exclusive rights to one magazine was to make the whole press side of things easier and to keep the rest of the media at bay. We'd had so much security around the hotel, too, it had to have been someone on the inside who had swiped the photo. Anyway, the fact of the matter was that the day after my wedding, when I was supposed to be basking in blissful afterglow, I was in a shit fight with a national magazine, trying to convince them that the leaked shot had been nothing to do with us, as they were now threatening to withhold the agreed fee and sue my father for allegedly failing to provide adequate security.

Meanwhile, I had bills from the wedding piling up around me, and I'd been counting on that money to pay for them. 'The pictures are no longer exclusive and that was the deal' was what they told Terry Blamey. To honour the agreement, my management had, in fact, organised intense security, and brought out a security expert from London to oversee the entire operation, but it wasn't enough. Despite the security at the wedding, investigations – that we paid for – later revealed that the negatives from the original film roll had been stolen from the photo-processing lab. We then took legal action against the lab for failing to provide adequate security. After a couple of stressful days and sleepless nights for all, the lawyers had a long lunch and agreed that both sides need not take any further action as *Woman's Day* had received at least twice as much publicity as they'd originally anticipated, and finally agreed to pay the fee.

The other twist at the end of the fairy tale was just as hard to take.

A day after the wedding, there were reports in a London newspaper that Lady McMahon hadn't wanted to attend our wedding at all, but was merely doing her duty. I was aware that she'd majestically swept in ten minutes late, and then point-blank refused to pose for any of the official wedding photographs. There had been quite a few raised eyebrows on the day, but I still hoped against hope things might turn around. It wasn't to be.

The report was full of quotes from close friends of Sonia, saying things like: 'Lady McMahon would have liked Julian to marry someone more socially acceptable' and 'she was never going to accept her son marrying a 'sexy' pop singer'. The paper even claimed that Lady McMahon had told a reporter she was 'hoping to break a leg' so she didn't have to go to the wedding. It was just a newspaper report, I know, but the substance of it was borne out by equally hurtful things she said about me to people who knew her over the course of my marriage to Julian. Nothing I did or said was ever going to change her mind.

Sonia McMahon had shown me that she was a lady in name only. In some ways, though, I feel I have to thank her. She helped me to discover a depth of character within myself that I never knew I had: a strength in silence – if you like, my inner 'Lady' – and it's an attribute I hold very dear these days.

Chapter 13

Fractures

I want to tell you now about the wonderful honeymoon period of my married life. I want to tell you about romance and togetherness and about the excitement of being newlyweds living happily together in Manhattan. Oh boy, do I wish I could tell you all of that.

During the first few months of 1994, I was back and forth between London and Manhattan, with Julian working steadily on *Another World* in New York. In May, Mushroom Records released a single in the UK, 'Get Into You', which had been written and produced by the One World production team. Once again, this single didn't set the charts alight, so the *Get Into You* album disappeared without a trace.

A month later, I was back doing another stint on *The Big Breakfast*, which led to hosting a show for the BBC called *Fan TC*. It was a TV pop quiz in which rival teams would answer questions about their particular idols. I was finding my feet as a TV presenter and I have to say I quite enjoyed it. The only downside to all this TV work was that I had to be away from Julian more and more regularly, and he wasn't happy about it. I knew only too well, though, that I needed to go where the work was at this point. My records hadn't been selling well and my savings were dwindling severely. I was still paying for virtually every-thing as far as Julian and I were concerned. I just kept telling myself, 'It's OK, Julian is going to be a huge television star *one day*, and then, *one day*, *he'll* look after *me* financially for a while.' As it turned out, only one half of that prophecy would come true – he did become a star.

As time went on, I started to feel guilty about being in London so much. Every time I had a few days free, I would fly back to New York to be with my husband. It got to the stage where I was flying across the ocean on Virgin Atlantic so often that I knew the names of almost all the cabin crew without looking at their name badges. Still, it was worth all the travelling to get back to Julian and our life in New York, and it would only be for a while, right?

A few months into our marriage, though, we started to argue when-ever I went back. I couldn't tell you what the rows were about; they weren't about anything specific or life altering, but they were there – niggling, angry fights that were growing more and more frequent. I heard alarm bells. I didn't understand it: why was this so hard? As far as I was concerned, the time we had together should have been so pre-cious, but it seemed that every five minutes we were bickering about something that wasn't important. Surely we hadn't been married long enough for these kinds of fractures to be appearing in our relationship already?

I decided that I needed to try harder. After all, I knew I wasn't per-fect. Maybe it was my fault for not being there enough; maybe I always seemed too tired when I was with him and he felt neglected. Whatever was going on, I gradually started to feel like I was juggling our mar-riage, our finances and my work in London, trying desperately to keep all the balls from crashing to the floor.

One of the problems was that while Julian had loved the romantic notion of proposing and all the anticipation and thrill of a wedding, he didn't seem prepared for the everyday nuts and bolts of matrimony. Marriage is not one event or a party: it's a whole life's work. But Julian was still a party boy at heart, and as much as I truly loved that side of him, it definitely wasn't helping matters as the rifts got wider. On top of all that, I had a nagging feeling as the months went by that there was something else going on, and that's when the fractures turned to chasms.

Julian was very friendly with an actress who worked on the show with him, and whenever I got back from London, I'd notice little things dotted around the apartment that I knew Julian would never buy: usually fresh flowers or little potted plants, but also little homely objects that I knew hadn't come from him.

'Oh, where did this come from?' I might say. Or, 'Nice flowers, who gave you those?'

The answer was always the same: they were from his female co-star. Some of these little gifts ended up in our bedroom, which made me feel even more uncomfortable, and it seemed strange to me that this girl would be buying personal little gifts for someone else's husband. Whenever I was away in London, dark thoughts started to occupy me more and more. I tried so hard to sweep them away, telling myself that you have to have trust in a marriage, but it got harder. Once you've set your mind on that train of thought, it's a ride that won't stop, and pretty soon I was driving myself nuts. Typically, I never voiced these concerns to anyone, although my London flatmate, Laura, could surely tell something wasn't right. I didn't want to talk about it – not even to my family.

What was stranger still is that I didn't confront Julian about it when I was in New York with him. I'd dip my toe in the murky water and casually ask the odd question about 'her' here and there. Whenever I did, there was such awkwardness between us that it would set my poor mind racing all over again. Then we'd spend some time together, have a nice dinner or do something romantic, and I'd tell myself I was being stupid and paranoid, and I had to pull myself together. Once away from him again, though, the feelings would creep back. Relationships conducted by long-distance phone calls are never a good idea, as I've found to my cost over the years. If one person says the wrong thing in the wrong tone of voice, it can mean a whole world of insecurity and sadness once the receiver has gone down, and an isolated voice on the end of a telephone is no substitute for being able to look into someone's eyes.

What I couldn't take was Julian's growing indifference to our marriage and to me. I'd hoped and expected to go into a life partnership in which we had fun together and enjoyed being in one another's company. If we had to be apart sometimes and it was tough, then we'd try that little bit harder to make it work. Sadly, in the end, Julian didn't seem to want to try at all.

After one particularly horrible fight over the phone, I remember thinking: 'This is *not* it! This isn't anything I wanted it to be and it's never going to be.' In addition to the fights, there was a great divide between us in terms of our differing notions of family, and I couldn't see that ever changing. So the cynics had been right after all – Sonia had been right after all – we were from two different worlds and we should never have tried to merge them. I guess at first I'd naively thought that marriage was about two people, but it isn't: it's about how two people fit into one another's worlds, and that encompasses their families and their careers and all that goes with them. Julian was never going to be able to share his world or his family with me like I had shared mine with him, and he didn't seem to want to anyway. It was time to walk away.

Now I had to face Mum and Dad – at least over the phone – and admit that my marriage had failed. I had to pick myself up and try to carry on working. There was so much to think about – a whole future, in fact, and not the one I'd planned. Mum and Dad said all the things that I'd expected them to say when we spoke.

'Is this really what you want? Are you sure you couldn't try to make it work?'

Dad completely laid it on the line. 'Dannii, if it's really that serious, then you're talking about divorce papers, and that makes it *very* official. You have to be certain about this.'

But I was certain. It was such an overwhelming feeling. I was in a bad place; it wasn't going to get any better and I needed to get out of it. I couldn't have been any more sure by then.

Back at my flat in Fulham I felt lonely. I'd sit and stare at the oppressive walls of my bedroom for hours, unable to figure out how or why things could have gone so wrong with Julian, unable to move and without any inclination to pick up the phone and call someone to ask for help. I felt like I was in an enormous hole that I couldn't scramble out of, and my work, as always, was my only salvation. Unfortunately, that particular rug was about to be pulled from under me as well.

Mushroom Records announced, halfway through recording a new album with me, that they were terminating my contract. People weren't interested in Dannii the pop star any more, and they didn't feel it was worth continuing. All at once I'd lost my husband and the only other thing that kept me going and made me feel alive – my music. What's more, after years of financial stability and careful saving, I got the wake-up call that not only was I completely and utterly broke, I was terribly in debt. I felt like an idiot.

Dad had warned me time and time again: 'Dannii, London and New York are two expensive cities and you're living in both of them and spending a fortune flying back and forth between them. You need to keep an eye on your spending.'

'It's OK, Dad. Don't worry,' I would reply. 'Julian is starting to earn now. The money will be there and we'll be OK.'

But, of course, it never was there, and now it was too late and my money was all gone. How could I have been so stupid?

It's still hard to put into words how I felt during the summer of 1995. It was as if somebody had drawn a huge black line under my entire life to that point; it was as if a bomb had dropped and blown everything around me to bits. When I finally came up to survey the damage, I found that there was absolutely nothing left.

I was twenty-three.

Chapter 14

Saved by the Bunny

In the months that followed the marriage break-up, I suppose you could say I was functioning. True, I felt like I'd hit rock bottom, but I wasn't scribbling suicide notes or about to jump off a bridge any time soon. I guess that's mainly because of all the hearty support I had from my family. What do people do when their world falls apart around them and they don't have that kind of love and support? I can't imagine.

When everything around me had gone, and the house of cards had fallen flat, it wasn't my career or the money I cared about, or even keeping a roof above my head – it was the heartache that was so hard to take. That was what kept me up at night and that was what tore me apart. I knew I could always get off my butt and make money at something – anything – but no one could help me put my heart back together.

I was all too aware that I wasn't looking after myself properly but it didn't really seem to matter. I was hardly eating and I couldn't sleep properly. I suppose I was struggling with the stark realisation that nobody wanted me: not my record company, not my husband and definitely not the public.

Sure, I tried not to get too 'woe is me' about it, but as the weeks went on the only time I saw my name in print or heard it mentioned on TV or radio was as the less successful Minogue sister: Dannii in Kylie's shadow, Dannii's bitter jealousy over Kylie's continued success, Dannii's fashion faux pas and Kylie's triumphs. Hey, isn't Kylie bloody fabulous, everyone? And isn't Dannii tragic? I can tell you, it's not easy to be publicly pitted against someone you love and admire. It hurts. The truth of the matter is that I never felt like I was competing with my sister. I'll say it again: *I NEVER FELT LIKE I WAS COMPETING WITH KYLIE.* I just wanted everything I did to be the absolute best it could be.

Although I got very tired of the constant comparisons, and doing interview after interview in which I'd be asked more questions about her than I would about myself, it wasn't because I hated her and felt jealousy towards her. It was the opposite, in fact. I was always the first one Kylie would excitedly play her new recordings to for an honest opinion, and she'd always invite me down to the dress runs of her concert tours, knowing she'd get a candid critique from me. The truth is: I am and always have been so very proud of Kylie, and she is of me. I think all the Dannii-bashing headlines often hurt Kylie more than they hurt me.

One Saturday night at around this time, I decided to go and watch Kylie play a gig at London's G-A-Y club. At the time, G-A-Y was the biggest gay club in Europe, and certainly one of the most popular. It was, and still is today, run by the well-known club entrepreneur Jeremy Joseph. I've played the club many times over the years, and it's always the most fantastic crowd. Getting my glad rags on and heading out to see my big sis strutting her stuff was just what I needed to drag me out of the doldrums. I remember picking out a favourite orange vintage maxi-dress and slipping it on, then doing my hair and make-up, trying to look forward to a fun night out for the first time in weeks. Once I got to the venue, there were a couple of press photographers around who took a few shots of me before I went inside and headed upstairs to Kylie's dressing room to wish her luck. Then I went back down to the VIP balcony to watch the show, and did manage to have a good time.

The following week one of the pictures snapped of me that evening appeared in a magazine next to a picture of me from a few years before in the same orange dress – and it sent me reeling in shock. On the left was a picture of a curvy, smiling young girl with so much hope in her eyes, while on the right was a skeletal, drawn, unhappy woman whose faint smile was a lie and whose eyes said nothing. Friends had told me I was too thin, but it was only when I cast my eyes over the two hugely conflicting images of myself that I fully realised the physical toll the past few months had taken. The lack of sleep, the lack of food – it was all there staring viciously up at me. I sat with my mouth wide open, unable to tear my eyes away from the page. It was, as they say, a real wake-up call.

I had to do something, and I had to do it fast. I needed to get a few good meals inside me and I needed to stick my head out of the door and find some more work. 'Show a bit of resilience, girl,' I told myself. But what could I do? Apart from presenting *The Big Breakfast* road shows around the country that summer, work offers were pretty thin on the ground.

Out of the blue, through Terry Blamey's office, came a very unexpected and, I have to say, somewhat surprising proposal. 'You've had an offer to do a magazine shoot,' Terry told me. 'A cover shoot, in fact – for Australian *Playboy*.'

'What?'

'You can choose the photographer, the location, the look of the shots – in fact, you can have complete artistic control, they want you to do it that much,' Terry said. 'And the fee is very, very good!'

Of course, this meant I'd be naked: however tasteful and beautiful the shots ended up, we were talking about getting my kit off for the whole world to see. Exposing my body in exchange for a large cash sum seemed a million light years away from being a smiling, all-singing, all-dancing child star. How had it come to this? Could I do it? Was this all there was from here on in? There were so many conflicting thoughts and feelings going around in my head. Naturally, Mum and Dad didn't want me to do it.

Dad, as ever, was the angel of conscience on my shoulder. 'You need to think about this, Dannii,' he said, sternly. 'Once you've done it – if you do it – these pictures will be out there . . . *for ever*. You should think long and hard about it first.'

When push came to shove, I was in the shit financially and that's all there was to it. I couldn't turn it down.

'I really don't have a choice, Dad,' I told him tearfully when I'd finally made my decision. 'This was my mistake and only I can get myself out of this mess. I'm so sorry!'

Still, on Dad's advice, before I signed on the dotted line with *Playboy*, I tried asking Julian one more time if he could perhaps see his way clear to paying me back some of the huge amount of money I'd spent on the two of us when we were together. After all, apart from keeping him afloat while he got his career got off the ground, I'd also paid for any little luxury he desired. Surely he would help me out now.

But it never happened. Dad eventually told me that he and Mum had met up with Julian at the Sunset Marquis Hotel in Hollywood some time after the break-up, because they were deeply concerned about my health and stability. Julian told them that he was very sad about the split. Afterwards, though, I never heard another word about it nor did I see any money, despite Dad providing Julian's agents with the details of exactly how much I'd spent.

I wouldn't ask my family for money. I felt like I'd be burdening them with the fallout of my own stupid mistake. The photos I decided I could live with; what I couldn't live with was the thought of adding to Mum and Dad's stress over the marriage break-up and my state of mind. My pride wouldn't allow it.

I chose a photographer called Adam Watson to do the shoot. He'd previously taken some pictures of me a year or so before for a very chic Aussie magazine called *Not Only Black and White*. I thought he'd captured me beautifully and in a way that I felt no other photographer had. I trusted Adam. When we got together to discuss ideas for the shoot, we decided that the confines of a studio weren't at all what we wanted. We both loved the idea of shooting in the desert: the rawness of the landscape and the sense of freedom we'd capture there sounded perfect.

We took a car from LA with a crew in tow, and eventually left the city smog behind us, travelling for hours through the gorgeous desolation of the Nevada desert. I remember we played Alanis Morissette's *Jagged Little Pill* album and the Oasis album *What's the Story (Morning Glory)* back to back as we went. Gradually, I began to feel like a mountain was being lifted off my shoulders. As I stared quietly out of the car window, the wonderful isolation of the desert washed over me, and it occurred to me that the landscape all around me looked like some sort of wonderfully fresh and blank canvas. Perhaps it was. Perhaps this was where I got to start all over again. Why not?

Of course, taking one's clothes off in front of a group of relative strangers is not the easiest thing I've ever done, but, strangely, as the shoot progressed, this feeling of shaking off the dust of the past year grew and grew. It was such fun finding all the great locations to get the best and coolest shots that we could, and I found the nudity surprisingly and wonderfully liberating.

We'd stopped in a very cool vintage store before we left LA and bought some cowboy boots and a beat-up cowboy hat. In one of the shots that Adam set up, I was wearing just the hat and boots while kicking along through the dust with the sun slowly setting behind me. It felt absolutely beautiful being in the middle of nowhere with the warm sunset glowing on my skin. When I closed my eyes for a moment, I was suddenly a little girl running around naked in our back garden in Wantirna, with the very same sun that had shone on me then shining on me now, and I felt such comfort, such relief.

When my issue of *Playboy* came out in Australia, it sold out so fast that the company almost went into meltdown trying to print enough copies to fill the shelves again.

I thought the pictures Adam took were tasteful and gorgeous. The thing I remember being most happy about was the fact that so many of my girlfriends, who, let's face it, wouldn't normally be buying a magazine like *Playboy*, rushed out to get it and all called me with the same reaction.

'Wow! These are amazing pictures. You must be so happy with these. You look beautiful, Dannii.'

And I *was* happy. Even Mum and Dad were relieved that the shots were not what they were expecting, and thought that their youngest daughter, despite being naked, looked rather lovely.

It's funny, isn't it? People say that magazines like *Playboy* exploit women, but in my case the exact opposite was true. Being able to get naked and look beautiful after feeling so worthless for such a long time gave me back my long lost self-esteem. The magazine gave me complete freedom to do what I wanted to do, and look exactly how I wanted to look, which is rare in any section of the entertainment industry. In addition, I had total control over what photos went to print. In the weeks leading up to the shoot, I hadn't had control over anything in my life – my thoughts, my feelings, my sleep patterns – absolutely nothing. Now I felt I was back; I could breathe again. Far from exploiting me, *Playboy* pulled me from the water just when I was about to go under.

I'd been saved by the bunny.

Chapter 15

Where the Hell Did She Crawl Back From?

Several months later, when I picked up the keys to my new rented apartment in London's Battersea, it seemed like I was moving on with my life and putting the spectre of the last couple of years behind me. It had been love at first sight the minute I walked through the door to view the place, and somehow I knew I was meant to be there. The apartment had panoramic views across London and a wonderfully airy feel about it. It was high up, which I always prefer, and I could look out over the river Thames – a real bonus.

I'd been pretty much flat out with lots of television work before that, which fortunately continued into 1996, with more *Fan TC*, more *Big Breakfast* road shows and a new children's Saturday-morning show called *It's Not Just Saturday*, which ran for sixteen weeks from January. It seemed that even though I wasn't making records any more, the bulk of my work was still in the UK.

I decided that if I was going to be staying around, I might as well find a place to rent where I'd be happy. There were too many bad memories associated with my flat in Fulham. Once Laura decided to move on, I couldn't bear to stay there any longer.

At the end of that year came two more TV jobs: a kids' adventure show called *Scoop*, and *Electric Circus*, a magazine-style entertainment show in which I got to interview people such as Val Kilmer, Diana Ross and Chris O'Donnell. I was working very hard, and was finally emerging from the financial wasteland I'd found myself in at the end of my marriage.

I managed to scrape together the money to buy a couple of what some might call 'luxury items' – as my friend Terry Ronald discovered when he came to escort me to the BBC one morning. I'd been asked to present *Top of the Pops* for two weeks in May 1997, which was very exciting after appearing on it so many times as a performer. Terry turned up at the apartment to accompany me in the car.

'Come and talk to me while I put my make-up on, Terry,' I shouted from the bathroom.

I hadn't seen him for a while so we had lots of gossip to catch up on, and, as usual, I was running slightly late. As Terry stood in the bathroom doorway, though, I noticed him doing something I wouldn't normally expect him to do – he was staring attentively at my chest. I looked up at him.

'What?' I said.

'What do you mean, what?' Terry replied. 'I was just looking at . . . noticing . . . Dannii, where exactly did *they* come from?'

He was now pointing directly at my breasts.

'Oh, these!' I laughed. 'These are brand new, darling, and they feel really natural. Do you wanna meet the girls and have a feel?'

Terry nodded, slowly, with a hint of fear in his eyes, and I pulled open my shirt. Then he put his hands, gingerly, on my bare breasts, and smiled.

'They're absolutely lovely,' he said, grinning. 'God, how many guys would pay good money to do exactly what I'm doing now?'

He was still nodding appreciatively and cupping my boobs when my manager, Terry Blamey, walked unexpectedly through the open front door of my apartment and stumbled upon what must have looked a rather bizarre situation.

'Fuck me, I've seen it all now,' Terry Blamey said.

Terry Ronald and I dissolved into fits of laughter.

I'd always been curvy before, you see, and I didn't mind it. Then, of course, my weight plummeted after the break-up with Julian. Once I got healthy again, I sort of found a happy medium. This meant I was a lot slimmer than I'd once been, so my boobs disappeared and, quite frankly, I missed them. While I was in New York the previous month, I did something about it – and that's all there was to it.

'Sorry about that,' I smiled as I breezed past my wide-eyed manager and exited the apartment for the *Top of the Pops* studio. 'I wasn't expecting you to walk in.'

Terry Blamey just laughed.

It wasn't only my body that had gone through a bit of a change in early 1997, my image had too. Now, with shoulder-length platinum-blonde hair, I felt almost like a new girl. To complete the revamp, I received an interesting and truly thrilling offer.

Steve Allen was the A&R manager at Warner Bros Records, and he approached Terry Blamey with the idea of me doing a new album with them. It had been two years since I'd done any recording. I was keen to hear what ideas they had about making Dannii Minogue a saleable commodity in the world of pop music once more. Steve was very enthusiastic and saw in me a ready-made pop star. He had real faith in me as a recording artist, which was refreshing. He wanted to make an album of up-to-the-minute electronic pop that nodded to the current trend in club dance music, using a team of young and as then unknown producers. It's amazing now when I think back on some of the producers who cut their teeth on that album: Brian Higgins, who went on to write 'Believe' for Cher and then founded Xenomania, who write and produce all the Girls Aloud records; Brian Rawlings and the team at Metrophonic, who have had huge success over the years; and Ian Masterson, a fresh-faced Irish boy who was to become one of my closest friends and colleagues.

Ian worked out of a studio in Bow, East London, that was dungeon-like, to say the least. He seemed highly intelligent and funny, and more than a little nervous when I turned up at the dimly lit studio with Terry

Ronald to record vocals on some songs he'd written. This was basically Ian's first proper production job, as he was fresh out of Cambridge University, and had come to the attention of Steve Allen after remixing a Pet Shop Boys record. Steve had decided that Ian's inventive approach was exactly what my new album needed, and he was right. Ian has a great pop sensibility and the two songs he wrote for me were truly great. The first was called 'Someone New', which was a huge, bouncy Eurodance number; the other was called 'Disremembrance', which has a beautiful, haunting melody and has remained a firm favourite with my fans across the years.

After only a couple of hours in the studio that first day, Ian, Terry and I were cracking dirty jokes and laughing together like old friends. Since then, Ian Masterson has remained my friend and musical director, and has written and mixed countless songs for me, becoming a kind of third musical musketeer.

I wasn't quite so sure about some of the other songs I recorded during that period. Producer Brian Higgins had written a song called 'All I Wanna Do', which I thought was OK when I heard it, but I wasn't exactly jumping up and down about it. Everyone else, however, thought it was a hit. Steve Allen and Brian Higgins thought it was the record that was going to put me back on the map, and even my manager loved it. I wasn't convinced, and I was reticent about singing it right up until the day of the recording session at a little studio in Berwick Street, Soho.

'I'm still not sure,' I said to Terry Ronald, while Brian set up the microphone and then started running the track. 'I like it. I'm just not sure it's right for *me*.'

'It's a hit, Dan,' Terry said. 'It's so good for you, and you should give it a go. I think it's going to work great with your voice on it.'

Brian nodded. 'Let's just try it,' he said.

Well, thankfully, I did try it, and 'All I Wanna Do' went hurtling to number four in the charts on its release in August 1997; my 'comeback' single was my highest chart position to date. You can't *always* be right, you know.

*

It was around this time that I dipped my toe back into the hazardous waters of romance. I started dating a handsome celebrity photographer from Manchester named Steve Shaw. Steve had photographed me for *Sky* magazine, and I found his down-to-earth, northern humour and unpretentious manner quite sexy. He was in the entertainment industry but seemed unaffected by it, and I liked that. Steve was tall and slim with spiky, light brown hair and twinkly eyes. We swapped numbers during the *Sky* photo shoot, hooking up to go to a party together a few days later. I guess that was the start of it. I was wary at first, I suppose, as I felt more than a little bruised after Julian, but I convinced myself that it was about time I had some fun again and I wanted to be with someone. Steve was very nice to have around, and very easy to *be* around.

I'm sure, though, that during our first few months of dating, Steve would have described me as difficult, to say the least. I was trying my best to relax into the idea of being in a relationship, but my war wounds made any sort of commitment to a man seem terrifying. Still, we did manage to have a lot of fun together and Steve got on with my friends, which is always a bonus with a new beau as far as I'm concerned. I admired his artistic eye and his talent for photography, so when he mentioned that he'd be interested in shooting the video for my upcoming single, I thought it was a fantastic idea – after all, I'd always wanted to have a crack at co-directing a video clip, too, and this could be the perfect opportunity.

The next single after 'All I Wanna Do' was called 'Everything I Wanted' and was a song I'd co-written. It was a moody, swirling, dark track and Steve and I had the idea of shooting the clip on old Super 8 film. Once again, I found myself back in the Nevada desert for the filming. This time, Steve and I decided to drive from LA to Las Vegas in a 1960s Mustang convertible – not especially clever in the middle of a scorching desert with no air-conditioning, I grant you, but at least we looked cool!

We didn't have much of a budget to speak of, so it was just the two of us and a cine-camera. We never knew how good or bad the footage was going to look once we got back to London. There was no digital playback or anything of that sort with this type of film: it had to be developed. I did my own hair and make-up and threw some clothes together from one of the vintage stores we passed; it was all very much ad hoc. I trusted Steve's eye, and his instincts, and we ended up with some great, grainy black-and-white footage of me diving into a motel pool, roller-skating along a desolate-looking side street, and, of course, driving through the desert seductively lip-synching the chorus of the song with my hair in pigtails. It was all very sensual and evocative, and I absolutely loved the end result. Of course, heading across the Nevada desert in a classic Mustang with your sexy photographer boyfriend isn't the worst way to spend a weekend, and I have to say the whole experience was pretty romantic and a lot of fun. Steve and I grew closer after that trip and, finally, I started to relax and get used to the fact that I had a man in my life again, and a good one, it seemed.

The new album, simply called *Girl*, was released in September 1997 and the reviews were great. The *Smash Hits* review said: 'If you like your dance music to come with a touch of jazz, a load of great tunes and bags of attitude, you'll love this!' Even in the States, tastemakers like Larry Flick – who was the dance-music guru on *Billboard* magazine – were really excited about the album. Suddenly, I was thrown into the limelight as a pop star all over again, performing on TV music shows and promoting the album all over Europe, Asia and Australia.

I found myself in Brisbane on one memorable day of promotion, doing a record signing in the large department store, Myer. I was with my manager and his then-girlfriend, Rachel, and it was a pretty hectic scene, with fans and press all trying to grab a few words with me and a picture or two. For some reason, the press seemed unusually forceful that day, all pushing to get to the front of the bustling crowd as I signed copies of *Girl* at a table that had been set up in the store.

Suddenly, one guy shoved a TV camera in my face and said, 'So what do you have to say about the death of Michael Hutchence then, Dannii?'

What was he saying? Michael Hutchence, the rock star, was dead?

Michael Hutchence, my sister's ex-boyfriend? I looked over at Terry Blamey and Rachel, who looked as bemused as I was.

'What the fuck are you talking about?' Rachel snapped at the reporter.

I couldn't even speak.

'He was found dead in a hotel room in Sydney an hour or so ago,' the enthusiastic hack went on.

I didn't believe it. I hadn't heard anything on the radio on the way to the store and Michael was a young man – he couldn't possibly be dead. I went on with the signing as best I could, but I was in shock. When we got back to the hotel, Terry Blamey made some calls and confirmed that it was, in fact, true, and I went straight to the bathroom and threw up.

Later, I tried to imagine what Kylie must be feeling, and I knew I had to call her as soon as I possibly could: she and Michael had been so close once. Then I thought about Michael's current girlfriend, my former *Big Breakfast* colleague Paula Yates, with whom Michael had a very young daughter, and I felt even sadder. What on earth must they be going through? And how could something like this happen to someone who supposedly had the world at his feet? It was as confusing as it was tragic, and very hard to come to terms with.

Around this time, I went on another trip with Terry Blamey – this time to Japan. I discovered that trying to accommodate the local customs sometimes came at a high price. On this trip, I was literally flying in, performing one gig and then flying out again to continue promotion somewhere else. The gig was at a club called Velfarre, which is in the Roppongi district of Tokyo and had proclaimed itself the largest disco in Asia. I'd heard great things about the place and I was looking forward to performing there with my dancers.

I'd heard that Warner Records in Japan were very excited about me coming over, which meant that almost as soon as we landed in Tokyo, we had a record-company dinner to attend. I was tired after the flight, but the place we were going for dinner was close to our hotel, so I freshened up and hauled it together enough to look as bright and fresh for my Japanese hosts as I possibly could: eyes and teeth, Dannii, eyes and teeth!

Anyway, all the heads of the company were there and it was very grand. Terry Blamey and I were escorted upstairs to a private area in the beautiful restaurant, where we were assigned our own waitress each for the evening, then we sat down at the table, surrounded by all the nattily dressed bosses of the record label. My waitress was stunningly beautiful: dressed in full kimono, her delicate features were painted like an exquisite doll. As she glided towards me, she smiled and bowed her head, gently asking what I would like to drink.

'I'd like some sake, please?' I said, and off she went.

Now, there are many customs surrounding the serving and drinking of this traditional rice wine, but one of them is you never pour your own – it must be poured for you, even if you are the host. So there I am with a tiny little sake cup, scarcely one gulp big, chatting away to the guys around the table and thoroughly enjoying myself, while my gorgeous waitress shuffles back and forth to the table, replenishing my sake as soon as I've finished it, which is basically after every sip. As the evening wears on, more and more people join us at the table, and every time somebody new sits down, there's yet another bloody toast and everybody gets their minuscule cups refilled.

'Kanpai!' someone seems to be shouting every five minutes, and, not wanting to seem rude, I'd have another sip of sake.

'How many people actually work at this record company?' I said to a slightly blurry-looking Terry Blamey at one point, but he just shrugged. I wondered why I felt so strange. It must be the jet lag, I told myself.

Quite suddenly, though, I decided that I simply had to go back to the hotel – right then and there. As Terry decided to stay for a bit longer, I headed off, alone and unsteady, to find the car that was taking me. Once back outside the hotel, things started to go horribly wrong. It was like a moment out of Hunter S. Thompson's *Fear and Loathing in Las Vegas* with the whole landscape moving violently around me, and me completely unable to coordinate my body in any way, shape or form.

'Okay, girl, pull yourself together,' I told myself as I entered the hotel lobby. 'It's a long way to those elevators at the end of the reception area and you have to get there without falling down.'

The carpet across the lobby was a ferocious pattern of huge coloured spots, and definitely not what you want to see spread before you when you're as drunk as I clearly was – looking down at it was making me want to hurl. I was also aware that the lobby was packed with people, so my next idea of crawling along the floor to get to the elevator was also a no-no. I took off my shoes, and followed my nose, most probably zigzagging across the hotel's luxurious foyer until I reached the lift safely.

Once I'd reached the floor my room was on, things didn't get any better. The corridor was very dimly lit and I couldn't remember where the hell my room was or its number – only its general direction along the corridor. Still, at least there was no one in the corridor as far as I could see, so I dropped to all fours and started to crawl along the floor, dragging myself up to each and every door to try the key as I went. Even if I'd been able to remember the number of my room, by this stage I couldn't see the numbers on the doors or the keys.

I found my room – God only knows how. The weight of my body against the door sent it flying open, leaving me prostrate and only half in the room with my legs sticking out like the Wicked Witch of the West after Dorothy's house has landed on top of her in *The Wizard of Oz*. I made one more concerted effort to crawl to the bathroom and I thanked God and all the saints when I felt the cold tiles beneath me.

I guess I don't need to go into too much detail about what happened next, but it wasn't pretty. The next day, when Terry arrived to collect me for a sound check at the venue, I couldn't move, see or function in any useful way, so the sound check wasn't going to happen. Terry ended up leaving me in my hotel room with a slab of Hi-C, which is a Japanese Lucozade equivalent, and told me to get as much of it down me as I could while he went to check out the venue with the dancers. I did eventually manage to haul myself up and do the show at Velfarre that night. Since I left Japan the very next morning, I didn't get to see much of beautiful Tokyo on that trip. I'd had my head stuck over a toilet bowl for most of it.

*

The promotion I did went very well but, to be honest, I was kind of shocked that I was back in the game and that the singles were so successful. I got the feeling people in the music industry were thinking, 'Crikey! Dannii Minogue! Where the hell did she crawl back from?' I felt more sure of myself though. This time, I had some life experience behind me, which is always a plus when you're an artist of any kind. I could contribute to lyrics and bring something more to the table creatively, and I felt good about that. I had stuff to talk about . . . *plenty* of stuff.

On a slightly more superficial level, the new platinum-blonde look was working well for me too, and I found myself back in the 'most sexy' polls, and appearing on the covers of magazines for the first time in a long while. It was the men's magazines like *FHM*, rather than the teen publications, that seemed to favour me now, which I guess didn't really surprise me, given my blonde locks and my rather prominent new assets.

Along with the change of image, I'd also decided that I wanted to put a live band together for TV appearances and gigs, rather than just having a bunch of sexy dancers behind me. Ian Masterson thought it was a great idea, and he and Terry Ronald called up some of their musical mates, including percussionist Steve Smith, guitarist James Nisbet and female backing vocalist Mitch Stevens. Terry and Ian decided that they both wanted to be in the live band as well, so they joined on backing vocals and keyboards respectively. When we played the Gay Pride concert on Clapham Common in the summer of 1997 under clear blue skies and in front of thousands of people, we went down a storm. I was overwhelmed by people's reaction to my new sound and my new songs. It felt fabulous to be back doing what I'd always loved more than anything else – music. To top off a great year, 'All I Wanna Do' went gold in Australia in November. It seemed like Dannii the pop star was well and truly back.

Chapter 16

Unleashed at Last!

Once I had my band together, Terry Blamey started to get more and more live gigs for me, and a lot of them were UK university balls, which was great fun. The audiences there were wild and enthusiastic, but predominantly testosterone-fuelled boys who had no doubt been pawing over pictures of me in *Sky* magazine or *FHM*, and weren't always as interested in the music as they might have been. The first thing that I always noticed at the university gigs was that the boys were all rammed down the front against the stage in their dinner jackets, grinning like sharks, while their party-frocked dates stood grumpily at the back with their arms folded. It made us all laugh.

'Jesus, it smells like a boys' locker room out there,' Terry Ronald remarked before we took to the stage one night.

'Well, you should know, love,' came the quick retort from Ian.

As well as the universities, we did some fantastic nightclub dates up and down the country, and I performed songs from the new album, as well as updated versions of some oldies like 'This Is It' and 'Love and Kisses', which always went down a treat. As my musical director, Ian found a way to fuse the club dance sounds of *Girl* with the live band, which made the shows sound exciting, and I loved getting up close and personal with the audience – all sweating and jumping up and down while singing along to the hits. I decided that as soon as I got the chance, I wanted to put on my own tour around the theatres and I approached my manager on the subject.

'It's very expensive, mounting a tour,' he warned me, but I didn't care.

'I really want to do it,' I said. 'I love playing live and we'll make it work – let's go for it!'

Before anything could get underway, though, there was something else in the offing that I couldn't say no to. SEL, a large sports and entertainment management company, had got together with a producer called John Frost to devise a new take on the musical *Grease* – performing it as an arena spectacular. The show was to travel all across Australia and play in all the state capitals' arenas with a centre stage, surrounded by a 10,000-strong crowd. There would be a live band suspended on a stage, high above the performers' heads, underneath which would be the lighting rig, and the main stage would have seventeen different moving hydraulic parts that went up, down and around.

Terry Blamey excitedly told me that I had been offered top billing, playing the lead role of Sandy.

I couldn't believe it, and my mind flipped back to the house in Wantirna, when Kylie and I would jump around the lounge, doing the dance routine to 'Greased Lightning'.

But Sandy? Sandy? Surely not . . . I was always the bad girl, no?

From the first meeting with the producers, I was adamant. 'But I don't want to play Sandy,' I told them. 'I want to be Rizzo! That part is much more me!'

The producers disagreed.

'No, no, Dannii. We want you to have top billing in the show, obviously,' they told me, 'and Sandy is the lead role, so that's the role you should take.'

I was adamant, though, and asked Terry Blamey to fight my corner.

'I see myself as Rizzo, I've always wanted to play her. So whoever's playing Sandy is playing Sandy, but if they want me to do the show, I'll be playing Rizzo, and they'll give me the top billing.'

I guess Terry didn't leave them much choice but to agree, and when I finally took on the character in rehearsals, absolutely everybody said I was right for the role: they couldn't possibly imagine me as Sandy.

It was one more childhood wish fulfilled.

There were some old friends working on *Grease*, too: Craig McLaughlin, whom I'd worked with on *Home and Away*, played the part of Danny, and another former *Young Talent Time* team member, Jane Scali, played the part of Sandy. In fact, the whole crew, from the musical director to the ensemble dancers and everyone in between, was fantastic on this production and we all worked together brilliantly. It was a very happy cast and crew.

Rehearsals and preparation for the opening of the show went pretty smoothly, but on the first night disaster struck big time. During the dress rehearsal on the afternoon of the opening, half of the moving stage wasn't working and everybody started freaking out – it was a catastrophe. We had press and TV people coming to review the show, as well as friends, family, ticket-holders and invited celebrities.

As the opening night was in my home town, Melbourne, Mum and Dad had booked a limo to bring my grandparents, who were excited about coming. Half an hour before the show, I was made-up, mic'd up, wigged-up and ready to go on, hoping against hope that the technical problems would be resolved before curtain-up. It wasn't looking good, though: one of the most fabulous and key pieces of the set was the car in the 'Greased Lightning' scene, which, theoretically, came onstage up a ramp and lit up during the number. Because the stage wouldn't move, they couldn't get the car onto it. The consensus among the producers and the crew was that the show couldn't possibly go on. By this time, there were 10,000 people in the arena, all cheering and clapping and dying to see what we had in store for them, so I marched up to one of the anxious-looking producers to have my say about the situation.

'This show is going on!' I said. 'My grandparents are on their way – in a limo – and I'm not going to disappoint them!'

Everybody in the cast felt the same. When it became clear that the mechanical stage wasn't going to budge for love nor money, the powers-that-be decided that we could go on and perform a broken-down version of the show. This meant it would be more like a recital of the script with all the songs and as much dancing and costume changes as we could do without any complicated stage blocking. There was no time to rehearse this, however, so we decided to do it as best we could. Craig went out onto the stage and addressed the eager crowd, explaining to them what had happened, but insisting that if they were willing to use their imagination, we were all dressed up and ready to perform for them. No, it wouldn't be the show they were hoping to see, but as well as tonight, everyone would get a ticket to come back and see the show again when it was up and running properly. Amazingly, nobody left the arena and away we went.

It turned into quite a night. Because of the situation with the set, there were lots of funny mistakes punctuated by giggles, plus some very comical asides and ad libs from the cast members during the show about invisible cars and the like, which had the audience laughing. The whole crowd was with us – we could feel it – and the support and reaction we got was truly incredible. The audience was there to have a good time and we had them in the palms of our hands. My friend Judy was there that night, and she came back to see the show a few weeks later and loved it.

'But that opening night was exceptional,' she told me. 'And I'm so glad I was there!'

During a very short break in the tour, I dashed back to London to perform with my band at the Royal Albert Hall, opening the show for the recently re-formed Culture Club. Apart from the thrill of being a supporting act for my childhood heroes, it had been a dream of mine to play at the prestigious London venue and I wasn't going to miss out, despite the fact that I'd have to fly to London, rehearse and perform the show, and then tear back to Australia for the next *Grease* performance, all in less than a week. Besides that, I'd also get to spend some time with my boyfriend, Steve. I'd been missing him terribly, despite having a great time on the *Grease* tour.

The Albert Hall show was phenomenal, and I had a blast, but the lightning return trip to Oz took its toll. It resulted in me spinning out and almost fainting during 'Look At Me I'm Sandra Dee' one night with horrendous jet lag and thousands of people around me. My palms started sweating like never before as the opening chords to the song rang out, and I felt dizzy. For the life of me I couldn't remember the first word or, indeed, a single lyric of the song. This sudden realisation sent me into a panic attack, with my heart thumping like it was going to jump out of my chest and my breath getting shorter by the second. I'd really, really overdone it.

Suddenly, though – and it still seems like a miracle to me – I opened my mouth and the words came out quite unexpectedly. I somehow managed to fumble my way through the rest of the show in what felt like a semi-conscious state. After the show, the director came into my dressing room and said it was my best performance yet, but to me the whole show was a blur. After that night, I promised myself never again to push my body unnecessarily like that, and never ever to perform with jet lag. Have I stuck to that promise? What do you think?

When I'd finished sixty-six shows of *Grease – The Arena Spectacular* in Australia, it was time to get back to London and to Steve and to my ambitious plans for my very own tour. Terry Blamey had found a promoter and we had a whole bunch of theatre dates lined up all around the country. This was going to be fabulous, wasn't it?

Just before we got the show on the road, I lost my record deal with Warners. Yes, I'd had a huge hit single with 'All I Wanna Do', and, yes, the *Girl* album had had some wonderful write-ups, but the critical acclaim didn't help the album sell. As a female pop singer, I was still being compared to my more successful sister. *Girl* was a commercial flop.

Losing my second record deal didn't hit me nearly as hard as losing my first one, and it was a case of 'pick yourself up and dust yourself off'. I'd had a great run with *Grease* and I was getting back on my feet financially. As far as I was concerned, it was onwards and upwards with the 'Unleashed' tour – aptly named, as it turned out.

*

Not having a record label or sponsors for the tour, we could afford only a very basic set plus minimal lights and a backdrop, but we had a marvellous tour bus with beds for everyone, crew and band alike. The plan was that we'd sleep after each show while travelling to the next theatre in the next town. The two-decker bus was fairly luxurious, with an area at the front where Terry Blamey and some of the crew usually sat, then down the middle there were the double rows of coffin-sized bunks, and the lounge was at the back. It was equipped with a TV, video and CD player to keep us amused, as well as a fridge with a constantly restocked supply of sandwiches, crisps, cakes, chocolate – and alcohol. This meant that each night after the show, while the crew were packing up the set, the band and I would head for the cosy tour bus and get the party underway. By the time we took off for the next town each night, there'd be a full-on mini-nightclub happening at the back of the bus in the band's lounge, with everyone completely hammered and not even vaguely interested in sleeping.

I think something strange happens to people when they go on tour. It must be something to do with the element of freedom, and not having the usual responsibilities of home life to worry about – they seem to let rip. My band was no different, and they seemed to embrace life on the road with alarming gusto.

Ian Masterson was my musical director, of course, and Terry Ronald was on board as one of my backing singers. By this time, the pair had become best friends and a loud and formidable comedy double act – particularly after several bottles of Chardonnay.

My other backing singer, a great girl called Mitch, would sometimes get so drunk and fall into such a deep sleep that no one could wake her when we arrived at our next destination. While the rest of us clambered out of our bunks and headed for nice soft beds in a lovely hotel, poor Mitch often woke up on her own on the bus in a theatre car park.

The other members of the band were Steve Smith, a cheeky South London boy with a dirty laugh, who later went on to front the dance act Dirty Vegas, and James Nisbet, who earned the name 'Fluffy' on the tour because of his blond flyaway hair (being a rock-and-roll guitarist, I expect he was ever so pleased with that particular moniker). These two boys knew how to enjoy themselves and both liked a beer or ten. Fluffy, in fact, was already a veteran of a few wild tours, and he showed the rest of us how to do it properly, with lots of blistering guitar solos on stage and lots of partying off stage.

My manager, Terry Blamey, had never been one to shy away from a bit of harmless revelry, and he came along on the tour too, bringing his semi-wild-child girlfriend, Rachel, who was in charge of hair, make-up and wardrobe, and who proved to be quite the party girl on the road. Blonde and voluptuous with pouty lips and Bambi eyes, Rachel was good hearted and professional, but often let loose once her Terry was safely tucked up in bed or was sitting down at the front of the bus: she'd often end up doing tequila shots and dancing up and down the aisle of the bus in various states of undress, which, of course, amused Steve, Fluffy, and the boys in the crew no end.

One day, Rachel had them all agog when she climbed up on the coffee table in the bus lounge in her six-inch heels and stuck the top half of her body out of the skylight. Arms in the air, she sang at the top of her voice while hurling toilet rolls into the stratosphere like streamers, wearing only a black peekaboo bra. It was a bit like the opera-singing drag queen on the top of the bus in *Priscilla, Queen of the Desert* – only instead of it being in the wilds of the Australian outback, it was on the M62 motorway heading towards Hull. Eventually and unsurprisingly, given her footwear, Rachel toppled down and landed on the table, sending drinks flying everywhere.

Sometimes I felt like I was on a school trip without any teachers. As the tour progressed, the constant partying got worse. Even on a rare quiet night, when we'd all decided to settle down in our pyjamas with a nice cup of tea and watch a romantic comedy, Fluffy would get bored and crack open the champagne, and, fairly soon, out of the window went *Pretty Woman* and on went the Pamela Anderson/Tommy Lee sex tape, which my percussionist Steve somehow inevitably had a copy of.

To be honest, I can't really commit to paper half the stuff that went on during the 'Unleashed' tour, as we promised to take it to our graves. 'What happens on tour, stays on tour!' as they say. Suffice it to say that some of the crew, who had been on the road with some pretty hard-core rock bands, told us on the last night that the Dannii Minogue tour had been right up there in the party stakes. They were relieved it had finished, because another couple of weeks might have killed them.

Each evening while on the road, someone would be landed with the title 'Witch of the Day' and presented with a mini witch's broom. This accolade was for the person who had, that day, been the grumpiest or most objectionable: it was a good, light-hearted way of letting people know that they might need to be a little bit more considerate to every-one else. After all, living together on a bus every day for six weeks, eating together and working together, the chances of one person get-ting on another person's nerves sometimes were quite high. It was always glaringly obvious to everyone when I was in a foul mood, as I tend to go deadly silent and let smouldering eyes do the talking – I've always found this method extremely effective when conveying my dis-pleasure at something or someone, and it saves me the bother of screaming my head off.

The tour took us all over the place, but it wasn't exactly 'New York, London, Paris, Munich': it was more King's Lynn, Hemel Hempstead and Rhyl. Being Australian, I hadn't heard of many of these small towns. Although I'd spent many weeks travelling up and down the country with *The Big Breakfast* road shows, half the time I had no idea where I was.

'Where exactly is Bridlington?' I asked Terry Ronald as we drove into a quaint little seaside harbour.

Terry peered out of the window and said, 'It's in the 1950s, dear!'

In one town, we got bored and restless on a day off, so we decided to go on a shopping spree with a difference. My whole band and me stalked from one end of the main shopping area to the other, popping into any stores that we fancied, and then dressing up in whatever it was they happened to sell. We went into a sports shop first and tried on dif-ferent football kits and grabbed footballs off the shelves, then we had a passer-by take a 'team shot' for prosperity. Next, we headed to the

Disney Store and, unsurprisingly, all wore Mickey Mouse ears, witches' hats and whatever else we could lay our hands on, and had another photo. We dashed into a furniture store and got some poor passer-by to take snaps of us reclining seductively in the display beds while we screamed with laughter. It might sound silly now, but it was the sort of childish thing I never got to do as a teenager in Australia because everyone knew me. Hidden within my band, people didn't seem to notice that it was Dannii Minogue acting up in their local high-street store. Caught up as I was in the spirit of the tour, I didn't care if they did. The final shop we visited was a lingerie store, where Mitch and I decided that we should definitely try on a couple of sexy baby-doll nightdresses over our clothes and model them for the boys. Unfortunately, the staff in the store didn't find our fashion show as hilarious as we clearly did, and consequently I was ejected from Ann Summers, followed closely by the rest of my band.

The theatres were lovely, as were the audiences. Whether we were playing to packed houses or half-full ones, I always managed to have a good time, despite the fact that I was missing Steve, being on the road so much. He came to as many of the shows as he could and I'd spend time with him if there were a few days off between dates.

The 'Unleashed' set list was a mix of my newer songs, plus oldies and cover versions of some disco classics I loved, such as Blondie's 'Heart of Glass' and Sylvester's 'You Make Me Feel (Mighty Real)'. I'd have my poor backing singers, Terry and Mitch, dressed up in all sorts of over-the-top disco get-ups to perform the songs.

At one show in King's Lynn, there was a fairly rowdy Saturday-night crowd in, and two loud-mouthed guys in the front row started heckling me and shouting some rather off-colour comments while I was trying to perform. After a while, they turned their attention to Terry Ronald, who, at the time, was wearing white platform shoes and a feather boa and dancing around a giant white handbag with Mitch in similar attire. I started to feel really uncomfortable. Everyone around them in the audience could clearly hear the sexist and homophobic comments they were hollering at the stage. As they were quite drunk and right in the front row, it was all a bit too close for comfort. Then my discomfort turned to anger when they both stood up at the end of one song, probably to hit the bar for more drinks.

I let the applause die down, walked right to the edge of the stage, leaned down in front of them and said loudly into the microphone, 'Off to the toilet together, boys? That's cosy! I thought it was only us girls who went to the toilet in twos.' Then I gave them a big wink. Well, the audience went nuts: laughing and clapping and cheering, and the two guys slunk off to wherever they were going with a look of abject horror on their faces, never to return. The moral of that story is, of course, don't fuck with somebody who has a live mic in her hand!

'Unleashed', which Ian Masterson ultimately rechristened 'Unhinged', went on for six long weeks, and at the end of it everyone needed a holiday, and, quite possibly, a drying-out clinic. After the tour, though, it was straight back to *Grease – The Arena Spectacular* for me, but now in New Zealand. And I was happy to be nominated for a prestigious Australian MO award for my portrayal of Rizzo.

At the end of 1998, I was invited to play at the Mushroom Records 25-year celebrations at the Melbourne cricket ground in front of 80,000 people, with my former label releasing *Dannii: The Singles* – a greatest hits album in Australia. I was a busy girl again – just the way I liked it!

Chapter 17

Fast Cars and Drag Queens

Gumball 3000 is a 3,000-mile road rally that takes place once a year on public roads, with a different route somewhere around the world each year. It's supposed to be more of a fun rally than a serious race, and every year all sorts of people enter in all sorts of cars. The first of these races took place in the summer of 1999. My then boyfriend, Steve Shaw, decided that he was going to enter in his new Porsche Boxter, and eagerly signed up for it. Never one to miss a bit of excitement, I agreed to drive the rally route with him, which was from London to Rimini in Italy and back, taking in parts of Austria, Germany and France. All sorts of people were going to be competing in the race, including celebrities and actors such as Jason Priestley and Billy Zane. The Gumball 3000 organiser, Maximillion Cooper, was combining the racing element of the rally with nightly parties and layovers in luxury hotels.

I was genuinely excited about taking some time out of a busy schedule and doing something with Steve that would be both exhilarating and romantic. At first, I couldn't wait to get on the road. However, as I said, the race was along public roads, and we were literally driving all day. Once we got underway, I realised that tearing around public highways at fast speed was definitely not for me. Cars would be hurtling through little French towns trying to get to the next stop, and I'd be anxiously biting my fingernails, worrying that there was going to be a terrible accident of some sort. Although all the competitors are supposed to keep to the speed limit, the thrill of the chase often seemed to override common sense, as far as I was concerned. Still, this was the first-ever Gumball 3000, and there was a great deal of excitement surrounding it, so I tried to have fun and enjoy it as much as I could, despite having to resist lodging my fingernails in the dashboard for safety. Sadly, a few years later, my forebodings were realised when an innocent couple were killed after being hit by one of the rally cars at over 160 kilometers per hour.

At one point, the rally made a stop in Monaco, and it was there that I met someone who was going to become a very important person in my life for so many reasons. Her name was Laura; she was on the rally with a friend, and was also helping to organise some of the parties surrounding the event. I'd bumped into Laura a couple of times throughout the rally but, to be honest, everyone was so bleary-eyed at the end of each day's driving that in-depth conversation was usually out of the question. When Steve and I attended a stunning party that the rally organisers had put on in Monaco one night, we finally got to talk at length.

The party was overlooking Casino Square. All the various and incredible cars were lined up with their Gumball numbers and stickers on. There was a real buzz among the locals about the rally coming into town. I remember thinking that the whole atmosphere, and indeed Monaco itself, seemed so glamorous and beautiful. I thought at the time how wonderful it would be to come back for a proper visit. It felt so romantic being there with Steve, looking at all the well-dressed people in the square checking out the Ferraris and the Lamborghinis and enjoying such a great evening. Laura explained to me that she lived in Monaco most of the time, and she told Steve and me that she was going to be organising another party in London at the end of the rally.

'It'll be at the Chocolate Bar. You guys have to come,' she smiled.

'We definitely will!' I promised.

I really liked this girl right away. She was quite striking, with long, curly, light-brown hair, smiling eyes and an infectious laugh. Her warm, enthusiastic manner drew me in as she spoke.

'Hey, if you're ever in Monaco,' she said to me, 'you must give me a call.'

And she handed me her number.

'Thank you, Laura,' I said. 'I will!'

I couldn't imagine what would bring me to Monaco again, beautiful as it was. Anyway, eventually, we said our goodbyes and departed the gorgeous soirée in Casino Square.

'She's really nice,' I said to Steve, as we headed back to our hotel.

Little did I know then how significant Laura was going to be in my life over the next few years.

It had been a fun year so far: apart from being surrounded by the glamour and fast cars of Gumball 3000, I'd performed for the second year running at the Mardi Gras party in Sydney, which is probably the biggest and most famous annual gay parade and party in the world.

The previous year, in 1998, I'd performed 'All I Wanna Do' at the party. The Mardi Gras show producer, Gary Leeson, decided to put me on stage with scores of gorgeous dancing lesbians in full, sheer body stockings with strategically placed fig leaves – the whole theme being the Garden of Eden. Kylie was performing that year too, so it turned out to be a spectacular show and a great family night for both of us.

In 1999, Gary invited me to perform again, and this time I got together with Terry Ronald and Ian Masterson to write a song especially for the occasion. The song was called 'Everlasting Night' and was a real high-energy disco workout that was set to be released by the Mardi Gras record label in Australia.

I was very excited when I arrived in Sydney to shoot the video for 'Everlasting Night', which I was co-directing, and thrilled to meet all my colourful co-stars: a whole gaggle of stunning drag queens who'd been rounded up by one of the Mardi Gras organisers, Glenn Horder.

The idea for the video, which we were doing on a shoestring budget, was a wild party on a rooftop in Sydney. As well as all the drag queens, I had a host of beautiful boy dancers, including my good friend Ben Pauley, whom I'd met when he was a dancer on *Grease – The Arena Spectacular*. Blond and handsome, Ben was my featured dancer in the video; he also worked on the choreography for my performance at the Mardi Gras party.

When the video was in the can and edited, it looked fabulous. It featured shots of me, now brunette again, getting up close and personal with a beautiful, shaven-headed girl – there was even a sweet little kiss between us. It was all gorgeously camp and frivolous, and it was a great warm-up for the main event a few nights later.

The pre-party street parade that year was spectacular. It's such a big thing in Australia that it's covered on national television. I can't think of another country where the gay and lesbian parade gets national coverage – certainly not back then, anyway. I remember meeting the designer Jean Paul Gaultier at a cocktail party on a hotel terrace that looked out over the passing parade, and he was completely overcome by the spectacle.

'All of these incredible dykes and queens,' he said to me as he looked down at the packed streets in awe. 'In France, drag is quite an underground thing, and here all these people are parading up and down for all the world to see – it's great! It's like a big family.' And I guess that's exactly what it was like, in a way.

The previous year, when Kylie and I had both performed at the party, Mum and Dad had come to watch the street parade too, and somehow we all had to get across town to the Hordern Pavilion for the party afterwards. Dad was very excited as we got in our car to find that we'd been given a police escort on motorbikes to guide us safely through the partying crowds. I think it was the best part of the evening for him, and he couldn't stop talking about it afterwards.

'Just think,' he said, looking at all the tough-looking leather queens and fabulous trannies in all their wildest get-ups, as we slowly snaked through the partying multitudes, 'ten years ago the police would probably have been arresting this lot!'

It was true. It was almost the start of a new century, and times were certainly changing for the better in so many ways.

The show, of course, was always the highlight of the evening. Aussie rock legend Jimmy Barnes was performing the Sylvester classic 'You Make Me Feel (Mighty Real)' the second year I took part. It was quite a coup as Jimmy was a real old-school rocker, and his over-the-top performance of a camp disco classic was not at all what people were expecting of him.

I was due to appear quite late in the evening, and by 1.30a.m. the party room was absolutely heaving with sweating, dancing bodies in various states of euphoria and inebriation. It was time to go on! Mum had come along to help me with my hair and make-up. When she'd finished, I ushered her out of the dressing room and delivered her into the safe arms of my friend Grant Gillies, who worked for the Mardi Gras record label.

'Look after Carol, please, Grant,' I implored him. 'Don't let her get lost among all those tall trannies; she's only little!'

And then I was on – with a huge explosion of pyrotechnics and a hundred beautiful dancers below me on a gargantuan white staircase. I came down from on high on a shimmering crescent moon in a white satin disco dress. Then I was duly joined by many of the wonderful drag queens from the video, including Amelia Airhead, Tess Tickle, Kitty Glitter and Atlanta Georgia – to name a few. It was, if I say so myself, a pretty spectacular turn, and after the closing number we all left the party at dawn with our sunnies firmly planted on our heads.

Mardi Gras was usually a whole exhausting week of parties, and the host of many of the best ones that year was the aforementioned rock star, Jimmy Barnes, and his lovely wife, Jane. There would always be a great crowd of us hanging out at Jimmy's place, including my friends and various dancers and drag queens from the show. These parties would usually go on all night and half the next day, with people heading off to find a bed when they got tired, and then getting up a few hours later to come and rejoin the fun.

Some of the characters I met on that trip were very outlandish indeed – particularly one drag queen called Kitty Glitter. Kitty was well known because of her thick, glittery lipstick, and the fact that she used to perform a certain 'personal service' on all the straight boys who fancied a bit of something different. The story goes that her favourite trick was to make a damn good imprint with her very sparkly lips, knowing full well that the poor guy's girlfriend, or wife, was going to be faced with the glittering evidence of his betrayal once he got home.

I remember one beautiful summer night, looking down into the swimming pool at Jimmy's place and seeing yet another drag queen splashing around in the water with boobs made from water-filled condoms that were bobbing about in front of her in a bra. She had a full face of make-up, a huge wig and a cigarette in her mouth, and she waved excitedly at me as I smiled down at her from the terrace.

'Hi, darling!'

It was not something you saw every day, but that was the beauty of the whole scene during Mardi Gras in Sydney. After all the partying that week, our whole gang packed up our suitcases and headed to a beautiful tropical retreat outside Sydney for a bit of rest and relaxation. But, of course, once we got there, we just started the party all over again.

Back in London in the spring of 1999, Steve took shots of Kylie and me together for the cover of *Esquire* magazine, which still adorn the wall of our family home today – they were real landmark photos as far as we were concerned, as the two of us hadn't done a photo shoot together before. Steve always captured his subjects beautifully on film, and he had become a very highly sought-after photographer.

He was now living with me at my apartment in Battersea, and I wasn't quite sure how well that was going. I always did like having my own space. Though I absolutely hate being apart from Kris these days, back then having an increasingly moody boyfriend around the whole time was starting to get on my tits, so to speak. It wasn't that I didn't love or care about him – and I'll hold my hands up and tell you that I'm not always the easiest person to live with – but for some reason I felt that something wasn't quite right with him. However, I told myself that it would pass. After all, we'd been together for almost three years: it was the longest relationship I'd ever had, and up until he'd moved in every-thing had been hunky-dory.

Suddenly, though, everything became clearer when Steve announced that he was going to move to LA. He had been working out there on and off and he was really starting to get a reputation as a hot photographer there, so it seemed a great career move. This came as a bit of a shock, to say the least. As it got closer to the time of his depar-ture, I could tell that he wasn't himself. He was quiet and uncommunicative with me, and I started to feel that there was some-thing he wasn't telling me.

'Look, Steve, if you're worrying about us not being together once you're there,' I said, 'don't! I'm coming over in four or five weeks and I've already booked some time off work. It'll be fine. We'll make it work.'

'I'm not worried,' Steve told me unconvincingly. 'Everything's fine.'

My instincts were telling me something else.

'Do you want us to break up?' I asked one night as we ate dinner. 'Is that it?'

'Of course not,' Steve said aghast. 'I don't want to break up with you!'

Once he was settled in Los Angeles, however, that's exactly what he did do – he unceremoniously dumped me over the phone one night. There was no fight, no particular reason, just the difficulty of distance – again. Yes, I'd known Steve had found our being apart hard when I'd been on tour, or working in Australia, but we'd always got past that. The fact that we were now going to be on opposite sides of the Atlantic, though, was obviously the straw that broke the photographer's back, and there wasn't much I could do about it. I was pissed off. I'd given Steve every opportunity to tell me to my face that he wanted to end it with me, but instead he waited until he was safely thousands of miles away, and left me to pick up the pieces.

Chapter 18

Showering in Sunglasses

When a girl's been dumped she can do one of two things: she can either take to the couch in a tracksuit and chomp her way through a jumbo pack of chocolate biscuits, or she can put on her war paint and go out and have a good time. Having already tried the first option when I broke up with Julian, I wasn't keen to repeat the experience, so when an intriguing invitation came through the post a week or so after my transatlantic telephone bust-up with Steve, I decided that it was just what I needed to steer clear of the doldrums. I got on the phone to my good friend Jules.

'I've got this invitation, Jules,' I said to her. 'It's something to do with car testing in Barcelona, and a big party hosted by some team sponsor. You're a racing fan, aren't you?'

'I am,' Jules said. 'What kind of car racing is it, though?'

'I can't remember,' I said. 'It's something with a One in it.'

'Formula 1?' Jules squeaked. 'Oh my God – I'm a huge F1 fan! And you've been invited to testing?'

'Yes, and a party. It's the British American Racing team sponsors, I think.'

Jules was nigh on hyperventilating.

'Look, Jules,' I said. 'I know nothing about racing, but I do know I need to have some fun. And if you're up for it, we could have a huge party, girly weekend away. I really need to go out and have a few cocktails and a bit of a dance – what do you say?'

'I say let's do it!' Jules said.

Jules Kulpinski was at that time my brother Brendan's long-term girlfriend from Melbourne. They were both now based in London, with Brendan still working as a cameraman for *9 News* in Europe. A gorgeous, savvy blonde, she'd handled all the press side of things on the 'Unleashed' tour, and we'd always got on really well. Jules's addictive sense of fun would make her the perfect companion for me on the trip to Barcelona, and I was very happy that she was so enthusiastic about coming along.

Lucky Strike were the team's title sponsors and they had invited quite a few celebrities over, first to watch the cars test and afterwards to attend the big party with the team, which was to be held at a large club in the city. It was a huge PR event for the team, and it sounded like they would be pulling out all the stops, so Jules and I packed up our very best party frocks and set off for the airport.

When we arrived at the track in Barcelona, testing was already well underway, so Jules and I headed straight for the hospitality suite above the garages to watch from there. After a while, we were invited by some of the team to go down to the garage to meet the drivers and see the Formula 1 cars close up. I didn't want to meet the drivers. I was clueless about Formula 1. What the hell did I want to meet the drivers for? I just wanted to head to the party and get some cocktails happening. However, Jules was extremely enthusiastic about meeting the drivers and seeing the bloody cars, so off we trudged for a personal tour of the noisy, bustling garage with one of the team members, who affably took pictures of both of us sitting in one of the F1 cars and posing cheerily with some of the team personnel. It was there that I spotted a rather handsome man whom I assumed was one of the drivers, or at least a team member, and I got the distinct feeling that he'd noticed me as well.

'That's Jacques Villeneuve,' Jules whispered excitedly.

'Who?' I said.

'He's a world champion! I'd love to get my photo taken with him. Will you take one if I ask?'

'Sure!'

I was none the wiser, but as he approached us, Jules duly asked if she might get a picture with him, and he agreed. Jacques wasn't tall, but he was certainly very sexy in all his racing gear with his white-blond hair. As I took the photograph, he flashed the most adorable smile at me. Hmm, I thought. Interesting. Then, he suddenly headed over to speak to me – me who knows nothing about racing! What should I say? I remember telling myself, firmly, as he approached, that I should say something both interesting and relevant.

'Do you drive round in circles?' is what I came up with.

Jacques gave me a look that could have meant only one thing: is she taking the piss?

But I thought that's what they did – drive around in circles, no?

'Er, no – not exactly,' Jacques said, looking somewhat bewildered. 'We drive around a track, but it's not exactly in a circle.'

'Oh. OK.'

And then I was lost. That was the best I could do and I had absolutely no idea what to say next.

'Are you coming to the party tonight?' Jacques finally asked me – his French-Canadian accent was heavenly.

'We are,' I said. 'So I guess we'll see you there?'

'You will,' he smiled.

When Jules and I arrived at the club for the Lucky Strike party – frocks on, heels on – it was already alive and buzzing. There was definitely an air of glitz and glamour about the affair, and everyone around me seemed to be happy and relaxed – it was just what I needed! One of the first things I noticed was the ice sculpture at the bar, down one end of which a waiter was adeptly pouring shots of liquor that eager revellers were catching in their mouths at the other. I thought this looked naughty and fun. Once Jules and I had relaxed and had had a couple of glasses of champagne, we started to grab people around us, encouraging them to try it while we looked on.

I remember, among other people, David Coulthard being at the party, and Jules spotted former world champion Damon Hill, TV presenter Jamie Theakston and model Kelly Brook partying the night away, too. There was a beautiful outdoor area to the club that the party spilled out onto, but it was a little cold, and Jules and I hadn't brought sweaters. Jules's idea was to keep drinking until we couldn't feel the cold any more, which, oddly, seemed to make sense at the time. Eventually, though, we hit the dance floor, and when we did, we danced for hours, really letting go and having a wild time. The more I danced, the better I started to feel – it was like some magical medicine.

During all this time at the party, Jules noticed that I had a little shadow in the compact and bijou shape of Jacques Villeneuve, who had pretty much trailed us all night. In fact, no matter what room or area of the party we went to, there was Jacques, back for yet another little chat. I didn't mind at all: I was quite captivated by him, if you want the truth. As the evening wore on, I found him more and more intriguing.

'You are definitely flirting with Mr Villeneuve,' Jules said, flashing a smile at me and handing me another cocktail.

'Am I?' I said, innocently.

But of course I was. When we finally grabbed a cab to go back to the hotel, Jacques walked Jules and me out of the party and then leaped, unexpectedly, into the back of the car with us – apparently he was staying there too. I remember Jules looking over at me as if to say, 'Oh great! I'm the gooseberry!' I didn't have an awful lot of time to think about it, because the next thing I knew, Jacques was kissing me – what a way to end the evening.

Jules and I were sharing a hotel room. The next morning, both of us felt truly appalling. Though I hadn't considered myself terribly drunk the night before, I now had a hangover that felt like I was teetering on the precipice of hell. The only way I could face getting out of bed was to keep my eyes tightly shut. In fact, I showered with my sunglasses on, which is a very good tip if you're ever in a bright bathroom with a bad hangover and you need to get ready in a hurry. Anyway, once I'd finished showering, Jules popped her head around the bathroom door.

'There's someone knocking at the door,' she said.

'No way! Who is it?'

'It's Jacques! He wants to come in and I told him he can't, but he won't take no for an answer, so he's sitting outside in the hall.'

Jules shrugged her shoulders, and the ridiculousness of the situation washed over me. There I was, showering in my Gucci sunnies, feeling – and most probably looking – absolutely rotten, while a French-Canadian world champion Formula 1 driver sat pining outside my room.

'Oh shit! Tell him to come back later.'

I couldn't possibly see him at that moment, surely – I could barely stand up, for Christ's sake. Then he started knocking again, so I whipped my glasses off, and Jules and I peeked through the little peep-hole in the hotel door, both giggling like schoolgirls.

'What are we going to do?' Jules chuckled. 'Shall we let him in?'

'I guess we'll have to,' I said.

I composed myself as best I could and swung open the hotel-room door.

'Good morning,' I smiled. 'And how are you?'

'I'm fine,' Jacques said. 'But I've been thinking – instead of flying back to London, why don't you both come to Monaco to my house with me? I'd really love you to come for a few days as my guests – will you?'

'Well . . . erm . . .' I was slightly flummoxed. 'We have tickets back to London, and we can't change them, can we, Jules?'

'We can't change them,' Jules repeated, shaking her head, dutifully. Jacques smiled.

'Well, that doesn't matter; I have the jet,' he said.

'The what?'

'The jet! I have a private jet,' Jacques said.

Yes, of course you have a jet, I thought. Why wouldn't you?

'I can take you both to Monaco on the jet, and then we can sort out some other flights back to London later.'

Jacques was clearly quite chuffed with his plan.

'Oh. OK. Well then . . . Jules?'

I turned to her, desperate for some sort of level-headed supervision. 'Let's go' was her only offering.

So that was that. Hungover and clinging onto a loose plan with someone we barely knew, we were off to Monaco.

Once there, Jacques couldn't have been sweeter to Jules and me. He took us on a tour of all the places in Monaco that he loved and made a complete fuss of us. Of course, I'd been to Monaco earlier in the year for Gumball 3000, but this time I was getting to see the whole place properly, and it was gorgeous. On the first day, Jacques drove us up to Le Rocher de Monaco (The Rock), which is where the Prince's palace is, and then he took us to a movie at the fabulous outdoor cinema there. The next day, some of his friends from the Canadian ice-hockey team arrived and we all spent the day on a beautiful beach, stopping for a wonderful lunch with rosé wine and sumptuous seafood – it was all completely divine and incredibly romantic.

Unfortunately, and predictably, I hadn't had time to digest and process any of my thoughts and feelings about Jacques before we were splashed across the pages of one of the British tabloids. Caught on the beach that second afternoon by a photographer, the next day's headline announced that Jacques and I were an item. All I knew for certain was that Jacques seemed like a real gentleman, and I was becoming more and more smitten with him as the days progressed.

I wasn't used to having boyfriends who had the wherewithal to romance me in the way Jacques did, with private jets and beautiful dinners in dazzling settings, and I guess I liked it. Why not? Up until then, I felt as though I'd done most of the wining and dining in my relationships. Jacques was also very determined: he knew what he wanted and he was going after it. When he took me in his arms and kissed me after dinner on my last night in Monaco, I finally let myself fall. What girl could resist?

A week later, Jules and I were back in Barcelona for the Spanish Grand Prix, and Jacques and I were very much together. I couldn't believe it had happened so quickly and so soon after breaking up with

Steve, but I told myself it was fate. I'd been crying my eyes out a few weeks before and had gone to a party with a girlfriend to try to make myself feel better. Now here I was on the arm of a handsome, charming French-Canadian, who just happened to be a world-champion racing driver – it was all very Jackie Collins. That trip was quite fateful for my dear friend Jules, too, as a year or so later she became Jacques' personal assistant. She's gone on to have a great career in the sport she so loves, now travelling the world working for another world champion, Jenson Button. So my theory is: ladies, always go to the party!

Chapter 19

Pit Stop

At the start of the new century, I was on a beautiful yacht in Sydney Harbour, surrounded by friends and family. Jacques had hired the boat for the week leading up to the New Year celebrations, which we knew would be spectacular. On the night itself, we threw a big party. My brother Brendan was there with Jules, who'd brought her sister along, and my mum and dad, Terry Blamey and friends; Glenn Horder and Gary Leeson from the Mardi Gras committee were also on board.

Jacques and I were having a great time. Although the weather had been shocking that week, at the stroke of midnight on New Year's Eve we kissed as we watched Sydney's spectacular firework display together in awe. We were in love. It was truly incredible to be on Sydney harbour that New Year's Eve with so much hope in everyone's eyes. For me, the year that followed was going to bring something that I'd never experienced before: anonymity, to the very point that I almost disappeared, both professionally and personally.

The second half of 1999 had flown past in a blur. When Jacques' racing team, BAR, threw a big party in London, I attended officially as his girlfriend. It was the first time many of my London friends got to meet him. Once again, I was dating a man who lived in a different country: this one spent his time travelling around the world racing cars for a living. One thing that was very different this time around, though, was that instead of griping about the fact that I wasn't around, Jacques would simply send his private jet to collect me and take me to him. It was a nice feeling.

During this period, things were pretty quiet on the work front for me, but unusually I wasn't really worried about it. For the first time, I felt that I could sit back and let someone look after me for a bit rather than be the breadwinner myself. I started going to all the Grands Prix around the world, supporting Jacques as much as I possibly could. I began to learn all the different Formula 1 rules and racing terms, and nowadays consider myself an aficionado. I found myself spending more and more time in Monaco.

At one of the races, Jacques and I met George Harrison, who was a big fan of F1. Jacques, in turn, was a keen amateur guitarist and absolutely obsessed with the Beatles, so he was thrilled when George and his wife, Olivia, invited us to dinner at their house in Henley-on-Thames. The house, of course, was absolutely incredible, but the dinner itself couldn't have been more relaxed: it was eaten not around a dressed baronial table in a formal dining room, but around the Harrisons' comfy, worn-in kitchen table with their son, Dhani.

After dinner, George drove Jacques and me around the huge grounds of his house on a little golf buggy, giving us a superb tour of his stunning garden, which he was understandably proud of. He had designed it all himself and had worked, hands on, with a team of gardeners to create and maintain it. There were pretty lakes and bridges and fantastic features everywhere you looked. Dotted around this amazing landscape were several little huts. Adorning the wall of one of these huts were a few well-worn ukuleles, which George loved to play. Grabbing a couple down from their hooks, he started to teach Jacques how to pluck and play a few chords, and then he played for us. It was quite magical – one of those moments when you have to pinch yourself and say, 'Yes, this is pretty special!' It was, particularly as George and Olivia were so wonderfully warm and down-to-earth. Before we left at the end of the evening, George presented me with one of his ukuleles as a gift, lovingly signed by him.

Some time later, when I took Dad to the Grand Prix in Melbourne, which was excitement enough with him being so into cars, I introduced him to George, and he was completely gobsmacked. I don't suppose for one minute he had expected his youngest daughter to introduce him to one of the Beatles at a racetrack.

During these first few months of my romance with Jacques, theatre director Toby Gough approached Terry Blamey to ask if I'd be inter-ested in appearing in a play he was directing for the Edinburgh Festival. Now, when you think of Dannii Minogue starring in some kind of theatrical production, I expect Lady Macbeth wouldn't be the first – or even the twenty-first – role that springs to mind, but that's exactly the character he wanted me to play in *The Road to Macbeth*.

'Why on earth would anyone want to do a Shakespeare tragedy with Dannii Minogue?' I asked him and his producer, John Lee, when we met up to discuss the idea. 'This is never gonna work.'

But Toby's point was that at the Edinburgh Festival you had to stand out, and this, if nothing else, would stand out.

'You just learn the lines like you would any other script, Dannii,' he said. 'I think it'll be great!'

Of course, Toby's version wasn't your run-of-the mill telling of the story: his was set in the seventies, with the entire cast in full disco regalia, and the character of Macbeth portrayed as a gangster who had got into a situation over his head. Our Macbeth was played by a statuesque black guy called Ade Separa. He donned an Afro wig, white suit and gold chains, like something out of a Quentin Tarantino movie.

The other twist in our tale was the stage itself. *The Road to Macbeth* was performed outdoors at the Royal Botanical Gardens, and the audi-ences were led by torchlight from one spot in the gardens to another for various scenes. It was more of an experience than a play. Once again, I played the bad girl, just as I had with Emma Jackson in *Home and Away* and Rizzo in *Grease* – I was typecast and loving it.

Toby had been right, too, about memorising the lines, which, incidentally, didn't change at all from the original play. I learned the lines of Lady Macbeth like I would have done for any other part. Once I'd taken them in and understood them, I had brilliant fun playing her, and I was really delighted to get good reviews too.

As 1999 trundled towards 2000, there was a big surprise on the horizon. I'd asked Jacques to spend Christmas with me in Australia and he'd excitedly agreed.

Once we got there, though, I was in for a bit of a shock – Jacques proposed.

This knocked me for six as we'd been together only a few months, but I assumed what he meant was that we would have a very long engagement – after all, Jacques was aware of my reticence about marriage after Julian – I smiled and said yes, not really knowing if it was what I wanted, but at the same time knowing that I loved Jacques and wanted him to be happy. Once I had agreed to marry him, and Jacques had gone to Dad and asked for his blessing, he wanted to forge ahead with the wedding plans.

'Let's talk about the wedding; let's start to plan it,' he would say.

I would be thinking: let's not talk about the wedding; let's not plan it. I didn't think we needed to get married. Although I'd said 'yes', I was very happy being engaged for a long, long time. Jacques was determined, and it was rush, rush, rush all the time – which was exactly what I'd had with Julian.

By the early spring of 2000, the millennium celebrations were a happy memory, and I was at a fork in the road with my career, not quite knowing which direction to take. For some time, I'd felt that Terry Blamey and I were coasting along as manager and client, and he didn't seem to know what to do with me any more. Sure, it was fine when offers were put on the table, and Terry always knew how to negotiate a deal, but I needed someone to get creative and find me some new

doors to open, and that just wasn't going to happen with Terry. I think
he felt the same, to be honest. To add to the problem, he was getting
seriously busy with Kylie all over again. After a slight lull during the late
nineties, my big sister's musical career had taken an exciting upswing,
with a new record deal and a big hit single, 'Spinning Around', which
sent her shooting back to the top of the charts where she belonged. For
Terry Blamey and me, though, it was time to say goodbye. With no solid
offers of work on the table, I headed off to Monaco to decide what I
wanted to do next.

Now I never thought I'd say this, but for a while I was revelling
in the fact that I didn't have any work,. Before, I'd have been fretting
horribly about money and feeling useless, but what the hell? I had
recently bought my previously rented apartment in Battersea, I'd finally
got myself together again financially, and now I had a gorgeous man
with several homes and a great job looking after me. I started to relax for
the first time since I was seven.

Apart from the apartment in Monaco, Jacques had bought a couple
of houses in Villars, Switzerland. One was in the town itself and the
other was a cabin up in the mountains above the town with only four
or five other houses nearby. We called that one 'The Love Shack', as it
was so isolated and a pretty little romantic getaway for the two of us.
We spent quite a bit of time in Villars that year, particularly in the winter
sports season, because Jacques loves to ski and he did a lot of his training up there. I bit the bullet and had some skiing lessons myself. While
Jacques would ski every day with the head of the Swiss ski school, I
would go with his wife for a three-hour private lesson each morning –
Jacques had bought me all the appropriate equipment and gear to do
it properly.

Nights at 'The Love Shack' were relaxed and romantic, and Jacques
and I would listen to music or he'd practise his guitar while I cooked up
a storm, preparing delicious dinners for us both. It was such a quiet
haven and a world away from my life of photo shoots and TV studios
and his life on the racetrack. We loved it.

When we were in Monaco, life was a little livelier. Jacques decided
that he wanted to move out of his apartment and buy the house that

he'd grown up in, which was a beautiful place on its own plot of land with a pool. This gave me a great project to work on: picking out furniture and designing the interiors. I completely threw myself into the idea of living in Monaco, with Jacques, full time. There, I wasn't Dannii Minogue the pop star, I was the racing driver's fiancé. It was great fun getting to know a new town and exploring a whole new way of life. The climate was beautiful, as were the surroundings, and Jacques and I would dine out with friends at gorgeous restaurants and go to amazing parties together. When the race season was on, we'd go dashing around the world on his private jet to some of the most fabulous cities in the world.

I got on tremendously well with Jacques' family – his mother and his half-sister – and I made a few friends of my own in the town, too, as time went on. I remembered the girl who had made such an impression on me when we'd met at Gumball 3000 the previous year, Laura. I still had her number, yes, but I wasn't sure whether to call. Why not, though? She had said if I was ever in Monaco to call her and I was living here now . . . so I did.

'Brilliant!' Laura shouted when I finally called and told her about my rather sudden change of location. 'You have to come and visit me!'

I made plans for a trip to see her as soon as I could.

A few weeks earlier, Jacques had announced to me that I could have absolutely any car that I wanted, and after much deliberation I chose . . . a Smart Car. This decision, of course, appalled my motor-racing world-champion fiancé, but I didn't care. I liked the cute little Smart Car and I thought it would be practical for negotiating the winding roads around Monaco, plus I could always get an easy park at the beach. Anyway, after I'd managed to sway a horrified Jacques with my well-thought-out motoring practicalities, a Smart Car is what I got. The funny thing is, once I got it, Jacques – although he pretended to despise it – would always take my Smart Car if he needed to run errands around town, claiming that I'd blocked his car in so he had to take 'The Smart'! I knew very well, though, that he secretly loved bombing around in my fabulous little wagon. Imagine Formula 1 ace Jacques Villeneuve tearing around Monaco in a Smart Car – what would his

BAR teammates say? The next thing I knew, Jacques' mum had bought one; then one of our very good friends, Mark, got one. I'd started a trend for Smart Cars in one of the richest and most glamorous principalities in Europe.

So there I was in my precious little car, one hot afternoon, heading out to visit Laura, who lived just outside Monaco with her mum in a very old village called Eze. The so-called 'easy' directions she gave me turned out to be a little more complicated than I'd anticipated. There was something about a pink wall and a fork in the road and a big tree – it was all quite confusing as far as I could tell, and more like a treasure map than directions to somebody's house. To top it all, I couldn't see any sort of street sign once I got close to where I thought she lived in the village.

'Where's the pink wall?' I said to myself.

Stupidly, I hadn't brought my mobile phone to call her, and I was late, so by this time I was flustered and horribly embarrassed, plus I still couldn't find the pink wall or her street. In the end, I had to drive all the way back to Monaco so I could call Laura and tell her that I'd driven out there but couldn't find her house, so my friendship with her got off to a somewhat slow start.

The next time we planned to meet, Laura came to collect me, and she took me back to her place to meet her mum, Tina. Laura was born in South Africa, and had spent her whole life moving between there and Monaco and England. She was bright and worldly and seemed to have travelled everywhere. On this second meeting, I liked her as much as I had when we first met. Although she'd led such a different life to mine, she was one of the few people I knew who'd travelled and lived in as many different places as I had. That afternoon, we talked and laughed about being 'semi-nomadic' and how we'd both always been ready to try something new and exciting if it was offered. I felt a real connection with Laura; as I got to know her more, we got closer still. I hadn't had a close girlfriend since Lori Lipkies. Lori was now married with children in Australia, so our paths sadly didn't cross that often.

Laura was great and I started to spend much of my time with her whenever I wasn't working or busy on the house, and whenever Jacques was away training. She had the loudest and most insane laugh in the world; in fact, when she let rip, people would either turn and look at her in disgust or helplessly join in the hysteria. She was wonderfully infectious and loved to play and have fun. The best thing about Laura was that she was just as happy looking really daggy in flip-flops with no make-up, wandering around a market, as she was dressing up and attending the grand Bal de l'Été (summer ball).

Laura also enjoyed entertaining and was great at bringing people together – that was something else I loved about her – so almost every week there would be a big dinner or a party for us to plan. In fact, we ran the gamut as girlfriends: from supermarket shopping together to driving to Bvlgari to collect a hundred grand's worth of diamonds to wear to a fabulous party or event. It was all great fun, and Laura helped make my time in Monaco a happy one . . . at least for a while. Things were about to take an ominous turn, though, and it was then that I almost lost myself entirely.

Chapter 20

The Ghost of Dannii Minogue

Throughout the rest of 2000, I stayed with Jacques. We split our time mostly between Monaco and Switzerland. Apart from a couple of charity fundraisers in London, I seemed to vanish from the public eye completely. We'd moved into the new house in Monaco, which I loved, and for the most part I was very happy. Towards the end of the year, however, things suddenly started to take a very different turn, and I felt like an old spectre was slowly coming back to haunt me.

During the winter months, when we were in Villars, I noticed a change in Jacques. There was nothing particular that I could put my finger on at first, but I started to feel the way I had when I'd lived with Julian after we were married. It seemed to me that although Jacques had pursued me with such romantic ferocity, now he had me – now I had essentially given up my whole life to be with him – that was it. There was nothing else for him to do: no nurturing, no romance, nothing. Just like Julian, Jacques appeared to love the idea of a romantic partnership, but appeared to have no idea what to do with one once he had it. More and more often, I would be waiting for Jacques to come home from training or testing, or even go-karting with his friends, only to find that once he did get home, he'd disappear to another part of the house and do his own thing.

I couldn't understand it. How had I ended up in yet another country, feeling completely on my own? It wasn't like I'd started dating the boy next door and given up a part-time job in a sweet shop; I'd stepped away from a very successful career and moved to a different country – again. Was it me? Was I being unrealistic and naive to hope that a loving relationship would last slightly longer than the honeymoon period? The irony of it was that we weren't even married yet.

As Jacques' seeming indifference went on, I felt increasingly isolated and alone stuck up in the mountains. With Laura away at her place in South Africa during the winter months, I couldn't head back to Monaco and spend time with her to alleviate my loneliness. Jacques had become totally hooked on playing an intricate online computer game, and he seemed to be playing it every second of the time he was at home; he played late into the night, scarcely stopping to eat. It got so ridiculous that we would end up arguing about it. I'd implore him to spend some time with me rather than sit there in front of the computer, but it was futile. I felt that I was dealing with a teenage boy rather than the capable man I'd fallen in love with.

I knew only too well that Jacques wasn't used to people saying 'no' to him and that he'd been pandered to his whole life. It was like he lived in his own little bubble, and everyone around him had always let him do exactly as he wished. I guess it wasn't really his fault.

I remember one occasion that summer when we'd been driving out of Monaco and heading for the airfield to take the jet out to a race. Jacques would always drive fast – much too fast, in fact – and I'd constantly nag him to slow down on the highway. Well, on this particular day we got pulled over by the cops.

'Now you're in trouble!' I said to him.

When the policeman poked his head into the car window and saw who the driver was, a beaming smile crossed his face.

'Oh, hello, Mr Villeneuve. Sorry, I didn't realise it was you,' he said, sending us on our merry way.

I kept reminding myself that Jacques' life as a Formula 1 driver must be exhausting, and that maybe spending days on a computer game was his way of unwinding. After all, if Jacques wasn't racing, he was testing; if he wasn't testing, he was training, and then there was all the stuff he had to do for the sponsors. I know only too well that when you work and work non-stop, sometimes it's hard to have the energy for another person when you do stop, as much as you love them. That being said, it was hard to stop my frustration from boiling over. I simply couldn't let myself become the voiceless little woman tiptoeing around someone who hardly acknowledged my existence. Jacques became so engrossed with everything else in his life that I don't think he noticed that I was slipping away from him; if he did, he certainly wasn't doing anything about it. He never did anything mean or horrible to me, he just wasn't with me. Eventually, when I woke up in 'The Love Shack' one morning, alone, I thought: there's a ghost haunting this house . . . and it's me.

I travelled back to London at the end of 2000, as I'd been contacted by theatrical agent Samantha Richards, who asked me if I wanted to audition for a part in the London production of *Notre-Dame de Paris*, a musical retelling of the Victor Hugo story *The Hunchback of Notre Dame*. Jacques and I had been to the opening of the show in London, because a friend of Jacques, French-Canadian singer Garou, was playing the Hunchback, and had invited us. Tina Arena, who was one of the *Young Talent Time* team members at the same time as me, and who had gone on to become a hugely successful recording artist, was playing Esmeralda, which was the part that I auditioned for.

When I officially landed the role I was thrilled: a London West End musical – how great is that? The thing I loved about the show was that instead of being some fuddy-duddy old-fashioned musical, it was very modern and stylised, and the entire show was sung, like an opera. This, of course, was going to be another huge challenge, and I realised that fully only when I listened to each of the songs properly. These weren't the usual pop melodies I was used to singing – they were huge, soaring, epic numbers, and some of them sounded semi-operatic. Could I do this?

I knew I was going to have to work really hard, but I also knew I needed to get away from Villars for a while to sort out my complicated feelings about Jacques. When Laura invited me to go to visit her and her mum, Tina, at their place in South Africa straight after Christmas, I jumped at the chance. I knew that it would have to be a working holiday, though, as I had so much to learn for *Notre-Dame de Paris*, which I was starting in February.

The first thing I did was to call my singing teacher, Russell Penn, who lives in London. Russell is a big, gorgeous bear of a man, who knows every trick in the book as far as proper vocal technique is concerned, and, more specifically, how to achieve what you might think is well beyond your capability.

'Can you come out to South Africa?' I asked him. 'Think of it as a fabulous working holiday. You're the only one who's going to be able to get me singing these songs, Rusty!'

Luckily, Russell was on board.

'Absolutely!' he said. 'You'll be tearing the roof off with that voice by the time I've finished with you!'

I wasn't convinced, but, as usual, having a question mark hanging over whether I can do something or not only spurs me on to want to do it even more. Game on!

Laura, of course, was a wonderful host, and her house in South Africa was as lovely as I'd imagined it would be. The pool house there was the perfect place for Russell and me to set up shop, so we turned it into our music room, with a keyboard and all the sheet music printed out ready to go. The first thing Russell explained to me was that I was going to have to learn to sing in parts of my voice that I'd never used before. Although I could already hit most of the notes I was required to hit, it wasn't with any real power and didn't sound particularly pleasant, so I had to work on strengthening the top end of my range so I could belt out those numbers and show everyone, including myself, I could do it.

Tina Arena was going to be a tough act to follow. She'd been the oldest member of the *Young Talent Time* crew when I was on the show, and I'd always looked up to her. Tina has a magnificent voice, and to step into a role that she had made her own would be no mean feat – I was going to have to work very hard indeed.

As I sang through the songs with Russell every day, I started to find more and more power in the parts of my voice that I'd struggled with before. He showed me how to go from my deep 'chest voice' to my higher 'head voice' without losing strength or tone. Pretty soon, in the bright, sunny pool house, I was belting out notes that I could only have imagined singing before, and Russell would clap his hands and say, 'That's all you! Amazing!'

The great thing about working out in South Africa was that after I'd finished all my singing tuition with Russell, we could relax and hang out with Laura and Tina, and for a while I could push aside all the heartache over Jacques. Laura had become such a wonderful and trusted friend; I really don't know what I would have done without her during that time.

Once back in Monaco, I knew in my heart of hearts that my life there with Jacques was coming to an end. It would have been an easy decision if Jacques had been a horrible, spiteful man, but he never was. I just couldn't live my life as a spare part any more, and that's what I'd been doing for the best part of a year. Working on *Notre-Dame* made me see what I was giving up to be with Jacques, and it wasn't worth it.

I called Ian Masterson in London in a real state one morning, shaking and crying as I spoke to him.

'Can I come to your place, please, Ian? I'm leaving Monaco today and I won't be coming back. I just need to hang out with people. I don't want to be on my own.'

I was quite distraught about breaking up with Jacques, and I think the pressure of learning the show on top of that pushed me over the edge. But I knew I had to leave, and I knew I needed my friends around me. Ian must have sensed my despair, as he got straight on the phone to Terry Ronald.

'You'd better get over to my place, Terry,' Ian said. 'Dannii has split up with Jacques. She's heading this way and she doesn't sound good. I think I'm gonna need some help with this one!'

By the time I got to Ian's waterside apartment in London, I was a wreck. Ian's partner, Dan, made us all some dinner, but I could barely eat. I just wanted to drink vodka and chain-smoke cigarettes. I could scarcely speak without tears falling.

'I've only ever seen you like this once in the ten years I've known you, Dan,' Terry said, holding my hand. 'After you split up with Julian, you broke down like this. I didn't realise things had got this bad for you.'

Ian nodded his head in agreement. How could they have known? I'd almost disappeared off the face of the earth as far as my friends in London were concerned, giving up almost everything to be with Jacques. I felt like a failure. It was the second time in my life that I'd all but lost myself in someone else and become a ghost. I vowed then that it would never happen again.

Chapter 21

Where Do We Go Now?

The days leading up to my opening night in *Notre-Dame de Paris* were lived on a knife-edge. I felt emotionally drained, and the vigorous rehearsals for the show had left me exhausted.

A couple of weeks before the big night, I had a lot of press interviews to do. I told my friend Tim Reed, who was one of the general managers on the show, that I absolutely did not want to talk about breaking off the engagement to Jacques. Any press I did was to be solely about my appearance in the show: if any of the press were unhappy about that, then it was best they stayed away. The break-up was too raw and private to talk about.

However, by the time all the interviews got underway a week or so later, the company Tim Reed worked for was no longer overseeing the management of the show, so all my requests about Jacques being a no-go topic went out of the window. It seemed that the PR company handling the show's press coverage completely ignored Tim's original instructions. Practically all that the interviewers asked me were questions about the break-up – nothing about the show. I suppose it was naive of me to expect any different – they are reporters after all – but at the time I was very upset. One of the interviews, a mere six days after the break-up, was for a cover story in a Sunday supplement, and the reporter was particularly zealous on the subject of Jacques.

'Why are you asking me these questions?' I eventually said to her. 'I'm here to talk about the show I'm performing in, not my private life.'

'Well, that's what the story's about,' the journalist said, flatly. 'The only reason I'm here is to talk about your break-up with Jacques.'

I was furious, and stared icily across the table at her expectant face – she was hoping for the big dramatic scoop.

'Do you really think I've come here to talk about that?' I snapped, tearfully. 'I'm still too upset. I'm opening in *Notre-Dame* and I've made it plain that I don't want to . . .'

The woman wasn't vaguely interested in the show or what I had to say about it. 'Well, that's going to be a big problem, I'm afraid,' she said. 'It's very nice that you're in a show and all that, Dannii, but I've been sent here to get a story about you breaking off your engagement to Jacques Villeneuve.'

By that point I was in pieces. I knew that the reporter thought I was a hysterical, bitchy diva, but I didn't care – I was seething. So I did something I've never done before. After curtly answering a few more of her questions, such as 'So, do you think you're awful at relationships?', I walked out. The photographer at the cover shoot, Sean McMenomy, happened to be a friend of my brother, Brendan, and he could see what sort of state I was in.

'Hey, Dannii,' he said, softly. 'Let's just shut everything down and go. There's a pub round the corner. Do you fancy a drink?'

I looked up at him, teary-eyed.

'I do, actually,' I said.

For once in my life, I threw professional etiquette out of the window and went to the pub with Sean and got pissed.

A day or so later, I was to appear on the Jonathan Ross show on Radio Two to talk about *Notre-Dame*. It wasn't a good idea. I was already feeling delicate, and though I'd met him before and liked him, his brand of humour wasn't what I was in the mood for at that point in time.

'I think you look great now, Dannii,' Jonathan said when I walked into the studio. 'I saw a picture of you in the paper last week and you looked really fat.'

'Oh, thanks for mentioning,' I said, slightly taken aback.

'It's all right,' he said. 'I liked you when you were fat too!'

I'm sure he was trying to be funny and endearing, but I guess I wasn't in the right frame of mind to laugh, and I think Jonathan realised it quite quickly. Still, I was there because I'd been invited on, and I had a show to promote so I thought I'd better get on with it. It's quite tricky, though, to navigate your way through an interview when the person you're speaking to is far more interested in what they have to say themselves. Although Jonathan clearly found himself hilarious, he didn't give a shit what I had to say about *Notre-Dame* – or anything else come to that, unfortunately – and he made very little secret of it. In the end I started to clam up, making the interview sticky, to say the least.

Towards the end of this painful encounter, he made a comment about people only tuning in to Formula 1 to watch the drivers crash, which also got my back up, as Jacques' father had been killed on the track, and I'd witnessed first-hand the death of a racing marshal at the Grand Prix in Melbourne very recently.

Every time he asked me a question about the show I was appearing in – which is why I'd been invited on in the first place – I barely got to utter two words before he was shouting over the top of me. It was exhausting. The interview went downhill fast after that, to be honest, and once I'd left the studio he was even ruder about me on air. It was a case of 'It doesn't matter; it's just Dannii Minogue'. Jonathan has since said that I was 'being difficult', which is unfair. I don't think it is something either of us remembers with any fondness.

All of this was a reminder of how long I'd been out of the limelight, and exactly what I'd turned my back on, albeit temporarily, to be with Jacques. Now I was coming back simply to get on with my job – the only one I knew how to do – and I felt like I was hitting a brick wall. I didn't seem to know what people wanted from me any more.

When the Sunday supplement piece came out, the paper printed an unflattering nine-year-old picture of me getting out of a car on its cover and the journalist entitled the piece 'Trying To Be Kylie' – and I'm supposed to be the bitch here?

My saving grace around that time was the show itself. The cast and crew and everyone involved were wonderful, and when my opening night arrived I was extremely excited. My brother, Brendan, and Jules and all my London friends, as well as loads of invited press and celebrities, were coming to my first-night performance as the ill-fated heroine, Esmeralda. Even Jacques came to support me that night, and though I knew there was no going back, I was very happy he did.

Half an hour before the show, I did my all-important vocal warm-up with Russell. Then, as I put the finishing touches to my make-up in my dressing room, which was filled with cards and flowers, there was a knock at the door.

'Kylie!'

I was overjoyed to see my sister. After she'd given me a big hug, she smiled and said, 'I can't believe how calm you are! I'd be shaking with nerves!'

And I *was* calm, considering all that had gone on recently.

'I can't be nervous, Kylie,' I told her. 'If I let one single nerve creep in, I'm likely to freeze! I'll tell you what – you be nervous for me, and I'll go out and do the show. Just knowing that you're out there supporting me will get me through.'

'OK, deal!' Kylie said.

And it worked. Every time a nervous thought or feeling tried to sneak its way into my brain, I told myself: 'No. Not nervous. Kylie's doing the nerves; I'm doing the show.' It was always the same when she was starting a big concert tour. I'd tell her that I'd do the panicking, while she got out on the stage and rocked it.

The show that night was nothing less than a triumph for me. As I stood on stage belting out the show's big number, 'Live For The One I Love', I felt some of the unhappiness of the past few weeks melt away . . . just a little. The subsequent reviews said things like: 'Minogue makes magic' and 'Excellent, phenomenal, fantastic!' It was a great start to my run in the show.

I worked hard over the next few months, and I learned more and more about the discipline of being a theatrical performer. On Saturdays, when we had a matinée as well as an evening show, I was always exhausted – it was five hours of singing – and after the evening show, some of the cast members and I would head for the Light Bar in St Martin's Lane Hotel, where we could have some good food, grab a martini and unwind. Then, as Sundays were always 'dark', which meant the theatre was closed, I would sleep almost all day.

I had to get used to keeping completely different hours to my friends. I found it hard to eat before I went on stage, so on most nights at 11.30p.m., when most people would be thinking about going to bed, I'd be heading out from the theatre to have dinner. Most days I'd end up sleeping until midday, and then didn't leave the apartment until I had to go to the theatre. It was a bit like being a vampire.

Around this time I was approached by Radio One DJ Pete Tong, who also ran dance label FFRR, to be a featured vocalist on a brand-new club track called 'Who Do You Love Now?'. Producer Jon Riva and songwriter Victoria Horn had written the track. As soon as I heard its haunting, melancholic melody, I loved it. Once again, though, I was left thinking: 'Why me? Why Dannii?' I wasn't what you'd call 'cool' – I was in a West End musical, for God's sake – and this track was very definitely aimed at a very hip club-dance market. Still, I loved the song and very much missed the recording studio, so I agreed to give it a go. I was missing something else – a manager – and with a new record coming out and all the promotion surrounding it, I was going to need one.

'Why don't you meet my manager, Hillary?' Terry Ronald suggested while we were in the studio recording vocals for the new track. 'I reckon you'd get on.'

A woman manager, eh? Why not? Hillary Shaw was, and is, very well respected in the music industry, and she has worked at various record labels and management companies over the years. Her most famous clients up until that point were the massively successful girl group Bananarama, but these days she manages Girls Aloud.

As luck would have it, we did get on: Hillary was no nonsense and immediately suggested that if the single did well I should be thinking about doing a whole album to follow it up. I liked her instantly – she was stylish and forthright, and I knew that I'd be able to relate to her as a woman as well as a manager. I signed with Hillary, or Hills as she is affectionately known, in the spring of 2001, and as soon as I did, things started to happen.

By the time my successful, five-month run as Esmeralda in *Notre-Dame de Paris* was over in July 2001, 'Who Do You Love Now?' was already getting a huge amount of club play as an instrumental track. The plan was for me to start promoting the vocal version of the song by doing some high-profile club gigs. Before I knew it, I was jetting off to Ibiza with Hillary and Ian Masterson to play at the famous nightclub, Eden.

The minute we landed on the island, I fell in love with it. Ibiza has such a natural beauty, and the dusty, burnt oranges and pale greens of the island reminded me so much of Australia. Even the smell of the trees reminded me of home – it was magical.

The beauty of the old town took my breath away. At night this bustling hub came alive with bars, boutiques and restaurants galore, and a parade of colourful fashionistas and freaks, who marched up and down the cobbled streets handing out flyers for all the various night-clubs on the island. They were on stilts, and in G-strings, decked out in mirror balls, or covered in glitter, and I found myself completely caught up in the spectacle of it. The energy and the vibe of the island were phenomenal.

Eden was a fabulous club: it wasn't the biggest in Ibiza, but its rep-utation preceded it. I remember thinking that the capacity crowd on the night I performed seemed so young. By the time I was due to go on they were ready for a party. The stage jutted out right into the centre of the club and the sub-bass from the huge sound system made everything shake as the kick drum to my brand-new song ripped through it. Then, as I sang the first line of the song, it couldn't have rung any truer . . .

'Where do we go now? I don't know . . .'

This was going to be a great gig, I told myself. I had a feeling it was going to be the start of another whole new era.

Chapter 22

Vagina Days and Neon Nights

During the summer of 2001, 'Who Do You Love Now?' became a huge club hit, but the commercial release of the single wasn't due until November, so it gave me time to start working on tracks for a potential album to follow the single if it was a success. My new record label was London Records, and my A&R manager there was a friendly and enthusiastic northerner called Phil Faversham, 'Fav' to his friends and music business colleagues. He had a very definite view of the direction my album should take.

Rather than sticking to the straight dance atmosphere of 'Who Do You Love Now?', Phil thought the way to go was a tough electro-pop feel, referencing early Madonna and eighties Prince, which of course I loved, and then fusing it with the more hard-hitting electronic beats that were happening on the European dance floors at present. He had a few producers in mind for me to work with, too: the famous Murlyn production team in Sweden, who were the biggest thing in pop music at that time; Neïmo, who were a young Parisian production team; and a London-based team, Thriller Jill, who were none other than my great friends Terry Ronald and Ian Masterson.

Meanwhile, as all this got underway, Sam Richards, my theatrical agent, called me with another intriguing idea. *The Vagina Monologues* was a play written by Eve Ensler. It had a rotating cast of three actresses who all played several different characters apiece. Each of their characters delivered a monologue relating to the vagina in some way, whether it was about birth, menstruation, rape or orgasm. The whole concept of the piece was female empowerment and a woman's varying and individual relationship with her vagina.

Most of the famous actresses who took part in the production usually did so for a three- or four-week run, and that was precisely what I'd been asked to do, alongside comedienne Meera Syal and actress Kika Markham. One of the monologues I was given was delivered by a rather posh British woman in her sixties – so again I was taking on an interesting challenge. Sam Richards hooked me up with a dialect coach to get the accent right. I also turned to my singing teacher, Russell Penn, who was fantastic at helping me vary my tone and speaking voice for all the various characters I had to play.

I relished this experience, and opening night in the charming New Ambassadors Theatre was an absolute scream. Hearing the waves of laughter coming from the audience was a true joy. During my initial set piece, when I got my first laugh, I was taken aback. It was like wielding some wonderful magic power and it was intoxicating: I can completely understand why comedians, who have the wherewithal to make a crowd roar helplessly with laughter, get such a kick out of it.

My run in *The Vagina Monologues* was short – nothing like the five months I'd done in *Notre-Dame de Paris* – but once again I got into the swing of living the night-time existence of a theatre performer: staying up late, eating late and lying in the next morning. Luckily, The Ivy restaurant was opposite the theatre, and I'd have supper and unwind there most nights after the show. I was even fortunate enough to come across a very affable London taxi driver called Steve, who was a regular outside The Ivy, and he would collect me there every night at the same time and drive me back to Battersea.

A few months after my run in the play, I was invited back to perform at a special, one-off event at the Royal Albert Hall, which was called

'V Day' – that's right, Vagina Day. Many women who had previously performed in the now globally famous play joined together that evening to perform the monologues – I was performing with actress and comedienne Nina Wadia. The particular monologue we were doing happened to be the one about the well-spoken British lady in her sixties who was discovering herself, i.e. having her first orgasm. Nina and I were to read a few lines of the monologue in turn, as if we were one voice.

As the applause died down, we began. The crowd was receptive and everything was going along nicely. As the piece reached its climax, so to speak, Nina and I had to voice the sounds of the woman's orgasmic cries, which we did with gusto. This, of course, had the audience in fits of laughter, and even Nina and I had to stifle giggles. I clearly remember my shoulders involuntarily jumping up and down as I tried to stay focused and suppress the laughter.

Then, at the perfect moment in our performance, Nina did a little aside and told the audience that her husband was sitting in the balcony, and that he was a big fan of mine, at which point Nina's husband spontaneously yelled from above, 'I should be so lucky!' Everyone in the audience broke into laughter, as this quip, of course, was a reference to my sister Kylie's worldwide hit of the same name.

I looked up towards the balcony and, with a sardonic tone and a poker-straight face, said, 'Lucky . . . Lucky . . . Lucky . . .'

It brought the house down.

By the time I'd finished my run in *The Vagina Monologues*, I hardly had time to turn around before I found myself making a video and starting promotion for 'Who Do You Love Now?'. It had already been a number one club hit; when it was finally released commercially in November 2001, it shot up to number three in the pop charts, giving me my first Top 10 record in over four years. Phil Faversham was so happy with the record's chart position that he decided to forge straight ahead and finish the album – I was back in the music business again.

I'd already recorded a few songs, but Fav wanted to have as many as possible to choose from so we could put out an absolutely killer album.

Over the next few months my feet didn't touch the ground. Apart from all the promotional trips I did for the single, I also did songwriting trips to Sweden, Paris and New York. This was the first time that I'd had a big hand in writing the songs.

As I'd been writing and recording with Terry Ronald for such a long time, he came along on many of the writing trips, too. It was wonderful to have a friend around to hang out with when we weren't recording, and because of the relaxed nature of our working relationship I found it easy to have fun and enjoy the process when we were.

In Sweden, I recorded at pop hit factory Murlyn, which was set in a beautiful old wooden house in a forest by a lake on the outskirts of Stockholm. I went there on several occasions at different times of the year, and it was wonderful to see the seasons change in those gorgeous surroundings: from snow-covered trees and ice skaters in winter to kids frolicking in the nearby lake in the summer. I was really excited about the tracks that the various Murlyn producers were coming up with for me. I worked with some wonderful people there: Korpi & Blackcell, who produced my next hit, 'Put The Needle On It', songwriter Karen Poole, and Jock-E, who collaborated with me on a song called 'Vibe On', which was rather rude. The other great thing about working in Stockholm was that my close friend from Sydney, Ben Pauley, was living there with his boyfriend, Mathieu. If I got bored with hotel living, I would go and hang out at their apartment and spend my evenings drinking wine, and sampling various Swedish delicacies fresh from the boys' kitchen.

My next stop was New York, where Terry and I worked with the superstar DJ and producer Roger Sanchez, whom I'd previously met in Ibiza. We would turn up at his apartment every day and try out ideas. Roger always encouraged me to push myself lyrically, and not to be afraid to be honest in the things I sang about.

The New York City of March 2002 was completely different to the city I'd known and loved for the past twelve years. Only six months after 9/11, there was a subdued sadness about Manhattan that I felt almost everywhere I went. It was like a blanket had fallen over the city, but with it came a sense of community and brotherhood that I hadn't noticed before either. It was evident in people's behaviour and demeanour on the streets and in the stores and restaurants. Everyone was much nicer to one another, and the sharp-tongued brusqueness that New York was famous for had softened greatly.

I think the most fun I had on my various writing trips was in Paris with the three young, talented boys who called themselves Neïmo. Neïmo are a band as well as a production team. They had sent Fav some backing-track ideas for me, which I loved, so he escorted Terry and me over to Paris to meet them, with a view to us all working together on the songs. The 'studio' was a set-up in the living room of one of the boys. It was small and packed with musical equipment, and all the vocals were done with me shut in the spare bedroom, sitting on the end of the bed holding a microphone. Of course, being young Parisian boys, they all smoked and drank loads of coffee the whole time, so I'd end up joining them and be on a complete caffeine and nicotine buzz most of the time I was working there.

The guys were very cool and extremely handsome: Camille, who played guitar and did lots of synth programming, looked so young and innocent, but was a real joker who kept me laughing the whole time. Bruno, who was the singer in the band, had dark, collar-length hair and bright blue eyes, and he was totally gorgeous. Then there was Matthieu, the keyboard whizz, who was always the quietest of the three boys. Despite that, Terry Ronald fell head over heels in love with him and flirted outrageously the whole time we were there. One day I had to stop Terry trying to hide a gay porn magazine in the bedroom under Matthieu's pillow so his poor girlfriend would find it. He was always funny but a total nightmare.

The Neïmo boys' musical equipment was all vintage stuff. They loved messing around with old synths, drum machines and amps. Camille and Matthieu were obsessive about getting the mix just right, with the finished item being a kind of tough electro-punk sound that I absolutely loved. Of course, for me, they toned down their sound slightly to make it a bit more 'pop', but the influence of their innovative style was still there and we wrote three great songs for the album during our sessions in Paris.

Every morning, Terry and I would head out to the local supermarché to buy bread and cheese for everyone's lunch; if we were feeling in the mood we might have a glass of red wine, too. Then, in the evenings, after a long day in the studio, the Neïmo boys would take us to some amazing Parisian restaurants and bars that we would never have found on our own. I have fond memories of working in Paris with those lovely, talented boys, and we are all friends to this day.

On our third trip to Paris, in May 2002, I noticed that Terry didn't look well and he seemed tired all the time; in fact, one day he didn't come to the studio at all, and stayed in bed at our hotel. This was very odd, as he had never missed a day of work before.

'I'm OK,' he assured me on the Eurostar back to London. 'Just working too hard.'

Two or three weeks later, our manager, Hillary, called me to tell me that Terry had been diagnosed with cancer, and that he wouldn't be accompanying me on any more of the writing trips. I was horrified.

'Can I see him?' I asked her.

Hillary said that Terry didn't want to see anyone. He was about to start chemotherapy straight away and wanted only his family around him. He was much sicker than anyone could have imagined – as I was to discover a few months later, on what should have been a happy occasion.

Both born on 20 October, Terry Ronald and I have shared pretty much every birthday since 1991, when I was twenty. Consequently, we've had to come up with quite a few different ideas to celebrate, and some of them have been rather interesting. There was the *Breakfast at Tiffany's* cocktail party at my apartment in Battersea in 1995, when we mixed exotic cocktails, played fifties jazz and Burt Bacharach, and dressed up to the nines.

This was the one where we popped to the supermarket to buy all the bits and pieces for the cocktails and I got photographed with a shopping trolley full of nothing but alcohol. The next day, in one of the papers, there was the picture of me with absolutely no make-up on, doing a wino's trolley dash around Sainsbury's with a headline that said something like 'Dannii's binge drinking nightmare!'

Then there was the Studio 54 party in 1998, which we spent the whole of the 'Unleashed' tour planning. This was going to be a tribute to the fabulous seventies nightclub in New York, and everyone was to come in the appropriate fancy dress. I decided to get a bright red colour put on my hair for the occasion, and had it styled exactly like Farrah Fawcett-Majors in *Charlie's Angels*, complete with the famous 'Farrah flick'. This resulted in me leaving the hairdressers and tearing down the street being chased by yet another photographer who desperately wanted a shot of 'Dannii's shocking new look!', not realising, of course, it was for a fancy-dress party. This, too, hit the headlines the next day and everybody thought I'd gone stark raving mad.

The party, at the trendy Notting Hill Arts Centre in London, was fabulous and one of our best, with all of our friends in full disco regalia, including my brother as Dirk Diggler, with Jules as Rollergirl from the film *Boogie Nights*. Terry and Ian came as Studio 54 bus boys with white knee socks, satin shorts and bow ties. Famous DJ Joey Negro came and played a set for us that night too – it was quirky and glamorous and just what we wanted.

In 1999, I was in Melbourne for my birthday, so Terry and I didn't get to celebrate together. I had decided to have drinks with a small gathering of close friends in a lovely little private bar in a club in the city. It was a divine evening and I'd invited along my former hyperactive nemesis, Bevan, and some of the *Young Talent Time* crowd, as well as some of my newer friends, and they all turned up with beautiful birthday presents, which we put on a 'gift table' at the back of our private area while we were enjoying ourselves.

Towards the end of the evening, when I went over to the table, I discovered that all the gifts had been stolen – every single one of them – apparently by a couple of guys who'd wandered in from another room in the club. I hadn't opened a single present or card, and the thought that somebody would do that made me sick to my stomach. When I called Terry in London the next day to wish him happy birthday and tell him about my stolen gifts, I discovered that he, too, had fallen prey to criminals. Terry hadn't reached his meticulously planned birthday dinner – he'd been violently mugged on the way there and ended up in hospital for the night.

'Let's not spend our birthdays apart again,' I suggested to him on the phone that day. 'It's obviously very bad luck!'

Our birthday in 2002 was another story altogether. Terry had undergone months of chemotherapy by this time. Though I desperately wanted to see him, he was adamant that he didn't want to face anyone feeling and looking the way he did. I was determined, though, so I had Hills call Terry's mum, Margaret, and arrange for Hillary and me to visit him at his apartment on the day of our birthday.

In the car on the way there, Hills told me that I ought to prepare myself, as Terry had not reacted well to chemotherapy. Even having had this warning, when we arrived I was completely knocked for six: this wasn't my friend I was looking at lying on the bed but a bag of skin and bones with no hair and absolutely no light in his eyes. I'd known Terry's mum and his Aunt Rose for years, and they were both there looking after him as he was too ill to do anything for himself. When I walked further into the darkened bedroom where he was lying, I had to fight back the tears. He looked yellow, and his Aunt Rose told me that was because of all the chemo he'd been having. I kissed him on the head and wished him happy birthday, and he smiled weakly at Hillary and me as we sat down on the bed for a chat with him.

I'd never had a friend or known anyone with cancer before, or seen first-hand the effects of chemotherapy. Seeing someone you know and love like that is heartbreaking. It brought home to me how fragile life can be. When I looked up from the bed towards Terry's mum and our eyes met, a conversation took place between us without words. She didn't have to say anything, but the look in her eyes said it all. It was a look I remembered well and was to see in the eyes of my own mother a couple of years later.

When Hills and I got back in the car, we were both quiet for a long time.

'What can we do?' I eventually asked her.

'We just have to keep going,' she said. 'And keep thinking positive thoughts. That's all we can do.'

*

The following day I had to throw myself straight back into work, as I had a record to finish, difficult though that might be. Terry had become a mainstay of my musical life: I always felt so confident about my performances in the studio when he was around to help steer me. It was going to be very strange and sad recording the rest of the album without him.

By this time I felt that the sound of the album was coming together. I was enjoying being so hands-on with the lyrics and production ideas, and I felt confident enough to tell the people I was working with exactly what I did and didn't like. I wanted this to be my best work ever, and it looked like I was going to get my wish.

When the next single, 'Put The Needle On It', was released in October 2001, it was an instant number-one club hit, then it went soaring up the pop charts too. The record had such a cool, sharp, original sound, and the video, featuring me languishing on a giant, slow-spinning record with an elfin-like cropped hairstyle, was dark, sexy and moody. I started to get much more fan mail then, too. Many letters were from people telling me that although they hadn't been a fan of mine before, the sound of 'Who Do You Love Now?' and 'Put The Needle On It' had converted them. People couldn't wait for the album, which now had a title: *Neon Nights*.

Chapter 23

From Russia with Cash

For the past year or so, throughout the *Neon Nights* writing and recording period, I'd been happily and quietly dating a guy called Craig Logan. He'd originally been in the eighties pop band Bros, and was now very successful in artist management, working for Roger Davies, who looked after artists such as Cher, Tina Turner and, a favourite of mine, Janet Jackson. Craig had known Hills and Terry for some years. After I'd first met him, briefly, at a television studio and we hit it off, Craig kept calling them both, asking if they thought I might be interested in going on a date with him.

'What do you think?' I'd asked Hills over dinner one evening. 'He seems really nice.'

'He is a lovely guy. You could do a lot worse,' she advised me, like a stereotypical Jewish mother. 'I think you should at least go out on a date.'

'Well, maybe we should all go out together,' I suggested.

So poor Craig had ended up taking me out on a date to one of my favourite London restaurants, Nobu, one Friday night, with Hills and Terry tagging along as chaperones – and he treated us all to a really lovely evening. Craig was charming, and pretty good to look at too, with soft brown eyes and fine, chiselled features. I got a few knowing looks from Hills that night: I think she could tell right away that I was hooked.

My relationship with Craig, as it turned out, was a hell of a lot more relaxed and under the radar than what I'd been used to with Julian and Jacques. After the public drama surrounding those two break-ups, I was more than happy to keep it that way. Craig was warm and kind, and he had a real romantic streak that appealed to me. Although we were both in the music industry, we hardly ever went to showbiz parties or big events. After all the craziness of travelling around and writing for the album, it was nice to come back to Craig, who was so laidback and normal. We'd spend weekends at his picturesque house in the country, going for walks, watching movies and cooking. I felt like I had something solid in my life.

Unfortunately, it wasn't to last. Geography once again put paid to what I thought might be a long romance when Craig was offered the prestigious job of running Roger's office in Los Angeles. Here we go again, I thought. We were both happy at the time, but I did what I always did, and told him that he couldn't possibly turn down such a fantastic opportunity. Although I didn't want him to go, I wanted to be as supportive a girlfriend as I could be, and not clingy and selfish about it. I knew from bitter experience that our relationship would not survive it, and sadly I was right. As it turned out, Craig would be my last serious boyfriend before I met Kris five long years later.

Luckily, though, there was a Mr Right of a slightly different variety round the corner in the shape of a devilishly handsome guy called Benjamin Hart. Benjamin had worked for the Storm modelling agency that I'd had a contract with for a while; we had met briefly at their offices one day, but that was all. Then Benjamin's boyfriend, who ran a club in Amsterdam, booked me to play a special one-off gig at the club, and that's where Benjamin and I really clicked. I remember very clearly, after finishing my show in that awesome, thumping monster of a nightclub, the two of us sitting at a table swapping risotto recipes like two old nanas, both yelling over the ear-splitting music to be heard. It was so uncool – but fun – and we laughed and talked late into the night.

Benji is an actor now, but back then he was a model, and I could see why: his neatly cut dark hair, muscular arms and ridiculously square jaw were sure to turn the head of anyone who appreciates a fine-looking man, but his rugged looks were tempered by a soft voice and sweet nature that captured me right away.

'We'll have to hook up once we're back in London,' Benjamin yelled at me over the din of thumping house music.

'I'm sure we will!' I said.

We became great friends and spent a lot of time together – in fact, before I met Kris, Benji was my date at countless awards dinners and premieres, leading him to refer to me jokingly as 'The Wife'. I didn't know it then, but Benjamin was going to play quite a major role in helping me to catch my real Mr Right several years down the line.

My next single release from the *Neon Nights* album was in March 2003, and it was my biggest hit ever. 'I Begin To Wonder' stormed into the charts at number two – only kept off that coveted number-one slot by Christina Aguilera's 'Beautiful'. The song had originally been a hit in Germany for an artist called J.C.A. For my version, Ian Masterson and I had added some new lyrics before I was 100 per cent happy with it. I loved everything about this record: the lyrics, the sound of the track and the edgy video, which I had fun shooting.

Hills arranged a little celebration party at the private club Soho House in London on the rainy Sunday afternoon when the chart rundown was being announced on Radio One. My London friends came to celebrate my biggest hit with me. Jules was there, and Russell, my singing teacher, Tim Reed, who had looked after me on *Notre-Dame*, Ian Masterson and my whole 'Unleashed' band, including Terry, who had now come through his chemotherapy and was in complete remission. It was a happy afternoon and we all got very merry listening to the chart countdown and then cheering and dancing when 'I Begin To Wonder' finally blasted through the speakers.

For me, everything was exactly right with the release of 'I Begin To

Wonder'. The *Neon Nights* album followed the single quickly and went gold in a matter of weeks. It seemed that the months of travelling back and forth from Sweden and Paris, writing and recording so many songs had paid off. What made me most proud about the success of this album, more than any other, was that I'd had such a big hand in writing the songs and giving it its musical sound and flavour. All the production teams I'd worked with had been fantastic, and Fav, my A&R manager, had guided us through the process brilliantly. The best thing about it was that not only did the fans love *Neon Nights* but the critics did too. With *Love and Kisses*, I'd had an album that the fans loved but the critics weren't that bothered about, while the critics loved *Girl* but not enough people bought it.

'I finally bloody got it right with this one!' I told Fav.

There was one more crowning achievement for the *Neon Nights* album when my next single came out. 'Don't Wanna Lose This Feeling' was one of the songs I'd written in Paris with Terry and the Neïmo boys, but Fav thought the chorus needed strengthening, so a pop writer called James Khari came up with a punchier new one. It was so good, in fact, that Fav decided it would be the fourth single from the album, which prompted the boys from Neïmo to do a new version of the song, fusing it with an instrumental mix of Madonna's 'Into The Groove'. In the music biz, we call it a 'mash-up', cleverly laying the vocals of one song over the backing track to another. When I heard it, being the Madonna fan that I am, I went nuts for it.

This version of the song was re-christened 'Don't Wanna Lose This Groove', and it flew straight to the top of the club charts. I couldn't release this cool new mix commercially without somebody's express permission – that of Madonna herself.

'Great!' I said to Hills. 'And how do we do that, exactly?'

Luckily, my record company, London, was under the same umbrella as Madonna's label – the umbrella being Warner Music – so I had my people contact her people, as they say, and ask very nicely if we could use the sample of 'Into The Groove' on my record. Of course, she wanted to hear what we'd done with it first, and we correctly assumed that she and the other writers of 'Into The Groove' would want a chunk of the publishing rights. Eventually, I heard back that Madonna liked the mix and would allow us to release it with the sample of her song intact. It was the first time she'd ever let anyone sample one of her songs, and when it came out 'Don't Wanna Lose This Groove' got as much airplay as the original. We even ended up doing a new version of the video cut to the Madonna mix.

Of course, with the success of *Neon Nights* and its four big-hit singles came an absolute frenzy of promotion, television appearances and photo shoots. I had fun shooting covers for *Elle* magazine in India and *FHM* in France and, once again, I started cropping up in all those notorious 'sexiest women' polls. I was comfortable with myself now, happy in my own skin. I wasn't 'fat' Dannii any more, or dangerously thin Dannii or naked Dannii or even Dannii with the new boob job . . . I was a 32-year-old woman who worked hard and always tried to look her best; if people found that sexy, then great. The thing is, all those previous labels had been stuck on me by other people anyway and I realised now that they had nothing to do with how I felt about myself. The most important thing at the end of the day is how you feel about yourself.

There were lots of gigs and club dates all over the world and *lots* of air travel. Hills and I seemed to be on and off planes every five minutes. If Hills wasn't around, her right-hand woman, Angela, would be there to take the reins. We did promotional trips to France, America, Canada, Australia, Ireland, Germany and Japan, and I performed at Capital Radio's 'Party in the Park' in London, the Berlin Dance awards and the prestigious Logie awards ceremony in my home town of Melbourne all in the space of a couple of months. We really racked up the air miles.

It could be a lot of fun travelling around with Hills, despite the hard work, and having a female manager was very different to what I'd been used to with Terry Blamey. Quite apart from the fact that Hills could understand all those 'girly gripes' I might have far more than a man ever could, we also got to 'ooh and ahh' over one another's newest bags and shoes, and wile away the many hours of travel picking out the best shots from the latest photo shoot I'd done. Hills was, and still is, meticulous about her appearance, and sometimes I think it took her longer to get ready than it did me – and we often laughed as I had to remind her that I was the one going on stage or in front of the camera.

Some of the private gigs Hills was offered at that time were very well paid, and one of them in particular was quite intriguing. Hills was approached by a rich Russian businessman asking me to appear at a private party for his sister's birthday in Turkey. Once all the details of the gig had been set and the flights and dancers booked, Hills invoiced for the money to be paid up front into her management account – but it never arrived. So she telephoned her Russian contact: 'The money hasn't been wired,' Hills told them, sternly. 'We are not leaving the UK until I have it in my account.' Hills wasn't a woman one messed with.

'It's coming, Ms Shaw, I promise you,' the Russians assured her, mysteriously. On the day before we were scheduled to leave for Turkey – which was a Saturday – the money still hadn't arrived.

Hills made one final call.

'Look! The money's still not here, so I guess the deal is off,' she told the Russians. 'I'm not letting my artist fly out there on a wing and a prayer without any assurance that she's getting paid for her work. I always insist on 100 per cent of the money before we do the show.'

'Don't worry, please, Ms Shaw,' her contact reassured her. 'The show will still go ahead. Later today a man will arrive at Heathrow airport and there he will hand you the money personally in cash. Then you and Miss Minogue leave for Turkey the next day for the party, yes?'

Hills was taken aback. It was a lot of money and they were telling her that some Russian guy was going to breeze through UK Customs with a briefcase full of cash and hand it over at the airport. It was a bit like a cheap sixties spy thriller, but we were all so amused by it that Hills agreed to the Heathrow rendezvous and sent our live booking agent, Shaz, to collect the money, which, after a few hushed mobile-phone calls and some concise instructions, he did successfully – mission accomplished.

When Hills and I arrived to perform at the party, which was at the gorgeous Kempinski Hotel in the swanky resort town of Bodrum in

Turkey, I was quite surprised, after all that fuss, to find myself performing for the birthday girl and her twenty-five or so guests for about twenty-five minutes. But I lived it, loved it, drank the champagne and basked in my James Bond-like adventure.

Towards the end of 2003 and throughout the following year, all the hard work and promotion for the album started to pay dividends. I'd racked up my biggest run of chart successes to date. As well as an Aria award nomination in my home country for Best Pop Album, I was crowned Best Female Artist at the Disney Awards. 'I Begin To Wonder' was ranked among the biggest selling singles of 2003 in the UK. In Australia, both 'Put The Needle On It' and 'I Begin To Wonder' were placed in the top twenty singles of the year. It felt like the Sun had started to shine and I didn't want it to end.

Chapter 24

Disclosure

Over the years, I'd been involved in several charity events and cam-
paigns that truly resonated with me and I was passionate about:
Funny Women at the Royal Festival Hall, in aid of the Women For Breast
Cancer Care campaign, several wildlife conservation projects and the
Unite Against Hunger campaign, which is a food crisis relief programme that took me back to South Africa. This charity, spearheaded
by food giant Tiger Brands, ensures that more than 10,000 children
across South Africa get much needed food every month, and the work
the charity does is fantastic.

In October 2004, I was appointed ambassador for young people for
the Terrence Higgins Trust (THT), which is the UK's leading HIV and
sexual-health charity; it is a position, I'm proud to say, that I still hold
today. I had been involved with several other HIV/AIDS charities in the
past: the Bobby Goldsmith Foundation in Australia, taking part in the
Walk for Life for Crusaid in London most summers, and performing at
a ball to raise money for The Lighthouse Foundation.

The THT position, however, was something I was especially passionate about as it was aimed at young people, and I felt I could bring

something to the table and reach out to a young crowd, particularly as I was so involved in the club scene now. My role as THT ambassador was first to highlight and then to try to stamp out prejudice, and to help raise funds to support people living with HIV. I was very keen to play a role in educating people, especially younger teens, about the disease and prevention.

It was through the Terrence Higgins Trust that I met a wonderful young HIV-positive girl called Sarah Watson. We did an interview together for a teenage magazine called *Sugar* to highlight her personal journey and to warn other kids of the dangers of unsafe sex. As she spoke, I found her totally inspiring.

In 1993, Sarah had been a typical young woman who was in love with her steady boyfriend and had fallen pregnant. Her boyfriend suggested that the pair went for an HIV test, which seemed reasonable enough to Sarah, particularly as he assured her that he'd been tested before and all had been well. When they went for the results of the test, though, they were given the shocking news that they were both HIV positive. Although, at first, Sarah's boyfriend convinced her that it could easily have been she who had passed the virus onto him, she later discovered that he'd previously been an intravenous drug user and had most likely contracted the disease from sharing needles. Despite the risk, he had recklessly opted to have unsafe sex with Sarah. It also turned out that he hadn't been tested earlier.

It was a terrifying time for Sarah. With things as they were in those days – before the advent of successful drug treatments – she decided, with the doctor's support, that keeping the baby probably wasn't a good idea. How could she think about bringing up a child who could be infected with HIV when she didn't know how long she had left to live herself? So, on top of this painful news, she had to have an abortion, which completely shattered her world.

By the time I met Sarah, she was busy campaigning and talking to kids all over the country to try to warn them about the dangers of unprotected sex, and to teach them how simple it is to be tested. She has to spend the rest of her life on HIV medication, which, although life-saving, often has a host of unpleasant and often debilitating side effects. Her story both touched and motivated me, and made me even more resolute to fulfil my role as THT's ambassador for young people. Sarah and I have stayed in touch ever since.

These days her life has certainly turned around. Sarah has a gorgeous, supportive husband, Matthew, and a healthy baby girl. The drugs have changed over the years to allow a woman to become pregnant and give birth to a healthy HIV-free child. It certainly shows how the research money is moving things forward, and that is exactly why I joined the fight.

One chilly evening at the start of 2005, I arrived home tired from work as the man at the security desk in my apartment building was buzzing me.

'Miss Minogue, there's someone trying to deliver flowers directly to your apartment,' he said. 'But I told them they have to leave them here at the security desk – is that OK?'

'Sure,' I said. 'I'll come down and collect them.'

The lovely bouquet of winter roses came with a handwritten note. Once I got back upstairs, I put the flowers down on the kitchen counter, sat down on my couch with a cup of green tea and flipped open the neatly folded paper. What I read sent me reeling in shock and complete confusion. It was from a female journalist at a very well-known tabloid newspaper, and her business card was enclosed. The note read as follows:

17 February 2005

Dear Ms Minogue,

I need to speak to you face to face as a matter of urgency. I understand that you are suffering from an illness particularly relating to your campaigning work.

We are planning to run a piece on this subject this weekend. However, I need to speak to you or an adviser of yours first.

It is a very serious matter – I cannot stress enough how important it is that you make contact with me as soon as possible.

I will wait in the car park for an hour, and will not, after
delivering these flowers, approach the security desk again.
Sincerely . . .

What? *What?* Suffering from an illness particularly relating to my campaigning work? Was this hastily scrawled document saying what I think it was saying? That this newspaper was about to announce to the world that I was HIV positive?

I sat completely numb on my couch for several minutes, staring out of my window at the glorious twilit London skyline. Should I go and meet this woman? Did she expect some sort of admission or denial? Where the hell did this come from? I stood up and walked quickly across the room to where the flowers lay, picked them up, walked across the kitchen and viciously smashed them head first into the rubbish bin. No, I wasn't going to speak to her. I was going to speak to my manager, Hillary.

I was frightened, though. All I could think was: why? Why would someone do this to me? It's not like having HIV is a crime, but it was completely untrue and I felt that I was being accused. I'd seen first-hand the kind of prejudice people who do have HIV have to face, and it wasn't nice. What if it had been true – what if I had been positive? Wouldn't that be the most horrible infringement of a person's right to non-disclosure? I felt like my private world had been invaded, and this faceless woman journalist, in just a few minutes, had become my mortal enemy. When I think about it in hindsight, I wonder if she might have been trying to help me out by contacting me, wanting to get the facts right. Maybe she'd been told to write the piece and was doing everything she could to seek me out in an attempt to warn me about it, or to let me have my say. Maybe she wasn't the bad guy. At the time, though, I assumed that both she and the publication she worked for were out to get me, and I knew I had to jump on it quickly.

When Hills called the newspaper, she got nowhere fast, and she recounted her conversation with the editor to me.

'What the hell is this about?' she'd asked. 'Dannii is really upset and I'd like to know where this has come from.'

'We have it on *very* good authority,' the editor had replied, flatly.

'What do you mean: "very good authority"?' Hills said. 'She's not HIV positive – end of story. That's from her management. That's from her!'

'Yes, I understand,' the editor said. 'But our information is better than that.'

Better than that? Better than the horse's mouth? Then who? But, of course, they wouldn't disclose their source, and the whole conversation was completely futile. Now I had to decide what I was going to do next.

Over the next day or so, nothing was resolved and I was getting more and more stressed. I was taking sleeping tablets to get to sleep and I couldn't concentrate on work at all. I guess I'm a bit of a control freak when push comes to shove, and this was definitely out of my control. No matter how many times we told the paper that the story wasn't true, they said they knew it was and were running it whatever. I knew only too well that even if they were proved wrong somewhere down the line, the size of the printed retraction would be about a tenth of the size of the original screaming headline. I thought about Sarah and some of the wonderful and inspirational people I'd met and worked with through the Terrence Higgins Trust, and how people with HIV must have this nightmare about disclosure all the time – at work and with family and friends. I suppose I had to be grateful that, at the end of the day, whatever some lying headline said, I didn't have HIV. I decided that the only thing I could do to stop the story running for sure was to prove that I wasn't positive. So I called my doctor to arrange for an HIV test.

It's hard to describe how I felt on the way to my doctor in the car that morning. Having to draw blood to prove that I wasn't lying about something that should have remained private was sickening, to say the least. I was on my own, but what I really wanted was for someone to hold my hand and tell me how outrageous it was, and how unfair, and to say out loud all the things I was thinking. When I got to my doctor's office and whacked my arm on the table, ready for the needle, I thought: I'm a pop singer. What the hell has this got to do with anyone else? But no answer came back.

The results of the blood test were sent directly to the desk of the editor of the newspaper, and they were negative. I almost wish I could have delivered the test results myself, slapping the paper on the editor's desk under his nose: 'There. Now . . . Leave . . . Me . . . Alone!'

I wanted it over and, as soon as they got the test results, it was.

After that, I had even more compassion for the people who worked for the Terrence Higgins Trust and the people they were trying to help. The fact of the matter is that a national newspaper was prepared to print something that, true or not, could quite easily devastate a family or destroy a career. The whole incident made me feel angry and very sad.

Spending time with Laura was always the best cure for the blues, a real pick-me-up. Whenever I was in South Africa hanging out with her and her mum, Tina, I felt completely relaxed and unbridled. Laura and I would talk and talk for hours, sitting around in shorts and bikinis in the sun, then cook a great meal in the evening, drink some wine and talk a bit more. Their house was in Hermanus, which is a gorgeous spot on the southern coast of the Western Cape. It is where the whales come to swim in spring. Every night while I was there, Laura and I would go to the beach at sunset and take a long walk with her dogs. It was a complete joy to be out in the fresh air. The lifestyle in South Africa is very similar to that in Australia. There was always a *braai* – which is Afrikaans for barbecue – happening somewhere, and there'd often be a casual invitation from someone Laura knew to 'drop by' if we felt like it. It certainly was a change from my usual hectic, pre-planned city life in London.

Whenever Laura and I went out on the town, whatever country we happened to be in, we were like the naughtiest girls at the party. She'd always cook up some mischief and drag me right into the thick of it with her outrageous laugh or her flirtatious nature. It didn't matter whether we went out with ten people or just the two of us, we always had the best time wherever we were. I spent so much time with Laura and Tina, in fact, either in Eze or in Hermanus, that Tina started to think of me as a second daughter. With Laura being an only child, I was more than happy to fill the role of a surrogate sister for her.

Tina is an amazing woman – just like her daughter. Born in South Africa, Tina had been a model when she was younger and was very beautiful. In fact, she has the highest cheekbones I have ever seen and an incredible zest for life that I find inspiring. Tina always sees absolutely every little sparkle in nature's beauty, and something as simple as a bird flying past or a butterfly fluttering overhead would have her utterly enchanted. She has a good eye and a natural instinct for decorating, too, and her homes were comfortable, cosy and fabulous. Antiques were placed with flair, and shots from her modelling days hung on the walls alongside cute black-and-white childhood pictures of Laura with long curly pigtails and the cheekiest grin you have ever seen.

Music always filled Tina and Laura's houses. We all enjoyed chilled-out dance music, and those cool Ibiza compilations that made such perfect summer listening. On her travels, Laura was always finding unusual and rare CDs that I'd never heard of but always ended up loving.

A favourite weekly pastime for the three of us was to go shopping at the local markets together. The food markets in Italy were always a weekly trip from Eze: Sanremo or Ventimiglia. We'd stock up on the wonderful fresh produce, then we'd stop for a long lunch, soaked with rosé and finished off with limoncello.

Sadly, though, the precious time I spent with Laura and Tina seemed to fly by. Before I knew it I'd be back in London working on yet another new project.

There *was* a new project, too. Believe it or not, I'd changed record labels again by the start of 2005, despite the success of *Neon Nights*. London Records had dissolved the previous year, and its umbrella company, Warners, had gone through a huge shake-up. By the time the dust settled, everybody who had worked closely with me on *Neon Nights* had gone, and it didn't feel like home any more. Warners then told Hills that because of internal politics, they couldn't release any of my records for at least a year; if I wanted to go off and find a new record deal elsewhere, I could. I could hold onto the rights to any new tracks I'd recorded with them after *Neon Nights*.

So, in the latter part of 2004, I signed with independent dance label All Around The World, which was a small but extremely successful dance label in Blackburn in the north of England, run by a pair of lovely guys, Matt and Chris. I was now starting to write songs for a new album, after I'd had one Top 10 record with All Around The World called 'You Won't Forget About Me', which had also topped all the club charts and become my eighteenth chart hit.

That summer I put together a team of friends and proudly took part in the HIV and AIDS charity Crusaid's Walk For Life again. Terry Ronald, Ian, Benjamin, Russell, Jules and many of my London family joined me on the walk. We christened our team 'In there like swimwear' – there was no rhyme or reason to the name, it just made us laugh and fitted the bill for our motley crew.

It was a truly great day. Although we completed the ten-kilometre stroll in a fairly respectable time, there had been a fair few stops along the way for the odd glass of Pimm's or fish and chips.

The blackest of clouds was hanging over me on the sunny Sunday afternoon of the walk, however. Although I wore a fixed smile as we strolled through the streets of London, my friends walking with me knew well that their laughter and support were all that was keeping me going.

Just a couple of short weeks before, I had heard some news that had not only devastated me and turned my entire family's lives upside down, it had also broken the music world's collective ear.

Chapter 25

My Sister

Long before she was the exalted pop goddess she is today – before the hits, the hairdos and the headlines; before the lovers, the feathers and the gold hot pants; long before the whole world owned a little piece of her – Kylie Minogue was just my big sister.

We've never been closer than we are now. In 2009, when she joined me as my special guest judge on *The X Factor*, I couldn't have been happier – for so many reasons.

Kylie first forged her way into the British and Australian consciousness when she appeared in the long-running Aussie soap *Neighbours* in the late eighties. Her astounding transition from soap star to pop princess to global icon is, of course, very well documented. Beneath all the stardust there remains a very caring, down-to-earth girl, with an enlightened spirit and a generous heart, who loves her home and her family deeply.

Ever since she was a little girl, dancing with me around the lounge in Wantirna to 'Greased Lightning', Kylie has been a showgirl. Sometimes when she steps out onto the stage of a capacity-filled arena and sings her heart out for the crowd, I can still sometimes see the little girl standing there and singing into a hairbrush on a swirly carpet stage with a flock-wallpaper backdrop.

Of course, if you believed the press over the years, you might think that Kylie and I are something more akin to Joan Crawford and Bette Davis in *Whatever Happened to Baby Jane* than the loving sisters we are. Ever since I'd arrived in the UK in 1991, the press and the media have pitted us against one another, first favouring my supposed 'cooler, darker' image over Kylie's girl-next-door, bubblegum sweetness, then turning on me with a constant deluge of unflattering comparisons to my sister. Never mind that Dannii has had ten Top 10 records – Kylie has had twenty! Never mind that Dannii's album has gone gold – Kylie's has gone platinum. I can't pretend that some of it hasn't been vicious and hurtful over the years: it has. Less success was no success at all as far as my critics were concerned. As much as it broke my heart at times, it never made me any less proud and supportive of my sister, and I received the same love and support from her . . . in spades!

Nowadays, the press appears to have settled down to the fact that I have a successful career in my own right. Consequently, Kylie and I had a fantastic time when she asked me to join her on her television special for ITV in 2007 and we sent up our 'legendary' sibling rivalry in a brilliantly staged cat-fight.

The sketch was set in Kylie's imaginary dressing room at the television studio. While 'Kylie' sits reading *The Racing Post*, sister 'Dannii' turns up wearing an identical shiny Dolce & Gabbana leopard-print frock, wrongly assuming that it is her TV special as well as Kylie's.

'Mum and Dad will be so proud,' the long auburn-wigged 'Dannii' purrs to a horror-struck 'Kylie', who tells her sister what she thinks of her.

'Don't you need talent to be a talent-show judge?'

And then, inevitably, a magnificently stunt-coordinated fight ensues, with us flinging each other violently around the room, screaming insults. The battle involves flying champagne bottles, Kylie being flung into a clothing rail and, of course, lots of hair pulling.

Beforehand, Kylie and I were quite nervous – after all, neither of us was a comedienne. We weren't sure we'd be able to do the scene justice. Kylie and I did come up with some ideas of our own about delivery and staging and added a couple of extra lines, but once we were on the set the nerves really kicked, as we had to show the director and all the crew our 'hilarious' ideas.

'What if we think it's hysterically funny and they all hate it?' I said to Kylie anxiously.

It was as if we were little girls play-acting in their bedroom, not two seasoned professionals who had both been on television practically all their lives. In the end, we decided just to have fun with it. We figured if we were having a great time, then so would the people watching us. Once filming got under way, we really did have fun, and we couldn't stop laughing at the comedy violence, carried off to perfection by our very own stunt doubles. Mum and Dad were in London at that time, so they had come along to the filming. I think they got a real kick out of seeing us together having such a great time.

Towards the end of the sketch, Simon Cowell – who played himself – walks into the dressing room, which is now pretty much destroyed, and catches 'the girls' mid-fight. 'The resemblance is remarkable,' he says to Kylie as she recomposes herself. 'You must be Dannii's mum!' The sketch ends with Kylie punching Simon in the face and knocking him out, and the two of us innocently looking to camera as if nothing had happened.

Poor Simon. He'd been so kind in agreeing to appear in the sketch, but he was so out of his comfort zone with acting. He had to say only those two lines, but he had to do it at least ten times before he got it anywhere near right, and he was mortified.

Not long after Kylie's TV special, the two of us got the chance to work together once again, recording our first proper duet together since we'd performed 'Sisters Are Doing It For Themselves' back in the *Young Talent Time* days. It was for the BBC TV comedy *Beautiful People*, written by Jonathan Harvey. As the musical director on the show was none other than my good friend Ian Masterson, an idea was hatched that grew and grew. The TV show was set in the mid-nineties and told the story of a very 'theatrical' teenage boy who longed to leave his dreary home town and find the 'Beautiful People'. It was based on the memoirs of the author and creative director of Barney's department store in New York, Simon Doonan.

A year later, on the second series, I got to flex my comedic muscle again. I had a cameo role on the show, playing myself as I was in 1998. Wearing a long blonde wig from the BBC make-up department and a replica dress from my 'All I Wanna Do' video, I got to send up the press portrayal of the ultimate 'Dannii delusion' in a scene where the director had me stick pins in a Barbie voodoo doll of Kylie – it was a scream.

For the first series, though, Ian had an idea for us to record a version of the ABBA classic 'The Winner Takes It All' for an appropriate scene in episode six. What started off as a simple idea snowballed into something rather more elaborate. Terry Ronald came on board to produce Kylie's vocals and mine, and Kylie's musical director, Steve Anderson, who by then had worked with her for fifteen years, was to co-produce the track along with Ian, who had big ideas about the production.

'I want to get the full BBC concert orchestra playing on it,' Ian announced to Terry and me one day at the studio. 'It'll be amazing!'

Steve Anderson was for it. As the musical director who had worked on all of Kylie's live shows and lavish arrangements over the years, he wasn't exactly renowned for his subtle approach to a musical number. Now we had two Minogue sisters, two gay men and one who might just as well have been, an ABBA song and the BBC concert orchestra – camp wasn't the word.

Before the recording dates, Terry and I flew up to Glasgow, where Kylie was due to perform on her 'Homecoming' tour, so that she and I could run through the song with Steve Anderson. We sang it in her dressing room with Terry doing all the Benny and Björn backing vocals. It was another one of those childhood-memory moments: Kylie in her dressing gown as one of the ABBA girls and me singing into an empty Coke bottle as the other. When I eventually heard the finished track with the full force of the BBC orchestra behind us, I was over the moon.

It's been wonderful to do those fun things with Kylie in the last few years, and I've learned to appreciate those moments all the more since 2005, when I might have lost her.

I was in London when Mum and Dad called me with the news that my sister had been diagnosed with breast cancer. When you hear something that terrible it's difficult to believe, or even absorb, what you're hearing.

'I'll get on the first plane home,' I told Dad.

Kylie was in Melbourne at the time, in the midst of her 'Showgirl' tour, so at least she had the family around her.

'I have to warn you, though,' Dad said. 'There has to be a public announcement because Kylie has to cancel the rest of the tour and the insurers will want to know why. We'll have to tell the public exactly what's going on, and I think this is all going to happen before you can get back to Melbourne, so you might be in for a bit of a feeding frenzy with the press over there.'

'OK,' I said.

I was in total shock, but I knew I had to organise myself as fast as I could. 'I have to get back home as soon as possible,' I said to my assistant, Nina. 'Could you book me a ticket?'

The word 'home' reverberated in my brain. I had to get home. I had to see my sister.

By the next morning, the story had hit the press and it was all anyone was talking about: you couldn't turn on the radio without there being a Kylie record playing, and every morning-television show had some celebrity 'expert' offering up his or her opinions about Kylie's prognosis, and what she must be going through and, indeed, what might happen next. I couldn't stand to hear any more: the speculation, the assumptions, the worst-case scenarios. I knew that everybody was only wishing the best for Kylie and trying to convey the public's love and support, but this was my sister they were talking about, and I needed to hear her tell me herself how she was feeling, and hear her doctor tell me what was going to happen.

I flew home with British Airways, and the staff at the airport couldn't have been more considerate and helpful. They obviously knew what was going on, and they were very gentle with me, helping me to get on and off the flight without any press bothering me and with as little fuss as possible. When we stopped to refuel in Singapore and I headed for the executive lounge, one of the British Airways staff told me that there was a Reuters film crew there waiting for me, and they were expecting an interview.

'No,' I said to him. 'I'm sorry. I can't. I don't want to speak to anyone until I've seen my family or my sister; I'm just not up to it. Could someone convey that to them, please? Is there any way you can help me get back onto the plane without them harassing me?'

'I'll do my best,' he smiled.

The next thing I knew, I was hurtling through the airport towards the gate on one of those little buggies usually reserved for the old or infirm. Unfortunately, the Reuters crew had spotted me and ran after the buggy, screaming questions at me across the airport. It was hideous, and a complete freak-show for the other passengers. Once I got to security, I had to jump off and put my hand luggage through, and the TV crew turned their cameras on and came at me, despite my evident distress. Luckily, the security guards at the desk started yelling at them to turn off their cameras, as it was against the airport rules to film anywhere near the security area. Only then was I able to get through to the other side unscathed, and, of course, the crew couldn't follow.

Once I was on the final leg of the journey home, I think the shock started to take hold. Practicalities had kept me going until then, but as the plane left Singapore, the gravity of what was happening suddenly enveloped me and all I could think about was how Mum and Dad must be feeling, how Kylie must be feeling . . . I wondered what the frenzied press attention must be like for her. Sure, we were used to having cars with dark windows hiding paparazzi photographers parked outside Mum and Dad's house whenever one of us girls was home, but what must it be like now?

When I finally got home, the security team that had been part of Kylie's tour entourage had decamped to Mum and Dad's place, but there were still so many television crews, reporters and photographers outside the house it was hard to take in. There was even a giant satellite dish that looked as if it could contact Mars on the nature strip right outside our front gate.

All I could think about was getting inside and giving my sister a hug, so I put my head down as my car sailed past the throng and in through the gates. Once I got inside the house, I found the whole family assembled there, still very much in shock. I hugged and kissed Mum and Dad and then Brendan. I felt completely heartbroken, particularly when I saw the absolute anguish on their faces.

I needed to speak to Kylie alone. The things we spoke about that day are things that I'd rather keep between us. Suffice it to say, I knew I had to lock eyes with my sister and let her know that I was there for her unreservedly, and that's exactly what I did.

Of course, once Kylie started having treatment, getting her out of the house and to the hospital was like some sort of covert military operation. There was a backlash of public opinion, however, against the way that the press and media were encroaching on the house and the family, with their huge vans and giant satellite dishes lining the street where we lived. At the end of the day, the media are only there to give the public what they want – a story – but many people thought that they'd gone too far. Candid photos of Kylie hiding her face on the way to undergo life-saving surgery angered her fans and all the people across the world who love her.

My friend Terry Ronald once told me that while he was ill he wanted everything and everyone around him to remain as normal as possible because it reminded him how things could be again. Well, we wanted that too – the garbage still had to go out, the grocery shopping still had to be done – but it was difficult to do these mundane chores without the fear of being snapped or being harassed for an interview.

Having the world's media camping on our doorstep made a bad situation much worse. In the end, the Victorian premier, Steve Bracks, stepped in and warned the ever-growing mass of media people that any disruption of our family's right to privacy would not be tolerated.

I tried hard not to let it get to me, because I knew that as bad as I felt, my parents felt a thousand times worse. I also knew that as well as supporting Kylie, I would have to make sure Mum and Dad were OK too – as much as I possibly could, anyway. It was terribly frustrating, nonetheless. I would have given my right arm to make it all go away, but I was helpless – we all were!

At no time during Kylie's illness did I let the darkest of dark thoughts enter my head: that I might lose her. It wasn't an option. As far as I was concerned, this was a nasty bump in the road, but she was going to come through it – I just knew she was. Her boyfriend at the time, Olivier Martinez, lived in Paris, so that's where Kylie opted to have her chemotherapy treatment. Mum, of course, decided that she would go and stay with Kylie for the duration, which would be several months, and Dad planned to get there when he could. Meanwhile, I knew I had to get back to Europe, too. I had a new single coming out, and hard though it was to consider, I returned to London at the same time, happy in the knowledge that Kylie and Mum were going to be a short hop across the Channel on the Eurostar.

Once they had settled into a wonderful old apartment that Kylie had rented in the Saint-Germain district of Paris, I would visit as often as I could. I felt as though I needed to see Kylie face to face regularly for a personal affirmation of how she was doing, because phone calls didn't seem to be enough. My most important job while I was in Paris was to keep her as occupied and as happy as possible and to do whatever it was she wanted to do, while giving Mum a bit of respite into the bargain. If Kylie wanted to go for a walk, we walked around the exquisitely pretty boutiques and shops on the streets around her apartment building; if she wanted to do a Sudoku puzzle and then fall asleep, I'd sit quietly with her; and if she wanted to watch *Ready Steady Cook* or *The Weakest Link* on TV every night, then we'd do that, too. Sometimes I'd put on some music, and I'd encourage her to get up and dance around the apartment's elegant, antique-filled living room with me. I was keen to get that little performance fairy inside her moving and telling her: 'Yes. You will get back on stage. You absolutely will, and then everything will be as it should be.'

It's quite tricky to feed someone who is undergoing chemo, as often their taste buds are all over the place. Kylie had to make sure she ate

as much as she could manage to keep her strength up for the continued onslaught of treatment. To this end, she hired a chef who came
twice a day and cooked. He was brilliant at coming up with *the* most
perfect lunch and supper menus. It also meant that Mum wasn't
spending her whole time in the kitchen and could spend time with
Kylie. Mum, Kylie and I would sit down to lunch together on giant sofas
around a big coffee table, eating and talking, and sometimes it was like
any other normal family lunch. Then I'd look out of the big windows in
front of me with the warm Parisian sun streaming in and remember
that what was truly normal was the everyday life going on outside
Kylie's safe little bubble, and I knew how desperately she wanted to get
back to it.

It's quite an incredible thing to watch someone you know and love
so well going through what my sister did. Mum and I had no idea what
to expect from one day to the next. It was as if my sister had been
stripped of all the ordinary, everyday things that made her who she
was. Her whole existence, her whole universe, in fact, was focused on
dealing with her illness, getting through the gruelling course of chemo,
and grasping as many simple pleasures as she could along the way. As
the days turned into weeks, my admiration for her grew and grew.

I wasn't the only one who found Kylie inspiring: she received thousands of letters of love and support from all over the world. She also
got letters from women who were going through exactly the same
thing as she was, or who had gone to their doctor for a long overdue
check-up, only to receive a potentially life-saving early diagnosis. This
meant a lot to Kylie, and I think it's what helped her to stay as strong
as she did. I was continuously bowled over at how much strength that
tiny little frame could radiate. Kylie never wanted anything she was
going through to affect other people in a bad way, and, consequently,
I never heard her complain – not even once.

Apart from the central core of our family looking after my sister, there
was another layer of people helping us through this difficult period –
an extended family, if you like. There was Kylie's boyfriend, Olivier, of
course, and her creative director, William Baker, who had been her best

friend and confidant for many years. She also had a really close friend called Kat, who lived in Paris. Kat would make sure that Mum and Kylie got out of the apartment and went for a walk or to a café whenever Kylie was feeling up to it.

I was lucky to have great friends to lean on as well, and boy did I need them sometimes! I remember once, when Kylie was going through a particularly rough patch, calling Terry and crying my heart out to him for two hours late one night. Having been through chemo himself, he knew how vile and difficult it could be, and a few weeks later he went over to Paris and stayed with Mum and Kylie on a week when I was unable to go.

My other great friend during this time was the Australian author Kathy Lette. I had met Kathy, her husband, Geoffrey, and their two beautiful children several years before – well before Kylie became ill – at a party at the Moschino store in London, and they were completely delightful. Being a huge fan of Kathy's books, particularly *Puberty Blues*, which was a seminal read from my teenage years, I was very excited to meet her. I was instantly drawn to Kath's fiery, funny and wonderfully dynamic personality. As we spoke, I took in her red hair, red lips and sparkling eyes, and I knew right away she was a real minx. We were laughing within seconds and our friendship was sealed.

After the party, her son, Julius, asked me if I might be able to get them tickets for Kylie's upcoming concert.

'I should think so,' I laughed. 'I'll see what I can do!'

Kylie had met Kathy before, but I knew she would adore meeting her lovely family, too, and so a week or so later, they joined me as my guests at Kylie's show in London.

Since then, both Kylie and I have become great friends with Kathy, who would often throw the most spectacular dinner parties with what she called 'a human menu'. This meant that you never quite knew who was going to turn up around the dinner table, from Salman Rushdie to Frida from ABBA, and in the case of those two, both on the same evening.

That big, fabulous house in North London ended up being quite a haven for me while Kylie was sick. It's such a warm family home, and

Kathy's such a lively, fun Aussie girl that it was a great place for me to hang out when things got rough. She's been a wonderful friend to both Kylie and me over the past few years.

As my sister bravely ploughed on with her chemotherapy, we suddenly had a piece of wonderful news as a family: my brother Brendan and his girlfriend, Becs, were expecting their first baby. It was such a joyous thing; it seemed like a chink of light in a very long, dark tunnel. Mum and Dad were over the moon about the prospect of becoming grandparents for the first time, and Kylie and I would surely be doting aunts. It gave us something to look forward to, especially as the baby would be born after my sister had finished her chemo.

Kylie, as you all know, eventually came through this horrendous experience with flying colours and has blossomed ever since. In June 2006, a short while after she'd finished her chemo and radiotherapy and was back in London, I was playing a gig at London's G-A-Y club. At the end of the show, club owner Jeremy Joseph invited Kylie on to the stage to present me with a bouquet of flowers. She looked so beautiful wearing an off-the-shoulder black dress, with her hair cropped like Mia Farrow, beaming a smile a mile wide, and, of course, the capacity crowd erupted. The atmosphere was electric and Kylie looked so radiant and happy to hear all the fans welcoming her back. Before the two of us left the stage, we burst into an impromptu, sisterly rendition of one of my early hits, 'Jump To The Beat', both belting out the line 'Everybody here say yeah!' It was a very happy moment.

Then, in November of that year, Kylie triumphantly took to the stage on her 'Showgirl: Homecoming' concert tour, and she invited me to come and perform the song 'Kids' with her as a duet for some of the dates. To be honest, I was reticent at first, because this tour was Kylie's big moment as far as I was concerned, and I felt like I might be muscling in somehow if I was up there singing with her. After I'd been to a couple of the shows, though, Mum said that Kylie was really tired. Although she was enjoying the tour, it was already taking a toll on her.

'She'd love you to get up there and sing with her, Dan,' Mum said after one of the Melbourne dates. 'She can't understand why you're not keen, and I think having you there will give her a real lift.'

'Of course I'll do it,' I smiled. 'I wanted Kylie to have her moment but I'd love to be there for her and do it.'

So the next night we strutted along a catwalk that jutted far out into the crowd of screaming fans: me in a black superhero-style corseted Dolce & Gabbana leotard with black fishnet stockings and boots, and Kylie in a leopard-print catsuit complete with ears – and we sang our hearts out together. It was an absolutely fantastic experience, and we did it again on the opening night of the tour in London – incredibly, with Madonna watching in the audience.

Chapter 26

Strippers and Cocaine

I learned a lot from seeing my sister go through what she did and come out the other side a survivor. It seemed to me that her whole life, like mine, had been lived from childhood on under the gaze of the public. When you work and work like she had, you sometimes don't have a chance to stop and think about how you feel about the things you're doing – you just get on and do them.

To go from that madness, suddenly, and to disappear into a private bubble where the only thing that matters is you – what sort of feelings must that evoke? Suddenly your life is at stake and you have a *lot* of time to think about all those things you didn't have brain-space for before – what then? For Kylie, I think it was like rebooting a computer. It seemed that she had the biggest 'spring clean' of her mind and her life possible, getting rid of all the unnecessary crap that might once have troubled her but now seemed totally inconsequential. Her priorities changed completely. When she emerged from that dark cocoon, she really was, as one of her song lyrics says, 'Like A Butterfly'.

It's a strange thing to say, I suppose, but I saw it with my friend Terry, and also with Sarah Watson from the Terrence Higgins Trust, and now

I'd witnessed it with my own sister: although a person with such a terrible illness feels physically destroyed, coming out the other side of it can be a rebirth and a blossoming. It's the kind of cathartic experience that Kylie would never have made time for otherwise, because she only wanted to make other people happy, never mind herself. If ever a positive thing came out of a life-threatening experience, then surely this was it.

Meanwhile, I'd had a wake-up call of an entirely different variety just after Christmas 2006 while I was staying at Mum and Dad's place, and a very expensive one, as it turned out. I was contentedly tucked up in bed one night when my phone rang, and I sleepily felt for it on the bedside table. It was Hills calling from London, and when I picked up the phone she sounded rather strange. I had received a text message from her earlier saying that she needed to speak to me urgently. As it was late, I thought I'd wait until the morning when I was alert – wrong move.

'Dannii, I'm going to ask you something and I need you to be absolutely 100 per cent honest with me,' Hills said. Her voice was measured and slightly clipped. This definitely wasn't a social call – whatever it was, it wasn't good.

'OK,' I said. Then I waited for the bombshell but I was *really* not expecting what came next.

'Were you snorting cocaine with strippers in the toilets of a lap-dancing club last September, Dannii?'

I sat bolt upright in bed.

'Er . . .'

'Please be honest with me. It's important.'

No shit! What the hell was she talking about?

'The lap-dancing club that I went to with Nina and Brett?' I gasped, and then I started laughing. 'Absolutely not! Why are you even asking me?'

Hills breathed a quick sigh of relief, but then went on. 'A Sunday newspaper here in Britain says they have evidence of you doing that and they quote some of the girls saying that you did.'

'Well, I can tell you hand on heart, Hills, there is no evidence of me doing illegal substances of any kind because it didn't happen. I went to the club with my assistant, Nina, and some friends. We had a few drinks and watched the stripshow – end of story. If there was anything else to tell, I'd tell you.'

'OK,' Hillary said. 'I think they're trying to call our bluff, but if you say nothing happened, then I believe nothing happened, and that's what I'm going to go back and tell them.'

When we hung up the phone, I snuggled back down under my duvet, wondering what the hell I could have done in a past life to deserve yet another ridiculous and utterly false press story hanging over my head.

Still, once Hills had telephoned the newspaper and put them straight, the story went away . . . for a while at least.

I suppose I should explain what I was doing in a lap-dancing club. It was all very innocent, really – honest!

Originally – and this was the only reason I even knew about the club – I'd been there to film a very light-hearted piece for *GMTV*, the breakfast-time news and current affairs show in Britain. It was during the promotion for my single 'Put The Needle On It' in 2002. For my *Top of the Pops* appearance, I'd decided that a bit of pole-dancing action for me and my dancers might be quite fun. Well, at the club in question they were running daytime pole-dancing classes, with some of the girls who worked there in the evening teaching anyone who fancied having a go and keeping fit at the same time. There was nothing seedy about it at all. So I went down there with the *GMTV* cameras to film a cute little feature about me learning to pole dance for my *Top of the Pops* performance – and that was that.

Cut to September 2005, and I was on a night out with my assistant, Nina, and a friend called Brett, who'd previously lived upstairs in my apartment block, plus my radio promoter, Charlie, a DJ from Capital Radio, and a couple of other people. We'd all had dinner at Nobu, and after more than a couple of glasses of wine and a fair few sakes, everyone was in high spirits and felt like going on somewhere else.

'Any suggestions?' the fun-loving Nina piped up, and suddenly I had a brainwave.

'I know somewhere that could be really fun,' I said mischievously as we came out of the restaurant into the cool Friday-night air. 'A club I went to a couple of years back that has pole dancers. I think I still have the number of the owner.'

I called the man in question, hoping that he would be able to put us on the guest list for the night. Unfortunately, and unbeknown to me, the club had changed hands and now had a completely new management team. Still, as luck would have it, the guy helpfully offered to telephone the new owners himself and tell them that Dannii Minogue was coming with some friends and to reserve me a decent table. Great!

Once we reached the club, we were well up for a good time. As soon as we hit the table, we ordered some vodkas and settled back in our seats to watch the show. The club was in full swing already and there were girls in incredibly skimpy outfits dancing around everywhere – performing to a very appreciative crowd, of course, including our table. Nina and I were fascinated by how the girls did what they did – writhing around half naked and being watched by so many different people while looking like they were having a good time. One of the strippers was happy to dance for us girls very enthusiastically without batting an eyelid, stripping off and writhing around in front of Nina and me while the guys looked on, giggling. At the time, we both thought it was a bit of a laugh and went drunkenly and laughingly along with it. One of our party was a gay guy who wasn't the slightest bit interested in catching a flash of boob or having a lap dance. He was thrilled, however, when a couple of the girls came over and he got to try on various bits of their costume, while we all fell about laughing. It was a spontaneous, fun night and we were all having an absolute scream.

Afterwards, I didn't think any more about it, until Hills called me to tell me about the newspaper's claims that they had proof of a salacious story. However, as I said, nothing came of it and Hills and I forgot about it until a month or so later, in February 2006, when the story raised its ugly head again, though this time in a slightly different form.

I was travelling back from a fashion show I'd been to in New York when the story broke in the same UK Sunday newspaper. 'Dannii's Lesbian CCTV Sex' screamed the headline – as I'm sure you can guess, it wasn't in the *Observer* culture section.

Inside, the paper had 'photos' of me that, I have to say, I wasn't thrilled about when I saw them in black and white. The shots were of the girl, writhing and gyrating around and across Nina and me. The lewd story that went with it, along with supposed 'eyewitness' accounts, made the whole thing sound dirty and scandalous, and was filled with ridiculous untruths, though at least there were no drug allegations this time. Suddenly a silly, drunken night out with friends was being treated like some kind of celebrity sex tape, and I was terrified that I was going to end up joining the infamous ranks of Pamela Anderson and Paris Hilton, which is *not* me.

I knew damned well it wasn't how it looked, but the thought of my parents and, worse, my grandparents casting their eyes over the photos filled me with sadness. I knew I'd have to call Mum and Dad to warn them, and I wasn't looking forward to it. I mean, what does one say to one's parents at a time like that? 'Hi, Mum, no need to worry, but there's a couple of shots of me floating around getting it on with a female stripper in public . . .'

What puzzled me about the whole piece was that the photos were supposed to be stills from CCTV footage, but a CCTV camera right above my head? Right above the place where I'd been seated by the club's manager? I smelled a rat, and I was right. When I finally got to look at the footage myself in a lawyer's office, it was clear that this was a normal video camera that had secretly filmed me and not CCTV. I'd been set up. The manager of the club had made sure I was in exactly the right place to be filmed and then made sure he got something worth filming. So *that's* why my stripper friend had been so enthusiastic.

That wasn't the end of it, though. After I'd spent a small fortune to get a legal injunction preventing stills from the film being printed anywhere else, and freezing the payment from the newspaper to the strip-club manager, Hills got a call from the industrious club manager himself. He was now, unsurprisingly, no longer working at the club. What sort of client wants to go to a lap-dancing club only to find themselves all over the Sunday papers the next day? It's hardly good for business. Not having received his payment from the newspaper because of the injunction, this charmer was now telling us that because it had all happened in public he had the right to sell the footage, and he was ready to do just that unless we wanted to buy it from him. He wanted a hundred grand and he wanted it right then and there.

Eventually, the only way we managed to get him off my back was to allow the newspaper to pay him the money he'd originally been offered by them in exchange for every single copy of the footage he had, with a guarantee that there were no other copies floating around *anywhere*!

I did all this via very expensive lawyers. One night out on the town with friends, albeit an unusual one, ended up costing me £50,000 in legal fees – and the club manager who had set me up still walked away with his filthy lucre.

Fifty grand for a night out – I guess you could say it went 'tits-up'!

Chapter 27

So Under Pressure

Towards the end of Kylie's chemotherapy treatment, Laura called me from South Africa to say that she had been unwell and was going to see her doctor for a quick check-up. Within three days of that appointment, Laura was in hospital having a full hysterectomy – she, too, had cancer. Apart from the horror of hearing that she had a life-threatening illness, Laura and her mum, Tina, suddenly had to absorb the brutal news that Laura would never be able to be a mum, and Tina would never have a grandchild through natural means. When I got the call to tell me what was happening, I was numb. I couldn't have imagined a bigger curve ball coming at me, and I couldn't believe that this insidious disease had once again returned to threaten the life of someone I loved – my best friend.

Laura, fortunately, was one of those people who always took what was thrown at her and faced it. It was a case of 'Right! This is what I've got to deal with – so let's get on with it!'

'It's all fine, Dannii,' she assured me confidently over the phone after she'd heard the news. 'I'm booked in at the hospital and it's all organised. I think it's best that I have this operation and get rid of the cancer in one go – it'll be fine.'

When I spoke to her right before the operation she was more delicate, however, and I saw a side to Laura I had never before witnessed:
she was scared. Once again, I went into protective mode, as I had done
with Kylie. Although I wasn't there with Laura, I tried to be as prag-
matic and supportive as I could possibly be. But the entire time I knew
I was helpless, and Laura's life was in the hands of her doctors and surgeons. The one thing that kept me going was that the people I knew
who'd been affected by cancer had come through it alive at the other
end. My dad had gone through treatment for prostate cancer a few
years earlier, Terry Ronald had survived lymphoma, and it seemed that
there was every chance that Kylie's was going to be another success
story the way her treatment was going. As far as I was concerned, positive thinking was half the battle. It had worked well for me before, so
that's the route I intended to take with Laura. I knew that she was
going to be fine, and I told her and myself that, loud and long. After
she'd come through the operation, it seemed like she was going to be
OK, but only after a very long recuperation period.

While Laura was recovering from her operation in South Africa, I was
writing songs in rainy Blackburn in the north of England. My record
label All Around The World were planning to release a greatest hits
package – a CD and a DVD – of all my biggest chart hits. I wanted to
put some new songs on there, too, so I'd travelled 'up north' with Terry
Ronald to work with a writer/producer called Lee Monteverde. I wasn't
in the mood for songwriting, but I knew it had to be done, as we
needed a big single to launch the hits album. After the first day, with
no good ideas flowing, Terry and I went back, defeated, to the beautiful old manor-style hotel where we were staying and drank vintage
port and played Speed Scrabble instead.

'My mind's not focused on writing upbeat dance tunes,' I told Terry,
as we sat in the hotel's gorgeous, oak-panelled dining room late into
the night.

'I'm never going to be able to think of bubbly, happy lyrics for a pop
single while I'm so worried about Laura – it's far too much pressure.'

'Just write whatever you're feeling,' Terry said. 'Not all up-tempo songs have to be happy. Look at "Who Do You Love Now?" – that was really melancholic, but it's one of your biggest hits.'

While the rain thrashed against my window that night, and I lay in bed unable to drift off to sleep, I came up with a title for a song that said everything about the past year as far as I was concerned – 'So Under Pressure'!

By the time we arrived at the studio the next day, Lee Monteverde had sampled a bit of an old eighties electronic pop record and had looped it up to make a fantastic sounding track. Then Terry started playing around with the chorus lyrics I'd suggested, singing 'I'm so under pressure' over and over across the dark, percussive track that Lee had created. The three of us thought it sounded great, and a couple of hours and four or five mugs of tea later, we'd written the whole song and were busy recording the lead vocals. The lyrics are about trying to carry on with your life while everything feels like it's falling down around you, about not having time to breathe before you turn around to face yet another crisis. It certainly seemed like there had been no end of disarray and sadness in the past year or so, and there was something magically cathartic about belting out my feelings on the subject over a thumping beat.

By the time my label managers, Matt and Chris, and two of the girls who worked in the office arrived, it was unanimous.

'That sounds like a hit single to me,' Matt said.

'Love it!' Chris agreed.

Job done.

The video for 'So Under Pressure' – due for release just before my *Hits and Beyond* album – featured me in some crazy but very beautiful outfits, performing the song in several visually 'pressure-filled' situations: spinning around in a deep white box while being filmed from above, which made me feel very sick; being entangled in a live giant albino python wearing a bikini and a pair of black-and-cream Chanel ankle-strap wedges, which is hazardous to say the least, girls; and being caged in a glass box that's slowly filling up with ominous black confetti. I put a lot of myself into that song and the video, and I was happy with the results. I'm still very proud of it.

*

For the release of *Hits and Beyond* in September 2006, a fabulous launch party had been planned at a chic cosmetics store in London called Becca. So many of my friends, dressed up in their best party gear, turned out to celebrate this milestone in my career, it was a great, great night.

All my favourite boys were there, of course: singing teacher Russell, Ian and Terry and their partners, my handsome pal Benjamin, Tim Reed, who had looked after me on *Notre-Dame de Paris*, and Glenn Horder from the Mardi Gras committee, who had now moved from Sydney to London and did a fantastic job of taking care of my apartment and my two cats, Floyd and Rabbit, whenever I was away.

My girlfriends were in attendance too: Jules, Hills and Angela from my management; my fun-loving assistant, Nina; Kathy Lette and her wonderful family; and, despite her recent surgery, Laura.

Although she'd been weak for a while after her operation, Laura's doctors were convinced that they'd got rid of all the cancerous cells and, unlike Kylie, Laura wasn't going to have to have chemotherapy or radiotherapy. Now she had to concentrate on resting and getting better; I wasn't entirely convinced that her flying over from South Africa was a great idea. Laura had decided that she had no intention of missing my big night – so typical of her – and she was determined to come over to stay with me in London for a few days.

'I'm all better,' she said. 'All I've done is rest and now I'm good to go! I want to be there for you, Dannii, and to be honest I'm very bored with being ill.'

I wasn't so sure, and we had quite a few conversations before the event about whether she was well enough to take an eleven-hour flight to London.

'I want to hear it from your doctor that it's OK for you to come,' I told her, 'or it's a no!'

But the word 'no' never seemed to sit well with Laura. Knowing how much she loved a party, it was ultimately hard for me to refuse her, despite my worry about her not being completely recovered from the operation. After she assured me her doctor said it was OK, I gave in.

'As long as you behave and look after yourself, Missy!' I warned her.

When Laura arrived at my place, before the launch party, I thought she looked a little thin, but I suppose that was to be expected. Her eyes still had the same sparkle and she looked as beautiful as ever, but I could see that the illness had taken its toll on my friend. Although this was supposed to be a joyful night, I was concerned for her as we left for the party. As the noisy, glitzy event got underway, and the room buzzed with excitable revellers, I noticed how quiet Laura was, sitting back and taking everything in without really participating, and that was not like her at all. Then I watched as she and Terry Ronald raised a glass of champagne together as two cancer survivors, and I smiled and told myself that she was bound to be a little tired, and not to worry so much. After all, I had an album to launch, and lots of eager press waiting to talk to me. Besides, Laura had promised me faithfully that she felt perfectly fine; in turn, I'd promised her that I wouldn't fuss over her all night, making her feel out of place.

Much drinking and dancing ensued, and the official *Hits and Beyond* album launch party went off like a rocket. DJ Steve Pitron was on the decks pumping out some amazing original mixes and mash-ups, and everyone was dancing, jumping up and down like crazy and really going for it. I felt like I was at a kids' birthday party instead of a serious music-biz bash – and that's just the way I liked it. When we finally headed for home, though, not too late in the evening, Laura came clean and admitted to me in the cab that she wasn't feeling very well and hadn't all night.

'I had such a great time catching up with everyone and seeing you,' she told me, 'but I don't feel quite right. I had only one whisky and I didn't even finish that!'

I took her hand gently, and smiled.

'Look, give yourself a break. You've been very ill, you've just flown eleven hours and practically dashed straight out to your first party in months. Of course you're going to feel tired and not yourself – it's completely overwhelming.'

By the time we got home, Laura was having spiky pains in her lower back and pains in her stomach, and I could see she was frightened. Still, she brushed it off.

'I think I've got a kidney infection and that's why I couldn't finish my drink,' she offered as I made us both a cup of tea in my kitchen. 'Perhaps we could get something from the chemist tomorrow.'

'Perhaps you could see a doctor tomorrow,' I suggested firmly, but Laura was having none of it.

'I'm fine,' she said. 'I'll be cool once I've had a good night's sleep.'

So we sat down quietly for a long overdue catch-up, looking out of the windows of my apartment over the river across a cheerfully lit London.

By late afternoon the next day, though, Laura herself was suggesting that she might need to visit a doctor.

'Can you call your GP, Dannii?' she asked. 'I don't have one here.'

Trying to get a last-minute appointment at a doctor's surgery late in the day was never going to be an easy task. In the evening, I was horrified to walk into the bathroom and find my friend curled up on the floor in absolute agony of the worst kind. Laura was sobbing and weeping. All she kept saying was: 'I'm going to die, Dannii. The cancer has come back and I'm going to die!'

I didn't know what to do. I was completely beside myself. This was my best friend, Laura: she was the strong one. I was the one who crumbled and then she would pick me up and look after me. That was always the way it had been – not this.

I have to admit, I was scared too. Hearing Laura cry those words with such conviction between gasps of breath shocked me to the core. For some reason, I still kept telling myself it wasn't true – it *was* just a kidney infection and she was in pain because of the surgery she'd had previously. When we finally got her to a doctor, though, he didn't tell Laura what she wanted to hear.

'You need to get to a specialist,' the doctor told her. 'I'm sending you right away.'

Things got worse from there on in. An immediate scan showed that Laura had a tumour the size of a grapefruit growing inside her stomach, pushing against all her organs – that's why she'd been in so much pain. It hadn't been that long since her previous scan in South Africa, which had shown no such growth, so this thing was aggressive and getting bigger by the day.

There was worse news to come. The doctors told Laura that they had no idea why it had happened, and no real clue what it was. Not only was she dealing with the panic and fear that her cancer had returned, she was also faced with the stark realisation that there was no viable plan to combat its progress. It was a nightmare.

Chapter 28

The Girl Who Followed the Sun

Laura's mum, Tina, was in London in what seemed like a flash, along with her best friend, who was like an aunt to Laura. Laura, meanwhile, was sent straight into hospital and prepared for immediate surgery, as we were told the tumour had to be removed urgently. Tina and I sat at the hospital together, nervously waiting for news of the outcome. The last twenty-four hours had been a complete and utter blur. Once the operation was done and the growth was gone, I breathed a somewhat tentative sigh of relief, hoping against hope that that would be an end to it, and Laura would get well again.

There seemed to be some confusion and, indeed, tension, between Tina's friend and the doctors, and she confided in me that she wasn't at all happy with what she was being told by the surgeons regarding Laura's treatment and her condition. As the day wore on, there seemed to be more and more doctors getting involved with the case and I could see that Tina's friend was upset and stressed, and was trying to take the pressure off Tina as much as she could. I decided to concentrate on Laura. I couldn't imagine how she must be feeling, and I was concerned that she might get wind of the nervous tension and medical discussions surrounding her.

Tina slept in a chair at Laura's bedside. I visited them every day, while still trying to get on with my work, which seemed ridiculous and trivial compared to what was going on with Laura. Every day she would want to hear only about what I'd been doing and where I'd been going; she didn't want to hear about anything medical. She seemed to want me to remove her completely, mentally at least, from the cage she was trapped in, so that's what I tried my very best to do.

After about a week, she was moved to the London Clinic, just off the Marylebone Road, and it was there that things took a turn for the worse. The next time I saw my friend, she was on a morphine drip with pipes coming out of her stomach, which were draining some hideous puss-filled fluid from the area where she'd had the surgery. Not only that, but she was swelling up like a balloon from the spot where the tumour had been, right down to her toes. She could hardly move at all any more – she was unable to use the bathroom or get out of bed – and it was heartbreaking to see.

The deterioration went on for several days. Each day I would turn up at the hospital and try so hard not to break down when she'd ask me to rub her feet gently, please, because she could no longer feel them. I wanted to be brave for Laura, so I chatted to her as I would have done if we'd been walking along the beach back in Hermanus with her dogs, making her giggle every now and then and trying with all my heart to keep her mind occupied with anything other than what was going on around her. The minute I closed that hospital door behind me, though, the devastation of seeing her like that took hold of me. She was so ill, so out of it on morphine – I broke down every time I left her.

Once outside the walls of the hospital, things weren't much easier to handle. At that time, the wonderful news of Kylie's recovery from breast cancer was the topic on everyone's lips. While I was overjoyed to have my sister back safe and well, having the whole world tell me how fantastic I must be feeling now her cancer had gone cut like a knife every single time.

'All right, love?' A cheery London taxi driver smiled at me as we left for the hospital in his cab one morning. 'Isn't it great about your Kylie? You must be so relieved! You know, my aunt had the very same thing recently – it was awful. She went through absolute hell for months, but now she's come through it as right as rain an' all – just like yer sister – so we're all celebrating, ain't we?'

'I guess,' I said, almost to myself.

The only thing I knew how to do was lose myself in my work, but even that turned into a trial. Promoting a single and an album, I was on a full round of press and TV interviews, but the moment I sat down to talk to anyone, the first words that invariably came out of their mouths were: Kylie is well again – you must be so happy it's all over! But, of course, I wasn't feeling happy. It was as if one vile and terrible sadness had merely been swapped for another. After beaming as many glowing smiles as I could find within myself, it got to the stage where I could hardly bear anyone mentioning the word 'cancer' in my presence. All I wanted to do was scream at the top of my lungs that it wasn't all over: not for Tina, not for me – and not for Laura.

One morning at the hospital, Laura's doctors came and delivered the news to Tina and me that they were now not simply draining the poisonous fluid from one area of Laura's body but from everywhere. They explained to us that her body was like honeycomb inside, and there were pockets of fluid everywhere. They would have to put a thousand drains in a thousand holes in her even to begin to get rid of it. It seemed that when the tumour had been removed, it had caused the cancer to spread all over her body, and now there was nothing they could do.

Despite the fact that her poor body was now terribly swollen, and she was on a morphine drip for pain relief, over the next week or so Laura seemed to adopt a 'taking care of business' stance from her hospital bed, and I was astounded by her mental strength. I wasn't sure, at first, if she knew that there was no hope of getting better, but whatever the case, Laura wanted to make sure that her mum was going to be looked after, and she wanted to organise all her affairs properly, which is no mean feat when you're that sick and in another country.

There was financial planning to sort out, and her properties and possessions to consider, which meant making a will. She also wanted to plan her own memorial. She did it all meticulously, utilising the time she had left to try to make other people's lives easier once she'd gone, and it was an amazing and inspiring thing to witness.

After several weeks, a steady stream of her many friends from all over the world came to see Laura and help support her mum. The doctors didn't seem to have any clear timeframe for how long Laura might be around. They were able to relieve her pain and keep her stable for as long as possible but nothing more.

Hills called me one morning and reminded me that we were scheduled to go over to Australia for a short working visit to promote the *Hits and Beyond* album, and she asked me if I thought I could make the trip.

'I'll speak to Laura and Tina,' I told her, sadly. 'She might stay like this for months – we just don't know.'

When I saw Laura that day, I stood at the end of her bed, softly rubbing her feet, just how she liked.

'I know you have to go,' she said. 'And it's not long, is it?'

'No, it's not long,' I said. 'And we'll speak every single day.'

Even then, in my head and in my heart, I felt that Laura wasn't going to be there when I got back, but I kissed her and told her I loved her, and assured her that I would see her again very soon.

My mum and dad now owned a beautiful farm an hour or so outside Melbourne, where they spent almost every weekend. During my short stay in Oz, I went down to spend a few precious hours with them on my one full day off. There was now only one more day of work scheduled before I was due to fly back to London to be with Laura, and I was relieved to be going because, by then, things were not looking good at all.

It was strange to think that not so very long ago I had been at the farm *with* Laura. A while before she first got sick, I'd brought her to Australia so that she could see exactly where I came from, and could visit the places that I loved and where I had grown up. Laura had loved the isolation and privacy of the farm most of all, and we'd spent many happy times there together, laughing and talking our way through the days, both feeling free and alive.

Now I was sitting there alone, staring out towards the bay as dusk slowly slipped into night. I let my mind drift back to one particular, momentous evening at the farm when the two of us got completely smashed on red wine, and danced and laughed into the early hours. Laura and I could have a party all on our own – we didn't need anyone else. The fact that we knew full well that we could lie in as long as we liked the next day, with no need to worry about work or life in general, made it all the more fun. Laura had told me back then that she hadn't felt well, but she'd shoved any thoughts of illness aside because she had been looking forward to the trip to Australia so much and didn't want to spoil it in any way. That visit seemed like only yesterday one moment, and a whole lifetime ago the next.

It was quite fitting and somewhat timely, I guess, that I was at the farm when I received the call to tell me that my best friend had passed away. She'd gone. While I was beside myself with grief and distraught that I wasn't there with her, I tried to find comfort in the fact that I was in a place that she loved and where I had so many beautiful memories of her. That's what I kept on telling myself: I wasn't meant to see my lovely Laura die, I was meant to be at the farm, safe with my family and filled with memories of good, good things. I had to believe that.

The next day, when I spoke on the phone to Laura's good friend Melchior, who had gone over to London from South Africa to help her organise her will and her estate, he told me that a couple of days before she'd passed away she'd suddenly come out of her morphine-induced haze and spoken to him with unexpected clarity.

'I need you to get me my passport and some money, Mel,' she'd said to him.

Melchior was, of course, taken aback.

'I've got everything you need right here,' he told her, softly. 'But what do you need cash and your passport for?'

'I need to see Dannii,' she said. 'I need to buy a ticket to get to Australia to see Dannii. She's over in Perth and I have to get to Perth.'

I don't know where she got Perth from, as we'd never been to

Perth together, but, as far as Laura was concerned, she was off to Perth.

'Honey, you can't travel to Australia, I'm afraid,' Melchior told her. 'You're too sick.'

But Laura was resolute. 'I don't care how sick I am,' she said. 'I know I have to get to Australia and be with Dannii and that's all that matters. I have to be with Dannii now.'

I guess Melchior thought I might find comfort in the fact that Laura was thinking of me before she died, but I was devastated to think that I wasn't there for Laura and her mum. It's something I'm still learning to live with – on some days I can, and on others I can't.

A few weeks later, back in London, I drove Tina to collect an urn with her daughter's ashes, then we travelled out of the city to Tina's best friend's house for a visit. It was only an hour or so outside London, but it was a lovely, quiet drive, and great to spend some time with Tina, talking calmly about all that had happened in the past weeks. Later that night, when we sat around the table at Tina's friend's house sharing a bottle of wine, I decided to take the urn containing Laura's ashes out of its box and place her on the table with us.

'She'd want to be here,' I smiled. Then I took off my new necklace and draped it around the urn.

'And she was always stealing any new bloody jewellery I got, so I guess she'd better have this.'

It was a strange evening, sitting there talking about Laura, with her ashes there and not her, but we found space to smile and even laugh a little as the tears fell, and it felt good to reminisce about the good times. When I got up to go to bed, Tina asked me if I'd like to have the urn in my room with me while I slept. As macabre as it might sound, I told her that I'd really like that. I guess I felt it was the only way I could get close to Laura, as I hadn't been with her at the end. With stuff like that, I'm normally the biggest scaredy-cat on the planet, but it just evolved naturally and felt right. The next morning when I woke up, I felt so much more at peace – like I'd had my own private time to say goodbye.

Several months after she passed away, Laura's special memorial that she'd planned from her hospital bed was held in Hermanus on what would have been her thirty-seventh birthday, 26 February 2007. I'd been an absolute wreck leading up to it, so much so that I'd gone to see a therapist a friend had recommended to help me wade through the jungle of conflicting feelings I had about losing Laura. I couldn't seem to visualise myself getting on that plane, because a memorial meant that it was final, and I wasn't ready to accept that. But I knew that Tina needed me there, so of course I did get on the plane, and when I eventually arrived I was happy to see the house full of friends and relatives who had come from all over the world to say their final farewells.

There were pictures of Laura everywhere that people had printed out or snatched from their albums and brought along for the day, and the house looked absolutely gorgeous. Once everyone was present, we left for the beach and headed to one particular sand dune with no buildings nearby and the most beautiful white sand. Tina gave everyone daisies – Laura's favourite flower – then we walked down to the water to scatter Laura's ashes, and float the pretty daisies on the ocean, just as she'd wanted. Once Tina had let some of the ashes drift out into the water, she invited other people to do the same. I knew it was what Laura wanted, but it's quite a challenge to put your hand into an urn of your best friend's ashes and touch them with your fingers – I really had to steel myself to do it.

Once I did, I held the ashes above the water for a moment and then slowly began to open my hand, acutely aware that as every one of my fingers curled open and every little flake fell into the sea, she was disappearing for ever. It was a very hard thing to do but so very Laura. She was drifting out to sea, slowly, and following the sun once again . . . just like she always had.

Chapter 29

There's No Place Like Home

You can't help but be affected by things that happen in your life, for better or for worse, but the really important moments can totally transform you. If you're lucky, that transformation will come in the form of growth and an appreciation of the richness of life, and a discovery of how beautiful and important it is. Kylie's situation, and Laura's, had taught me that I needed to make every day count, and grab every opportunity that came my way. I wanted to let good things back into my life after all the sadness and stress of the last two years. I wanted to let love back into my life. At the end of 2006, I felt it was time to make a few not so small changes.

I'd recently recorded a version of the Sister Sledge song 'He's The Greatest Dancer', which I loved performing on the BBC TV charity extravaganza *Children in Need*. I hadn't wanted to record a cover version, but the idea was that my new version of the song was to be used for a massive TV advertising campaign for a mobile-phone company, and there were all sorts of clever marketing ideas surrounding its release. Unfortunately, the deal with the phone company fell through, and the record only ever got a club release. Although 'He's The

Greatest Dancer' quickly became my eleventh number-one club record – giving me more number-one club records than any other female artist – basically the whole thing was shelved.

This wasn't the way I'd envisaged my music career going at all: random one-off dance singles, cover versions and records by DJ so-and-so 'featuring' Dannii. Yes, it was great being crowned 'Queen of Clubs', and I loved Chris and Matt, who ran All Around The World – they had clearly perfected the art of making those big, one-off dance hits – but they didn't have a history of recording artist-led albums. They didn't seem especially keen to rectify that with me, and there was nothing I could do to change that. I realised that I'd been lost for longer than I could remember. After the golden era of *Neon Nights* and all the fun I'd had performing on stage in *Notre-Dame de Paris* and *The Vagina Monologues*, it occurred to me that I'd been scraping by and accepting what was thrown at me without any real purpose. It was time to rethink.

On top of that, I'd become more and more frustrated with the way my relationship with Hills and Shaw Thing Management was going. Hills was now managing the biggest girl band in the country, Girls Aloud, and that was proving to be more of a full-time job than any one person could handle. It didn't help matters that the girls and I weren't the friendliest of stablemates after a rather public spat, which was played out in the British tabloids. One newspaper reported that one of the girls had accused me of being rude and stuck up after we met at a TV studio, and another paper said that I had retaliated, branding them 'a bunch of chavs', after which there was a kind of unspoken cold war for a while. Whatever had or hadn't been said, though, when Hills had come to me to ask if I was OK with her taking on the girls, I'd blindly agreed, not realising it was going to take up practically all of her time. I decided that my long friendship with Hills was much more important to me than having her as a manager. Besides, Hills' area of expertise had always been music, and I felt it was time for me to move away from that.

So that's exactly what I did: I walked away from my management *and* my music all at once. And guess what? I *did* feel free to discover that elusive richness of life. I *was* ready to grab every fabulous new opportunity that came my way – yes!

OK. Good. Right. Don't panic, Dannii. You might not have a music career any more, after – what, fifteen years? And you might not have a manager either . . . or a boyfriend . . . but you have friends . . . and you have . . . cats . . . Something new and exciting is bound to turn up – it always does. New! Exciting! Just you wait . . .

Thankfully, I didn't have to wait long. Melissa Le Gear at Profile Talent Management, who are my Aussie-based television and acting agents, got an offer through for me that completely threw me for a sixer. The job, as a judge on the brand-new Simon Cowell-created TV show, *Australia's Got Talent*, was exactly what the doctor ordered. The format had already worked well in the USA. I'd seen the show myself and thought it was fabulous. There were plans for a British version too. For me, the prospect of being back on prime-time Australian television gave me a special buzz, and I couldn't wait to get started.

Once I started filming, I felt the show was my saviour. I was going back to my TV roots, back to what I'd been used to as a kid: family entertainment, singing, dancing, the whole variety package – and I loved it. There were even a good many of the crew whom I recognised, who'd worked on *Young Talent Time* and other TV shows I'd been involved in, which made it feel like coming home. The fact that it was filmed in Melbourne, which meant that I could go home for real, was the icing on the cake. To be honest, after all that had happened in the last two years, I felt that I needed to be around my mum and dad, and I wanted to get to know Brendan's new family too – this job meant I could do that. It was the perfect situation.

Presented by Aussie TV reporter and motor-racing driver Grant Denyer, *Australia's Got Talent* is essentially a talent show featuring a mix of professional and amateur singers, dancers, comedians, magicians, jugglers and all sorts of other performers of all ages, shapes and sizes, competing for a $250,000 prize. The whole thing is presided over by a panel of judges, who were, that first season, the brilliant actor and singer Tom Burlinson, me and veteran musician and TV personality Red

Symons, who was seen as the deadpan and slightly Machiavellian Simon Cowell-type of character on the panel.

Red had been playing that particular role for years, originally with his own slot on an Aussie show called *Hey Hey It's Saturday*. This was a Saturday-morning kids' TV show that ultimately moved to a Saturday-evening slot and ran for almost thirty years. I had been a guest on the show with a young Johnny Depp in the late eighties. Red's slot on the show, entitled 'Red Faces', involved him cruelly judging all sorts of ridiculous and funny acts – he was playing Mister Nasty way back then, just as he was doing on *Australia's Got Talent*. The three of us judges had a great laugh together and I thought it was a really good team.

Friends told me that they felt they were seeing the real me on the show, which was something they hadn't seen for quite a while. I could be relaxed, have a laugh, dress up and look glamorous, and I got to speak my mind without having the constraints of a written script or a dance routine to encumber me. It's funny, because I'd never have pictured myself as a panellist of any sort, but a year or so before Kylie had astutely pointed out my destiny for me. 'Dan, you'd be great on one of those TV shows as a judge,' she'd said. 'Whenever you come to one of my show previews with your little notebook, I know I'm going to get a real honest opinion on how to improve the show.'

I wasn't convinced at all. 'What?' I laughed. 'I can't imagine it in a million years. What are you talking about?'

'Listen, you know what it's like to get up there and do it,' Kylie said. 'You know what the contestants are going through and you've got a knack for being constructive without crushing someone. You're made for it!'

I guess the producers of the show, Fremantle, must have thought the same.

At the end of a day's filming, early on in the season, one of the Fremantle producers tracked me down afterwards and congratulated me.

'You've been excellent, Dannii,' he smiled. 'I'm heading over to

London and I'm going to make sure Mr Cowell and everyone there
gets tapes of the show so they can see for themselves how good you
are.'

'Thank you,' I said, blinking at him.

I was taken aback, I suppose. I'd been so used to work situations
being pressured and tough in the last couple of years, I'd almost forgotten what it was like to be complimented on what I was doing. It was
a nice feeling. I hadn't realised quite how much I'd needed to hear
someone tell me: 'Dannii, you know what? You're all right, girl.'

Soon after the first few shows aired, Melissa Le Gear and Mark
Klemens from Profile Talent told me that they wanted to look after me
not just as agents, but as my worldwide management, too. I'd been
happy working with the dynamic Melissa. She was sharp and committed to work, but she also had a wry sense of humour that I liked.
Mel seemed to know exactly what I needed at that time and I eagerly
accepted the management offer. I was ready to start anew now, and this
was the next step.

After the taping of one show, a member of the production team, a
guy called Rob, rapped on my dressing-room door and asked if he
might have a word.

'Sure, come in,' I told him.

'When you get home tonight, Dannii,' he said, 'get on your computer and Google the BBC News website and have a look at the
top-five news stories.'

'OK,' I said, rather intrigued. 'What am I looking for?'

'You'll see,' he said, smiling. 'I think there's something very interesting there for you. When you've done that, here's the telephone
number of the person you should call if you think it would be right for
you.' Then he handed me a card with a name on it, Claire Horton, and
her phone number.

'Well, that's very cryptic,' I laughed. Later that night, after I'd
returned home, I got on to the BBC News page and scrolled down it.
What on earth could Rob be talking about?

Suddenly, a headline caught my eye, and I saw exactly what he
meant. 'British TV talent show, The X Factor, is looking for a new

celebrity judge.' Until then there had been three judges; now they were shaking up the format and looking for a fourth.

'Oh my God!'

I knew damn well that *The X Factor* was practically the biggest show on TV in the UK, and I never missed it when I was in London. I was a huge fan. Rob, of course, would never have given me the number to call if he hadn't had some sort of insider information about the possibility of me getting this gig. I was excited, and after a few deep breaths, I dialled the number on the card.

'Hi, Dannii, thanks for calling me,' Claire Horton said.

She sounded warm and friendly but I felt like jelly inside.

'ITV are looking for a new judge on *The X Factor*,' she went on, 'and we'd love to talk to you about it. We think you might be the right person for the job.'

'Oh, right.' I said.

I genuinely thought that somebody must have been having a laugh. *The X Factor* is Simon Cowell, Louis Walsh and Sharon Osbourne. What the hell do they want with me? This has got to be a joke. Even after I'd hung up the phone with Claire, who was ready to meet my new management team and me as soon as possible, I was in a state of shock. But there it was: I was being offered one of the biggest TV jobs in Britain.

Girls day out at the Melbourne Grand Prix. Nina, me, Laura and Jules

On the set of
Australia's Got Talent

Performing
'I Begin To Wonder'

With my idol, Olivia

'The Hits & Beyond' press shoot in London

On set with the adorable Twiggy for a Marks & Spencer shoot in Cape Town, South Africa

On holiday with
'the husband' Benji

With my manager, Melissa
Le Gear, off to lunch at the
House of Lords in London

With Nathan Smith at the
MTV Awards in Sydney

My sister joins me as special guest judge for *The X Factor*'s 'Judges Homes' in Dubai

Kylie presents me with 'Best TV Star' at the *Elle* Style Awards in London

Pulling on one another's wigs on set of *The Kylie Show* in London

My first live show at *The X Factor* – Sharon plays nice

In the hot seat

Louis throws out all the rules

Backstage with Cheryl at *The X Factor*, Fountain Studios, Wembley

Our first family portrait – with my boyfriend and baby bump!

Meeting the future 'in-laws', Elsie and Eddie, in Manchester

On holiday in Dubai: baby bump swims with a dolphin – pre-school has a lot to live up to!

The National TV Awards, baby bump's first red carpet

Snorkelling with Kris on the Great Barrier Reef

Attending our first family event, Storm Rugby match at AAMI stadium in Melbourne

Kissing in the sun at the Australian Open, Rod Laver Arena, Melbourne

Chapter 30

Mother of the Year

Once it had been announced in the press that Dannii Minogue was the new judge on *The X Factor*, all sorts of eyebrows were raised.

'What sort of credentials has *she* got to be a talent-show judge, let alone a mentor to the acts?' certain journalists and TV pundits were asking as I arrived back in London. 'Why Dannii?'

Although I was very well known in the UK – and had been for the past fifteen years – much of the British public didn't know anything about my earlier career in Australia. They didn't know that I, too, had got my start on a show in which I'd had to sing in front of a judging panel. I think some of the shock came from the fact that people don't like change. I suppose they thought that if *The X Factor* was working as well as it was, why shake it up?

One morning, as I perused yet another article questioning my wherewithal to be the new *X Factor* judge, I thought back to what judge Evie Hayes had said about me on *Young Talent Time* all those years ago, when I sang 'On The Good Ship Lollipop' in the little sailor outfit that Nain had made me: 'Danielle is a darling little girl, who, with proper coaching and tuition, could have a very fine future.' If only she could have known.

To be perfectly honest, I was sort of in agreement with some of the more disparaging press. I didn't know whether I could do it or not either. Rather than upsetting me, the comments about me not being worthy of the position on the judging panel made me shrug my shoulders and smile.

'You know what? Let's wait and see.' I'd tell them. 'While I'm completely blown away by having been given the opportunity, I don't know if I can do it myself yet. Yes, I've now done *Australia's Got Talent*, but this is a whole different ball game: now I've got to mentor the acts as well as critique them, and that's something I've never had to do before. So, yes, the cynics might well be right. If they are and I'm crap, I won't want to stay anyway. Trust me, you won't have to kick me off; I'll be the first one to hold my hands up and tell you if I can't do it!'

And I meant every word of it.

The one person who seemed absolutely confident in my ability was the show's creator, Simon Cowell. He'd seen tapes of me on *Australia's Got Talent* and was convinced I was the right woman for the job. He didn't ask me to screen test or audition or anything, he just told me to do exactly what I'd been doing on *Australia's Got Talent*.

'I want you to bring us your experience as a performer,' Simon told me once the filming got underway. 'There's no one else on the panel who has been a pop singer or a performer, and I think it's something we need because none of the other judges has experienced that.'

'I feel like I've got so much to catch up on,' I told Simon. 'You guys know it all backwards but for me it's a lot to take in.'

'Well, don't let anyone tell you that there's a right or wrong way to do it either, Dannii: you are there to give an opinion and yours isn't always going to be the same as everyone else's. If all the judges have the same opinion, then there's no show.'

I knew Simon was right, but I also knew that I had a lot to learn. As with everything else I've ever done, I was being thrown in at the deep end – I wouldn't have had it any other way.

I'd first met Simon a year or so before, when I was with Hills at the *GQ* magazine awards. That night, I'd been seated next to him, so we got chatting. I remember even back then him mentioning that he'd like to work with me. After that night there were all sorts of stories in the press about Simon saying he fancied me, and how he thought I was the sexier of the two Minogue sisters. It was all very silly and it made me smile. I found Simon intriguing too: he had a cheekiness about him that I found appealing, and you couldn't help but be in awe of everything he'd achieved in the entertainment industry.

On my first day of work, I was officially introduced to the other judges, Sharon Osbourne and Brian Friedman. Brian was also a newcomer to the show as he'd been brought in to replace pop manager Louis Walsh in a further shake-up to the show's format. Brian is a charming and flamboyant American dancer and choreographer who had worked with artists such as Beyoncé Knowles and Mariah Carey. He, like me, had been drafted in to give the new season of *The X Factor* a slightly different flavour. Sharon, meanwhile, had been a long-time hero of mine. I'd religiously watched her family's reality show, *The Osbournes*, on MTV, and had huge admiration for her, both as a TV personality and as a woman. How could this not be great fun?

I'd met Sharon briefly a couple of days before we started filming, when I'd been shopping in Bond Street. I spotted her on the street heading back to her car. When she saw me, she smiled and came towards me.

'Hi, Dannii,' she said. 'I'm so excited that you're coming to join the show. It's gonna be great!'

'Thank you,' I said. 'I'm really looking forward to working with you, too.'

I was pleased to have bumped into her like that, and relieved that she'd been so welcoming, because I was quite nervous about my upcoming first day's shoot, despite my excitement about the next few months.

On that first day of filming, we all gathered for the auditions. We had a lengthy line of hopefuls to critique before the end of a long, twelve-hour stretch. The idea was that we would sit on a panel together in a large room into which the contestants would be led, one by one, to sing for us. The four judges would then, in turn, comment on, evaluate, praise or criticise their performance, before moving on to the next person.

Brian and I – the new kids on the block – practically had chattering teeth we were so nervous. His dressing room was next to mine. Before we headed out for the filming, he came into my room for a pre-match pep talk.

'Are you as scared as I am?' I asked him.

'I sure am,' he said. 'But let's just enjoy it. What's the worst thing that could happen?'

Sharon popped her head round the door to say hello and wish me luck too, and then we were off.

It seemed to be going well but halfway through the day Simon called an ominous production meeting with the show's executive pro-ducers, including the Head of Entertainment at ITV, Richard Holloway. What was going on?

'Sharon's not happy,' one of the crew whispered to me, nervously. 'She's just not coping with all the changes, and she's not coping with the fact that Louis isn't here either.'

Great! A disaster on my very first day.

We continued through the rest of the afternoon with nothing else being said. Nervous though I was, I tried my very best to keep up and be as calm and natural on camera and with the people auditioning as Sharon and Simon clearly were.

Unlike *Australia's Got Talent*, where contestants can pretty much do whatever they like as long as it comes under the umbrella of enter-tainment, *The X Factor* is all about singing, and there were some amazing vocalists who sang for the four of us during that first audition day. There are also, as anyone who watches the show knows, some truly horrendous 'performers' who come up before the judging panel. Try though I might that day, when some poor deluded soul was cater-wauling so very far out of tune, it was extremely difficult to keep a straight face and some semblance of composure.

At the end of the day, Brian and I felt uneasy because we knew that something wasn't right. Being the two new judges, we figured that the problem must be with one of us – or perhaps both of us. The consensus among Simon and the executive producers seemed to be that the judging panel wasn't working well without Louis Walsh, and I had no idea exactly what that was going to mean as far as my place on the show was concerned. I'd have to wait and see.

During that whole first week of recording, I had convinced myself that I was being 'punked' for the MTV show of the same name, and that it was all a big prank. I couldn't really believe I was part of *The X Factor* judging line-up. With all the drama on day one, I tried to keep a knowing sparkle in my eye, as if I were ready for the cameras to jump out from behind a wall and say: 'Sorry, Dannii, it was all a wind-up, love.'

What eventually transpired was that Louis did come back to *The X Factor*, and Brian was duly shifted off the judging panel, taking over as the show's creative director, which he and everyone seemed very happy about. This, of course, left little old me as the only newbie. I realised fast that I had a lot to learn about how the auditions worked, and what, as a mentor, I should be looking for in prospective finalists. There seemed to be cameras coming at me from every angle and so much information to take in as well. The whole production was fast moving, and I guess it had to be, but for the first few days of auditions, I felt flustered and worried that I might not be able to keep up.

Everyone else seemed so relaxed. What was wrong with me? Simon was the one who, in due course, put me right: encouraging me, gently supporting me when he felt I was on the right track, and taking me to one side and giving me a little guidance when I wasn't.

Eventually, as the days and days of auditions went on, I started to relax and enjoy it. Once that happened, I felt my personality start to come through in my on-camera comments and critiques.

'You're doing all right,' Simon told me. 'In fact, you're doing really well.'

At first, with Louis Walsh back on the panel, everyone's mood seemed to be better and there was a lot more laughter on the set. Many of the in-jokes between the other three judges went over my head, but

I guess that was to be expected, as they'd all been through the auditioning process three years running. I was glad to see that everyone was in much brighter spirits, as it made me feel less anxious and more settled as the filming went on.

There would be times when the four of us would laugh so hard about something that had happened, or at someone who had auditioned especially dreadfully, that we'd have tears streaming down our faces, and for a while it felt great to be working in that kind of environment. I only wish it could have remained that way, but unfortunately my presence seemed to be upsetting a dynamic that was long established, and I slowly got the feeling that Sharon and Louis might have preferred things the way they had been. I couldn't blame them. I was still finding the concept of me sitting on the judging panel instead of watching on TV as a fan slightly bizarre, so it had to be doubly difficult for them. I decided to be as affable as I possibly could, and to keep my head down and do my work in the hope that eventually everyone would get used to me being there.

No such luck! As *The X Factor* hit the TV screens of Britain, and the audition episodes began to air, the press started to print story after story about a supposed feud between Sharon and me. It was completely untrue but so predictable: after all, you couldn't possibly have two women sitting together on a television show without bitchiness and bitter rivalry between them, could you? Well, that's what they were all implying, anyway.

The truth of the matter was that I was such a big fan of Sharon that I was excited just to be sitting next to her. She was strong and smart and had so many of the attributes that I admire in a woman. I did my best to ignore the stories, and I refuted them in every interview.

'There's no bad blood between Sharon and me,' I'd hear myself saying during an interview, knowing full well that wasn't what the journalists wanted to hear and it wasn't what they were going to print, either. That wouldn't make a juicy, sensational headline, would it? 'We're friends!' No, that won't do at all. 'Sharon's jealousy over a younger and more attractive co-star.' Now *that's* a headline!

I don't think it affected me as much as it did Sharon, and why would it? I'd had it all my life – being compared to Kylie and reading stories of our 'furious sibling rivalry' – and I was used to it. Sharon obviously hadn't been through anything like it before, and it was upsetting her. She seemed convinced that I was personally dashing round from magazine to magazine to tell them that I was younger and prettier than she was. Naively, once again, I believed that it was all a storm in a teacup and would blow over. How wrong can you be?

On *The X Factor*, each judge is given one of four categories to mentor: boys, girls, groups or over-25s, then the judges compete against one another to keep their acts in the race until the final. I was overjoyed when I got the boys category, as I'd been really excited about the potential of a couple of the young talented male singers who had made it first through the audition stages and then through the tougher bootcamp round. I now had to whittle six boys down to three finalists who would appear on the twelve weeks of live rounds. Eventually, twelve finalists would become three for the live final, screened on ITV just before Christmas.

Meanwhile, I was in need of an on-screen guest judge to help me pick my final three boys, so I decided to ask my long-time collaborator, Terry Ronald, to do the job – we'd worked together for so many years on so many different projects, and he knew pop voices better than anyone else I could think of.

Terry married his partner, Mark, in the summer of 2007, and I went to the wedding along with my mum and dad. It was a great day, and I was very happy to see the person who had been my very first friend in London, sixteen years before, so content after all he'd been through.

'No time for a honeymoon yet, though, love,' I warned Terry before he and Mark had even cut the cake. 'You're coming with me to Ibiza!'

It was fabulous being back on my favourite Mediterranean island to film the 'judges' houses' section of the series – I felt it was my little part of the world. By the end of the two days in Ibiza, I had to decide which of the three boys was to make my first-ever *X Factor* team. I'd had T-shirts made for all of them with 'Team Minogue' emblazoned across the chest: I was getting involved in the fun of it now. We shot in a stunning white villa overlooking the sea, and it was all very glamorous. As I didn't have to rush back to work straight away, I planned to stay on once the filming was done and catch a few days of much needed sun and girly chill-out time with the show's executive producer, Claire Horton, and JJ, the make-up artist.

On the first day of filming, I called an old friend and songwriting partner, Roger Sanchez, who was also in Ibiza for the season as a DJ.

'Dannii, come for dinner tonight at El Ayoun,' he said, happy to hear from me. 'It'll be great to catch up with you!'

I took Claire, Terry and *The X Factor*'s new presenter, Dermot O'Leary, and his girlfriend, Dee, along to meet Roger, too, and we had an absolute blast. It was so great to hook up with Roger again, and we spent a lovely evening together, laughing, drinking and eating the most divine food, while reminiscing about past times working together in New York. Afterwards, we all headed to the club, Pacha, where Roger was playing, and danced the night away. You'd have thought we were on holiday instead of there to work.

By the end of the second day's filming, I had chosen my three boys: Rhydian Roberts, Leon Jackson and Andrew Williams – all good-looking boys and great singers, though very different from one another. I was happy with my 'Team Minogue', and so were the show's producers.

'I really think you're actually going to win this,' Terry confided in me before he returned to London.

'I hope you're right!' I smiled.

I was now all ready and very excited about the prospect of the upcoming live shows, and I couldn't wait for the first one to get underway.

When the Saturday of the first live show arrived, however, things didn't exactly get off to a good start. It began to look ominous about two hours before we went live to air, when Sharon Osbourne's personal assistant breezed into my tiny dressing room while I was having my hair and make-up done.

'Sharon wants to see you in her room,' her assistant told me. 'Could you pop along now?'

My hair was in rollers, I was wearing a dressing gown and slippers and I only had half an eye made up, so I wasn't especially keen to go wandering up and down the corridor to see anyone.

'Of course I'll come and see Sharon,' I told the assistant, 'but can I go when I've finished getting ready? It's my first show and I'm really up against the clock.'

So the assistant smiled and left. I decided to see Sharon once I was fully glammed-up for the cameras. It was my birthday that day, so every five minutes somebody from the production team bustled into the dressing room to say 'Happy Birthday', which slowed my progress even more. I was now very definitely running on 'Minogue Time' and getting quite flustered as a result. Consequently, half an hour later, the assistant was back in my dressing room with a slightly more urgent tone.

'Sharon really is keen to speak with you, Dannii,' she said, 'before the show goes to air.'

What on earth could have been so urgent? It wasn't a birthday gift – I'd already received a beautiful bag from her and her daughter, Kelly, which I loved. I turned to Sharon's assistant, who was now clearly hovering and waiting for me to accompany her back to Sharon's room.

'Sorry, I will see Sharon before the show,' I assured her, while my hair and make-up girl, Karen, continued frantically with the job in hand. 'I'm just really, really running late now, and I'm starting to panic!'

Off she went again, looking more than slightly tense. I finished having my hair done and started getting dressed.

By this time, Terry and his husband, Mark, had arrived in my dressing room, which was now filled with flowers. Terry poured me a glass of champagne to toast our mutual birthdays and calm my nerves. I'd invited a few of my good friends down to see my first live *X Factor* that night, and I was planning to have birthday drinks in my room after the show.

Suddenly, about thirty minutes before the live broadcast, there was another urgent knock on my dressing-room door, and in bowled Sharon – still in her dressing gown – with her assistant tagging along behind her. She was not happy, and she was demanding to know why I hadn't gone to the press to tell them what a nice person she was.

'All this bollocks in the press is ruining my life,' she snapped. 'You could be telling them that I'm a nice person but instead you're adding fuel to the fire by saying nothing.'

'Sharon, I have never said anything bad about you, and I wouldn't say anything bad about you,' I told her.

But she didn't seem interested in what I had to say.

'I don't need this!' she squeaked. 'I'm a mother, for fuck's sake, do you think I need all this shit in my life?'

I froze in my chair as she came towards me, gesticulating as she shouted, and I tried reasoning with her, calmly, once more.

'Sharon, they are just stupid press stories about a non-existent feud. All I've ever done is tell people how much I admire you, but they don't want to print it. I know what it's like – I've been through it enough times myself. But I have no idea why this is happening now, because I've never said a bad word against you and I want you to know that.'

It was true: stories were rife in the papers about how Sharon was utterly distraught about my appointment as a judge on the show, and how she feared that she, as the older woman, was on the way out. Everyone knew damn well that the stories had absolutely nothing to do with me, and I couldn't understand her fury towards me.

'Oh, don't play the innocent,' Sharon spat. ''Cause if you wanna play games, Missy, I'll play . . . Don't you worry, I'll play!'

I turned, fleetingly, to look at Terry and Mark, whose mouths had fallen open in horror, and then I caught a glimpse of my make-up girl, Karen, who was frozen, holding a mascara wand in mid-air. By now, Sharon was screaming at me, furiously, and I was starting to get a little worried. It's hard to remember most of the abuse she yelled at me in the ensuing five or ten minutes because I was so shocked, but there she was, looming over me in her dressing gown, shouting and swearing – the 2006 Celebrity Mother of the Year.

My palms were clammy and my chest was tight, as I sat there in disbelief, listening to Sharon sound off. I noticed Terry had disappeared out of the door, and then, seconds later, he reappeared with Claire

Horton and one of the other producers, Mark Sidaway, who both tried to calm Sharon down.

'This is not the time or place for this – twenty minutes before we go on air, Sharon,' Claire said firmly. 'Let's talk about this later, shall we?'

But Sharon wouldn't leave, and finally, with about ten minutes to go before the broadcast started, the show's producers had to remove Sharon from my dressing room, still ranting as she went.

The minute she left, I burst into tears. I'd managed to hold it together while Sharon had been there, but once she'd gone I couldn't hold it in, and I wept quietly into my hands. I wasn't crying because I thought there was any truth to what she'd said; I was crying because someone whom I had previously looked up to and admired greatly had relentlessly bawled in my face for twenty minutes and ruined not only what should have been one of the best nights of my life but my birthday as well. It was now five minutes before I was due to go on live television in front of twelve million people, and I had make-up streaming down my face.

'What the fuck am I supposed to have done?' I said, trying to catch my breath.

'It's not you, babe,' Terry said, angrily, jumping to my defence. 'I think she knew exactly what she wanted to do just then, which was screw with your head five minutes before your first live show.'

My fabulous make-up girl, Karen Alder, suddenly took charge and cleared the room completely. Then she sat me back in the make-up chair, still shaking, and turned me around to face her.

'Right, Dannii,' Karen said, poised with a loaded bottle of eyedrops. 'You've got to go on in five minutes. Whatever happened just then was bullshit and you know it, so you're not going to let someone who isn't making any sense ruin your big night, right?'

I shook my head. 'No.'

Karen was right: the abuse was bad enough, but to let it wreck something I'd been looking forward to for so long – no, I wasn't having that.

'Good,' Karen said. 'So stop crying, pull yourself together and let's get you out there!'

She literally threw some more make-up on my face, fixed my hair and ushered me towards the dressing-room door.

When we reached the backstage area, I joined the other judges, Louis, Simon and Sharon, ready for our first grand entrance of the series. I could hear the studio audience going crazy and the music blaring out across the studio floor. Then, when the sliding screen opened to reveal the four of us to the nation, I put my hand out to Sharon, who was standing beside me, and she took it. Whatever had gone down before the show, I knew that she was upset. I wanted to try to show her that there was no truth in what the papers were saying and that we could be friends, or at the very least work together. As we moved down towards the front of the stage, Sharon lifted up our joined hands in front of the cheering crowd, and I felt relieved. Maybe that's the end of it, I thought. Maybe it's some kind of first-night nerves for her? Maybe now we could get on with the rest of the series?

But later that same night, when two of Sharon's acts got the least votes, she took off her shoes, ripped off her eyelashes and stormed off the show, swearing – in front of the studio audience and live on camera – announcing that she was going home and refusing to take part in the final decision about which act should be eliminated. I was stunned, and I turned to Simon, who was sitting next to me, expecting him to know exactly what to do or say in such an awkward situation, but he comically shrugged his shoulders and looked as puzzled as I was.

I did know one thing for sure: whatever was going on with Sharon, this certainly wasn't the end of it. In fact, I had a feeling it was just the beginning.

The rest of that first season of *The X Factor* was a rollercoaster of great highs and rotten lows. While I loved being a judge on such an exciting show, I started to grow weary of Sharon and Louis's clear and united front against me. Though Louis and I are good mates these days, he'd be the first to admit that back then he felt a sense of duty towards Sharon, taking her part in what had become a feud, albeit a one-sided one. Simon, thank goodness, was a great ally through all of it. I felt I could rely on him for support when things got rough – and boy, did it get rough. It didn't matter that I met with Sharon and Executive Producer, Richard Holloway, in an attempt to smooth things out. It didn't matter that my management company tracked down the recordings of press interviews I'd done and gave them to Sharon's agent so that she could hear what I'd said about her. Sharon had decided that I was her mortal enemy and therefore I had no voice.

I'm a tough cookie when I need to be. What could have been a dream job was at times a complete nightmare. I had more than one sleepless night trying to get my head around it – nothing made sense. I had to put up with insults flying at me both on screen and off. In fact, when I sat on the judging panel next to Sharon each Saturday, having seen her publicly destroy me on yet another television show or press interview that week, I felt like I was back at my old primary school, when I was forced to sit next to the school bully, Fat Billy.

Over the course of the next year or so, Sharon endlessly and publicly announced to anyone who'd listen that I was impossible to work with – but never explained why – that I was only on *The X Factor* because of my looks, not any visible talent or contribution to the entertainment industry, and Simon Cowell employed me only because he wanted to sleep with me. She adopted a ludicrous cod-Aussie accent, imitating me as if I were an airhead who knew nothing. She said I'd had too much Botox and plastic surgery and looked ridiculous, and I was nothing more than a mosquito that she wanted to flick away. On one memorable chat show, goaded by an almost salivating Graham Norton, Sharon Osbourne rolled around on the studio floor, pointing at her backside, and comparing my face to it – in front of millions of people – and to this day she hasn't stopped verbally attacking me.

The best course of action for me was dignified silence, and looking back now maybe that was a mistake. People sometimes saw me as 'icy', and I guess I can understand why, but what can one say to all that, anyway? When we were both on *The X Factor* panel together, it was either 'keep schtum' or a slanging match every other week, and I wasn't interested in that.

At the end of *The X Factor* 2007, the two finalists were Welsh classical singer Rhydian Roberts and the young Scottish jazz crooner Leon Jackson – both from the category I had mentored – with Leon ultimately going on to win the final. I was so over the moon that one of my boys had won, especially with it being my first series. At the end of the final show I was elated.

'Dannii kicked our arses!' Simon told the press afterwards.

In truth, it felt like it was mine that had been kicked, despite walking away as the winning judge. Was I going to have to go through all this again next year if I did the show? There was no telling. I would have to wait and see.

I don't know what happened between Sharon Osbourne and me. When I consider it now, I still feel sad about it, because when I met her I wanted so much to enjoy being part of the gang and for us to have a laugh together. I also secretly wanted to meet her rock-star husband, Ozzy . . . But I guess that's never gonna happen now, is it?

Chapter 31

Three Days in Flat Shoes

I still felt that I needed to make sense of Laura's death, and what I called the 'cancer madness'. After Laura, I'd lost another close friend, called Nigel, a driver who had worked for Kylie and me since we'd first come to London. He'd died of lung cancer, leaving a wife and two children. It seemed that the only way I could swallow the anger and the shock over losing Laura and deal with the pain of how much I missed her was to try to do something proactive. In April 2008, that's what I did.

I was contacted by a charity that was run by my childhood idol, Olivia Newton-John, who, like Kylie, was a breast-cancer survivor. She was raising money to build the Olivia Newton-John Cancer and Wellness Centre in Melbourne on the site of a former antiquated and impractical hospital building that was going to be demolished. The facility would provide world-class clinical care for cancer patients, and research facilities for important clinical trials to develop future cancer vaccines and treatments. It was Olivia's vision.

She had rounded up a team of cancer survivors, nurses, doctors and celebrities who had some link with or passion for the cause, and was planning a charity-sponsored, three-week, 228-kilometre walk across the Gobi Desert along the Great Wall of China. Olivia asked me if I would come on one section of the walk with her, which was what many of the other celebrities were doing, to raise as much money and public awareness for the cause as possible, and I jumped at the chance.

The only trouble was the walk came right in the middle of the second *Australia's Got Talent* season, and I'd have to complete my three-day walk in between two long studio days one week apart. This would mean flying out from Melbourne to Beijing and back again – about twenty-seven hours in total – in a very short space of time, but I was determined to do it and to get as many sponsors as I could along the way.

There were plenty of other celebrities who had signed up for the walk too: Cliff Richard, Joan Rivers, Didi Conn, who played 'Frenchy' in the movie *Grease*, Leeza Gibbons from US TV, Ian Thorpe, the Aussie gold-medallist swimmer, and singer and TV presenter Toyah Wilcox, to name but a few. We were all joining Olivia on one or more of the six different stages of the 21-day trek. Every one of us had been given firm instructions about having exactly the right equipment and walking gear, so I had to make sure I was kitted out with absolutely everything I'd need while I was there, especially shoes – no Christian Louboutins on this excursion. Some of my friends had already expressed their concern about the footwear situation when I'd told them what I was about to undertake.

'Dannii, we totally understand that you want to do something for charity, but three days in flat shoes? It just doesn't sound possible for you!'

After two flights from Melbourne, I ended up in the beautiful Ritz Carlton Hotel in Beijing – not exactly roughing it, I know – and there I met some of the team who would be joining me on the walk. Beijing is a city of twenty-two million people and has smog so thick it cuts out the sun. When I walked out into the air the next morning, leaving the comfort of the hotel, I had butterflies of excitement and nervousness about what the next few days would bring. I mean, let's face it, I had never been camping before and I was usually never more than a few feet away from a power socket to plug in a hairdryer.

The flights took me first to Xian, and then on to Jiayuguan, which is a desert city in western China. After almost two days of continuous travel, I was finally ready to start walking, although I don't think I was quite prepared for what I eventually faced.

It would not be an exaggeration to say that the first day of walking was a vertiginous climb. As most of my pre-walk training consisted of me wearing my trekking boots while typing a few emails the previous week, I was slightly apprehensive about my ability to conquer it. This was the mountainous part of the Great Wall, sitting between the Black Mountains and the snow-capped mountains of Qilian. The walk was several kilometres up to the highest, northern viewing point, and then a nine-kilometre descent to the Jiayuguan Pass. While the scenery was breathtaking, it was tough going.

I couldn't wait to meet Olivia properly on the walk. We had met briefly before as I'm a friend of her niece, Tottie, but I didn't know Olivia well. I was excited to be doing this momentous thing with her for her special charity. In truth, I wouldn't in my wildest dreams have thought that I'd ever end up hanging out with my childhood idol. If I'd imagined a scenario of Olivia and me hanging out together, we would have been doing something in fabulous outfits and platform shoes under a disco ball; we wouldn't have been in hiking boots with blisters in the middle of the Gobi Desert. Olivia was great, and I was amazed at how much time she spent with all the sponsored walkers – making sure everyone was OK, singing with us as she walked, and giving a hug and a few words of encouragement to anybody who needed it.

Walking that first day, I met some incredible people, and all of them had stories of loss and survival that moved me and helped me make some sense of the feelings that I'd experienced with my friends' and family's illnesses. There was a firefighter, Scott Morrison, whom everyone called Scotty, who had spent most of his life putting himself at risk to save others and had then suffered not one but two major brushes with cancer. Scotty had originally had treatment in the hospital we were raising money to rebuild, and he told me that the old site had not had anywhere near the standard of equipment and facilities they'd needed. When Scotty had desperately needed an isolation ward, there wasn't one, so he was on the walk to help build a better hospital. Scotty always stayed at the front of the walk and was a big hulk of a man. When I got the chance to talk to him about his experience and everything that he and his wife had been through, he cried like a baby. As one of the best-loved people on the walk, we were all devastated to learn later that Scotty had returned home afterwards only to discover that his 17-year-old son had leukaemia.

I also met a great guy called Adam Sutton, an Aussie cowboy who had written a book about his very colourful and often sad past. He told me all about his life, mustering cattle in the outback, and how tough it was for him to grow up gay in that sort of environment. I listened in awe.

'I'm a real gay cowboy, Dannii,' he told me, smiling.

'Well, Adam, it doesn't get much gayer than taking a stroll through a desert with Olivia and me, singing "Xanadu",' I said.

Dinner on the first night of the walk was quite an event, particularly for Olivia and me. We were quite high up in the mountains towards Mongolia and a special, traditional banquet had been organised for us in some large tents in what seemed like the middle of nowhere. There were about forty walkers sitting down to this meal, and we were all starving by the time we got there. I sat down next to Olivia at the big wooden table and awaited the first course. The first thing that was set down in front of us was some raw, peeled garlic, and Olivia and I looked at one another in bewilderment.

'Is this an appetiser?' I said.

'I don't know,' Olivia replied. 'Should we just eat it as it is?'

'Well, I'm going to have to eat something soon,' I said. 'I'm absolutely starving.'

So Olivia and I ate the raw garlic, thinking that although it seemed strange and tasted rather hot, if it was the custom there to eat raw garlic, that's what we would do. It all seemed fine when it first went down, but five minutes later both of us began to turn green and feel incredibly sick.

'I'm going to have to run outside,' Olivia said, holding her hand over her mouth, and I wasn't far behind her.

Within seconds we were both outside, behind an adjacent little tent, hurling up garlic together in very unladylike fashion, and it was coming out pink. Yes, I was spewing pink vomit with Olivia Newton-John in the middle of the Gobi Desert – definitely one for the scrapbook.

Afterwards, Olivia looked over at me, still trying to compose myself, and said with the cutest little laugh: 'Welcome to China!'

Once back inside the banqueting tent, we discovered that the garlic was, in fact, supposed to be eaten with the main meal, which they were now serving.

Now, I've been vegetarian since I was a kid. I always liked the smell of meat and I didn't mind the taste of it, but it never sat right with me once I'd eaten it. It always made me feel slightly ill, as if I wasn't digesting it properly. So, when I was thirteen, I marched into the kitchen and announced to Mum that from then on I was going to be a vegetarian. I'll always remember the look of horror on her face on hearing these words. She told me, in no uncertain terms, that if I wasn't going to eat what the rest of the family were eating, I would have to start cooking for myself. I guess that's when I started to learn about food, and developed a passion for cooking, because I have not eaten meat from that day to this.

Imagine, then, my joy at being a non-meat eater when I was faced with some of the delights being served up at our Mongolian-style banquet under canvas that night: donkey, dog and something that looked vaguely like a chicken. I stuck to salad and noodles.

The locals looking after us that night wanted us to enjoy the whole experience of being their guests, and to present us with the ceremony of a traditional banquet, which was something I did appreciate. After the dinner, we watched some dancers from the region, then we travelled to our next hotel, where I practically inhaled the vegetarian buffet and threw down a few glasses of *vin rouge* with some of my fellow walkers.

*

Any sort of vanity and, indeed, hygiene go out of the window when you're in such places. On the long trek across the desert plain, surgical masks were needed to protect our faces from dust, but each night I was covered in a thick film of it. I have to confess to finding dust in places I never thought I would – and certainly would have preferred not to. As the water in the showers there had a murky brown tinge to it, I tried to get as clean as I possibly could as quickly as I could.

Toilets, too, were an interesting prospect. We had to set up our own desert-trek toilet periodically, which was nicknamed 'The Throne'. Other than those in the hotels, this was by far the cleanest and most hygienic toilet we came across, as most of the public ones were literally just holes in the ground. It also seemed that people went to the toilet straight onto the road, whether there was a hole there or not, and in certain places human faeces adorned both sides of the public highway. A local guide explained to us that this was normal, and that in some parts of China the roadside is used as an open toilet, with men going on the left of the highway and women on the right. This was a real culture shock for all of us on the walk, so 'The Throne', makeshift as it was, provided a virtual oasis once it was erected.

On my last day in China, we arrived in Dunhuang after a five-hour bus trip, and I was so happy to see some greenery. The day before had been a desert trek and pretty tough going. Even though Olivia had been sick with flu, she'd taken every single step with us without a word of complaint. She had the strongest willpower I'd ever seen, I think, and to witness her carry on even though she was struggling was quite amazing.

After all that desert, my eyes felt like they'd been starved of colour. Arriving in Dunhuang, it was as if we were stepping out of an old black-and-white Western movie and into a 3D Bollywood one. There was quite a fanfare for our arrival, with pretty young dancers wearing full performance make-up, and costumes of bright pink and yellow, then a fantastic Chinese feast for lunch, with the tables covered in plates of steaming food. It was wonderful.

That final day's walk was a gentle stroll in comparison to the other days. After lunch, we went for an excursion to the Mogao Grottoes, which are also known as 'Caves of the Thousand Buddhas'. These are a maze of temples in the side of a mountain, with a magical backdrop of the most perfect sand dunes surrounding them. We visited three of the larger caves, which were filled with the most exquisite Buddhist art and hundreds of statues of the Eastern god, and I was quite sad when we were told that no photos were allowed, because it was one of the most breathtaking sights I've ever seen. Inside these desert caves, it was freezing cold, and I stood, mesmerised, at the foot of one Buddha, over 100 feet high. The walls and ceilings were decorated with thousands of intricate murals that were patterned like tiles, and I simply stared, wide eyed, all around me, taking in the absolute beauty, stillness and serenity of my surroundings. This had been a place of contemplation for centuries. Buddhist monks had lived here, while artists and pilgrims had come and sculpted and painted these deities to inspire and span hundreds of years – through wars and earthquakes and whatever else time had thrown at them. I felt small and humble among them.

While I tried to process the many reasons I was there, all I could hear in my head was the same word repeating over and over again: acceptance. Perhaps now, just over a year after her memorial on Hermanus beach, I would finally start to accept that Laura was gone – to accept it without anger and remain full of good memories. Some days are harder than others.

Chapter 32

The Lady Next Door and the Man from Space

I now felt I had a great management team of people around me, but, with Melissa in Melbourne most of the time, I needed someone on the ground in the UK before *The X Factor* started. I'd known Nathan Smith since the late nineties, and Mel and I agreed that he'd be the perfect candidate. Nate had been instrumental in helping me put together and oversee my website back when he was a fresh-faced twenty-year-old, and over the years I've come to trust his opinion and creative input.

He was great at keeping me informed and updated about what all of the fans talking on the website forum were saying and would always be sure to let me know exactly what they liked or didn't like. This was important to me because so many of the people who described themselves as 'Dannii fans' had practically grown up with me. The older ones had followed me since *Young Talent Time* and their very first vinyl copy of 'Love And Kisses', and many of them had stuck with me through whatever, and that meant a lot to me. Of course, as time went on, I've gathered many more supporters through the *Neon Nights* album and now *Australia's Got Talent* and *The X Factor*, and I've never for one minute take them for granted. Those people are the ones who enable you to keep going, and I'm very fortunate to have the fans that I do.

Nathan, who already had a handle on what was going on with me day to day through running the website, seemed the perfect person to step in and take over management tasks while I was in Europe. Melissa Le Gear back home in Oz handled all the bigger, contractual and legal stuff. Mel had worked for Terry Blamey from the beginning, over twenty years ago, in the Australian office and she'd continued working as my acting agent all through those years. She knew most of the people in my life including my family. I also had a personal assistant called Tori, who kept me organised, helped me sort out my clothes for the show and was a steady support whenever things got rocky at *The X Factor* studios. It was great to be around people I trusted.

My home life was on a pretty even keel too. Because I was working on two different television shows – one in Melbourne and one in London – it meant that I was getting the best of both worlds and not missing either place too much. I even had a substitute grandmother living right next door to me in Battersea in the form of a wonderful lady called Jo.

I first became friends with Jo and her husband, Kenneth, not long after I'd moved into my apartment building, and over the years we've become closer and closer. The first time I met them was after a birthday party when I had been presented with far more bouquets of flowers than I had vases for – so I decided the best idea was to give the extra bunches to my neighbours who lived on the same floor as me. After knocking on one of the three doors, I was greeted by a tall, elderly man with a scowl and a sharp tone.

'Yes?' he snapped. I peered, nervously, over the absolutely massive bunch of flowers that was weighing me down, so that he might get a better look at me.

'Er, sorry, I don't mean to disturb you,' I said, 'but I live next door and it's my birthday, and I've been given so many flowers – which I can't find vases for – so I wondered if you would like to have some of them.'

I proffered the bouquet and waited for an answer, but the man said nothing for ages and just glared at me. Then, all of a sudden, he took the flowers and said: 'All right then,' and shut the door.

Not even a thank you, I thought.

The next day, I bumped into the man in the corridor, but this time he was smiling at me and looked a lot friendlier. 'Thank you so much for the flowers,' he said, his voice now kind and soft. 'My wife, Jo, has been in bed with a very bad case of asthma, and it was very sweet of you to bring them, but you took me by surprise, I'm afraid, and I didn't know what to say.'

'No problem at all,' I said. 'It was my pleasure and it's nice to meet you.'

After that, I became good friends with Kenneth and his wife. When we first met they were in their late seventies, and we spent lots of fun times together. They didn't have kids or grandkids, and seemed to love having someone to fuss over and look after; as my grandparents were in a different hemisphere, I was more than happy to be on the receiving end of all their love and attention.

Jo was originally from Cambridge and even in her eighties, as she is now, she is extremely elegant and glamorous. Her voice is the first thing you notice, as she speaks beautifully. I love the way she says 'orf' instead of 'off'– just like the Queen. She always laughs at my Aussie brogue and the way I gesticulate, wildly, as I talk. In the fifties, Jo had been one of the top fashion buyers in London, working for companies such as Debenhams and Jaeger, and by all accounts was as chic and fabulous as you could get. With a petite, Audrey Hepburn-like frame, she was always immaculately turned out in gorgeously fitted suits and beautiful frocks, and she lit her cigarettes with a pink jade lighter, and smoked them through a long holder.

Back then, Jo had an assistant and a driver and she travelled all over with her work, just like I do now; I guess, when we met, she saw a little bit of herself in me. Consequently, whenever I have a beautiful couture dress or fabulous outfit turn up at my place, all ready for me to wear to an event or TV show, I always like to knock on Jo's door before I go down and get in the car, so that she can check out the frock and eyeball every tiny detail and hand stitch while I wait for her seal of approval. On the other hand, she also tells me when I don't look my best or when she doesn't like the outfit too, which is the mark of a true friend, and she always makes me smile. The comment I most like to hear from Jo is: 'That is full of fashion, duckie.' Then I know I've got it just right!

There have been other moments, moments I've already spoken about, when I haven't been feeling quite so glamorous, and I'm unable to face the world. It's still Jo's door that I'll go and knock on even then. Because she knows me well, she'll take me inside and let me crawl into her bed; then she brings me a hot-water bottle and a nice cup of tea and, if she thinks I need it, an iced eye-mask. When I need the cuddle that only a mother or a grandmother can give, the kind where I don't have to say anything at all, she gives me that too.

Since Jo lost Kenneth a couple of years back, we have become even closer, if that were possible, and despite her age, Jo comes out to parties with me, and to the theatre – she even visits me at *The X Factor*. She loves to socialise with a glass of champagne or two, and all my friends and family adore her. Despite our age difference, Jo is one of my best mates – like a mum and grandma all rolled into one, the fabulous 'lady next door'.

The only thing I didn't have going on was a love life. Apart from curling up in front of a romantic comedy with my two cats, the only mention of romance I'd had was when a 'scandalous' photograph of Simon Cowell and me apparently holding hands in the back of a car came out in the press and got tongues wagging, but it wasn't that interesting.

No, I was far more likely to be found in the company of my surrogate husband, Benjamin Hart, the handsome model I'd met in Amsterdam during the *Neon Nights* promotion. When the two of us decided to meet up in Ibiza for a holiday in the summer of 2008, I was unknowingly set on a path that would in due course lead me to the biggest shake-up of my life yet.

Space nightclub in Ibiza is not the place you would immediately think of if you were planning to meet the love of your life. When I turned up there to see my good mate Carl Cox play a DJ set, an encounter of that sort couldn't have been further from my mind.

When I arrived at the club with Benji and another friend called Lindsay, Carl and his tour manager, Ian, led us up to the VIP section of the club, which was right next to the DJ console. Carl was scheduled to play two sets that night, one earlier in the evening and the other one at 3a.m., and I was fairly certain that by that time I'd have long gone home to bed, leaving the boys to party on their own. But it was still early and we were all dancing in the VIP lounge, which gave us a fabulous panorama across the rapidly growing crowd, who were dancing and looking towards Carl, as though they had reached their musical Mecca.

At one point, we were leisurely scanning the room, when my eyes came to rest on an absolutely gorgeous-looking guy in a white tank top dancing with a few other people very near the area where we were standing. He was looking right up towards us.

'Wow!'

I turned to Benjamin, and pointed, discreetly, at this handsome vision, as we danced.

'Do you think he dances at my end of the ballroom or yours?' I said.

'It's hard to say,' Benji said. 'He's looking over at us but it's difficult to tell which one of us it is he's looking at.'

Now, as I've said, Benjamin is an extremely good-looking guy, so I thought there was every chance that this beautiful man, with close-cropped hair, strong, chiselled features and a body to die for, was checking Benji out.

'Well, I don't really fancy him anyway,' Benji said, 'but if we just keep dancing I'm sure it'll become obvious which one of us it is he's looking at.'

For the next ten minutes, Benjamin and I staged a little dance-off, both farcically competing with one another to see which of us could grab this handsome guy's attention, with him looking over at us and us looking over at him. And still we were none the wiser.

I felt I was looking good that night: I had the frock, the heels, the eyelashes, the hand-held fan to keep me cool. I was feeling great and having the best time. But after another five minutes of tirelessly shaking my stuff to the best of my ability, I still had no idea if the handsome man in the crowd was checking out my legs or Benji's arms, and I would never have had the guts to go over and ask him – I wasn't that brave. Suddenly, though, Benjamin caught the guy's eye and beckoned him to come over, and I squealed like a teenage girl at a pop concert. What was Benji doing? What on earth was he going to say to this hot guy? I wanted the ground to open up and swallow me whole.

When the mystery man – who was even taller and sexier close up – finally came over, I could see him and Benji in deep conversation only metres away from me, but the noise in the club was so blisteringly loud that I couldn't make out a word they were saying. After a minute or so, though, a grinning Benji brought Mr Handsome right over to where I was standing, and introduced us.

'Dannii, this is Kris. Kris, this is Dannii.'

And then with a wink and a cheeky smile, Benji leaned over and said quietly into my ear: 'All yours, love.'

Then I knew which one of us he'd been looking at.

Once the two of us got chatting, it transpired that Kris hadn't wanted to be at the club at all that night.

'It's my birthday tomorrow,' he said with the strongest, sexiest Mancunian accent I've ever heard. 'I've got a whole big day planned so I didn't want to come out tonight, but my mates dragged me out. Plus, before your mate Carl Cox, whoever that is, started, I had to sit through a Portuguese DJ playing two hours of Spanish house music, and it's not really my scene.'

Kris was in Ibiza on holiday with his mates and he'd apparently had a scowl on his face all night because he wanted to go home. By this time, however, he seemed more than happy that he'd made it out to Space and I was too. While we chatted over the music as best we could while Carl Cox continued his noisy 11 o'clock set, I discovered that Kris was as charming as he was handsome.

Meanwhile, I was wondering whether or not he'd noticed the fact that although we were standing pretty much face to face, I was perched a whole two stairs up from him, *and* in high heels. But I stared into his kind, sexy eyes anyway, and watched his lips moving. The more I listened to his soft, lilting voice, the more taken with him I was becoming.

'When Carl finishes his set, we're going to go backstage for a while,' I said to him eventually. 'I'd love you to come along with us.'

'OK,' he smiled – and what a smile.

'I'll just have to tell my mates that I'll see them later – back in a minute.'

What I didn't know then was that Kris had absolutely no idea who I was until his mates teased him about it, or even when they told him, 'That's Dannii Minogue you're chatting up.'

He said: 'Who? Dannii Minogue, the singer? Is it?'

It took a while before the penny finally dropped, and I found that even more charming.

'I wondered why all me mates were making rude hand gestures at me while I was talking to you,' he laughed when he got back.

In the backstage area, the champagne was flowing and Kris and I were having a great time, along with my pals, Benjamin and Lindsay, and all of Carl's other invited guests. Kris told me that he'd once been a professional Rugby League player, but after a couple of bad knee injuries he was now a sports development officer, coaching high-school kids in Manchester: not an actor or a celebrity photographer or a record-company executive or a racing driver but a teacher – how refreshingly normal that seemed.

When it was almost midnight, I don't know what came over me. 'Can I be the first person to kiss you on your birthday?' I asked him.

It was so forward and so 'not me' – and I wasn't even tipsy. I had such a strong feeling about this guy. Although I felt nervous, the words came out before I had time to stop them.

'Absolutely,' he said, flashing that smile again.

So, on the stroke of midnight at Space in Ibiza, that handsome mystery man kissed me and, just like a nightclub Cinderella, I fell for him then and there.

The rest of the holiday was, of course, magical. Kris and I got to know one another, day by day, and my friends, Benjamin and Lindsay, made it clear they also approved of him. Thank God for Benji: Kris and I have both since admitted to one another that we wouldn't have summoned up the courage to go and talk to the other one if it hadn't been for him.

A couple of days after that first night at Space, we all met up in the old town with Kris's friends, and I was so happy that they were all funny and down to earth – just like him.

Once we were back in London, I couldn't wait to see him again. After I did, I was on a high that I never wanted to come down from. When I looked into Kris's eyes each time we were together, I absolutely knew that he was the man for me. It was that fast. For the first time in so long, I was in love again, and everything about it felt right.

Chapter 33

Learning Curves

It's a strange thing being a so-called celebrity. You know what you're sign-ing up for – and if you don't, you learn fast – and the rewards and lifestyle it brings can often be wonderful. What you always have to keep in mind, though, is that everyone has an opinion about everything you do and say, both in your working life and your personal one. If that's some-thing you can't put up with, then you're better off working a regular 9–5. There *are* much tougher jobs than the one I do, certainly – it's not like I work down a mine – but I have bad days like anyone else, days when I feel like the canary who just keeps on singing sweetly until something goes terribly wrong, then falls off her perch while everyone else escapes.

There are no handbooks on dealing with the pressure of fame, and no instructions explaining what to do and how to behave when certain difficult moments arise. You have to learn it for yourself and get on with it, hoping to God that people will give you a second chance if you get it wrong.

Just before I signed on the dotted line for my second season on *The X Factor* in 2008, there was a rather interesting turn of events. Sharon

Osbourne decided that she wasn't coming back to do the new series and Girls Aloud singer Cheryl Cole was announced as her replacement. I didn't know Cheryl that well, and had only come into contact with her when we were both managed by Hills at Shaw Thing Management.

Right away, as always, the media at large decided that this was the perfect scenario for a whole new 'cat-fight' saga. Cheryl is beautiful and twelve years younger than me, so the tables were turned. I was in Sharon's shoes, and made out by the press to be the older, bitter woman.

Unfortunately, though, their plans for a juicy story fell somewhat flat, because I was more than happy that Cheryl was joining the team. I told my friends, 'I don't care who the hell it is on the panel next to me, as long as it's not Sharon sitting there. I just wouldn't be able to cope with another series like that.'

I meant it. Still, the rumours of behind-the-scenes friction were rife, so Cheryl and I had to do our best to ignore them, and Nathan did his best to make sure the press got their facts straight as much as he possibly could.

It did appear, however, that having been flavour of the month on the 2007 *X Factor*, in 2008 I couldn't seem to put a foot right. I was mentoring the over-25s, which is always a tough category, and it seemed that every decision and choice I made for my contestants was coming under vicious fire, both on the show and in the press.

'Dannii's a useless mentor,' people were saying, despite the fact that I'd taken first and second place with my acts the previous year. I started to doubt myself after a while, and it was making me miserable at work all over again. This was coupled with the fact that back then Louis was still smarting about Sharon's departure, and the two of us weren't getting on at all. After several unnecessary and rather personal snipes at me on one show, Louis accused me of cheating, live on air, saying I'd unfairly stolen the song that he had planned to do with one of the acts that he mentored. Unbeknown to the audience, *The X Factor* judges take it in turn each week to have the first pick of songs. That week I was first and Louis was last, and he wasn't happy about it – it was as simple as that.

I suddenly had to defend my character in front of a jeering studio audience on live television with ten million-plus people watching, and I felt myself shaking. I started to speak, to try to explain the rules and that I would never cheat or steal a song. Louis shouted me down, yelling at me that I *had* stolen his song and I wasn't playing fair. A couple of minutes later, when the show's host, Dermot O'Leary, came to me to introduce the next act, I couldn't speak or even open my mouth. My eyes began to fill with tears. Under the desk I felt Cheryl, who was next to me, take my hand, and I swallowed hard.

'Dannii?' Dermot said again, expecting me to pull it together.

But I couldn't do it, and consequently, there was a minute or so of very awkward airtime. When I look back on it now it all seems so stupid, and I know Louis feels the same.

'You stole my song!'

'Oh no, I didn't!'

'Oh yes, you did!'

But honestly, when you know the whole nation's eyes are on you, and you're feeling like you're being cajoled and bullied and accused . . . well, I'm only human.

Cheryl, supposedly my new arch-nemesis, was very sweet and supportive to me that night after the broadcast, but I put it to the producers of the show that while I was more than happy to join in with the show's legendary competitive judges' battles, I certainly wasn't prepared to be a punch-bag, and neither should anyone else. After that night, a Facebook page was set up called 'PETDM' – 'People for the Ethical Treatment of Dannii Minogue'. That, at least, made me laugh.

Halfway through that second season, I did consider throwing in the towel when it got to the end of the series. Instead of looking forward to the recording of the show each week, I would sometimes dread it.

One chilly November Saturday, snuggled down in the back seat of the car on my way to the Fountain Studios in Wembley, I told Terry Ronald, who came to *The X Factor* with me every week, 'Terry, it's a cold rainy night and I'd much rather be at home curled up watching TV.'

'Well, you can't stay at home and watch telly, dear,' Terry said, 'because you're *on* it!'

It made me see the funny side, and we both giggled all the rest of the way there.

What did keep me going through all that was my gorgeous man, Kris. He came up to London to the studio nearly every weekend to support me. Every time I walked into my dressing room after a hairy moment in front of the cameras, Kris would be right there, smiling and holding out a glass of champagne for me, telling me how great he thought I was on the show, and letting me know how beautiful he thought I looked on camera. What more could a girl ask for?

We were going from strength to strength, and Kris was completely relaxed and unaffected by the idea of coming in to my world, which, let's face it, is sometimes an odd place to be. He took it in his stride when photographers snapped us every time we stepped out in public, or when someone in a restaurant came and asked me to sign their serviette while I was holding my knife and fork in midair, just about to eat. And while he couldn't quite grasp the concept of people being so obsessed with celebrity, not ever having had an idol himself, he wasn't fazed by it either. Kris thought that the whole entertainment industry was rather hilarious and a little crazy too, and sometimes it was hard to argue with him.

Towards the end of the year, I asked Kris if he would like to travel home to Melbourne with me at Christmas, and he excitedly agreed, telling me that he would have three weeks off work to come and visit. The only dark spot on the horizon was that I knew Kris was going to have to go back to his job as a sports development officer in Manchester right after the New Year, but I would be staying in Australia for at least another five months, with a third season of *Australia's Got Talent* keeping me on my home turf. An eerie feeling of déjà vu descended on me.

I knew that although Kris enjoyed his job, and was great with the kids, it was a job and not a career or passion for him. He was working where he'd grown up, but with some tough teenagers, and he told me that coaching sports wasn't something he saw himself doing for ever. Kris had been a successful professional Rugby League player, first in the UK with the Leeds Rhinos and Salford City Reds and then in France, and he missed it. So, with all this in mind, I decided to take drastic action before we left.

'I think you should stay in Australia with me,' I told him one night over dinner, and I couldn't believe the words were coming out of my mouth. 'I've got to be there for the next five or six months and I can't imagine being without you.'

I'd thought long and hard about my past and what I'd learned from it. I thought about what had happened to my relationships with Julian and Steve and Craig – all because of distance, and all because I was always too afraid to voice my concerns. I wasn't going to let that happen again – not this time. This time it was going to be different.

'I think you should stay out there with me, and let's work it out as we go. I'm sure you'll find something you like doing there.'

In fact, Benji Hart, who'd previously been both a model and a talent scout himself, had recently suggested to Kris that he'd make a great model.

'Maybe that's something you could try?' I said. 'Would you consider giving it a go?'

'Maybe,' Kris said, and I could tell he was seriously considering it.

'You know it makes sense,' I smiled.

After we'd thought about it seriously, it did make perfect sense – for both of us.

I wanted to meet Kris's family before I whisked him off anywhere, for however long he was coming with me. After all, he'd never taken a flight longer than four hours before. Suddenly along comes this famous Aussie girl whom he'd met on holiday a few months before, whisking him to the other side of the world and away from his mum and dad. I wanted them to meet me and for them to know who I was and how serious I was about their son, so we arranged a trip to Manchester.

Of course, from past experience, meeting a potential 'mother-in-law' was a bit of a nerve-racking prospect for me, but Kris's mum, Elsie, was completely laidback and friendly, as was his dad, Eddie, and they welcomed me into their home warmly and without reservation. It meant such a lot to me to see that Kris was from a happy, loving family just like I was. Not once while I was there did I feel they were thinking: 'Goodness! That's Dannii Minogue.' It wasn't important to them in the slightest what I did for a living, or what my public persona was. To them I was simply their son's girlfriend. As long as we were happy, that's all that mattered. It said so much about the way Kris had been with me ever since I'd first met him: natural, grounded and loving.

Kris did hand in his notice at work, and although it was tough for him to leave his family and friends, when he got to Australia he completely fell in love with it – even more than I imagined he would. He instantly clicked with the more relaxed lifestyle, the outdoor living, the laidback people, the space, the food and, of course, the weather. At Mum and Dad's place, he was part of the family right away, and I was so happy that they seemed to approve of him so unreservedly.

At Christmas when Kylie, Brendan and the rest of the extended family arrived, they, too, got on with Kris like a house on fire. One morning, when Kris was bouncing Brendan and Bec's new baby, James, gently on his knee, I was walking through the kitchen when I heard Dad say purposefully to Kris, 'So . . . you like kids.'

Kris slowly looked up until his eyes met mine as I crossed the room, and I think I saw a twinge of something approaching panic, but I just smiled and kept walking. Don't get involved, Dannii, I told myself, and I breezed out of the door without saying a word, leaving Kris to sort that one out for himself. Kris *was* great with both of Brendan's kids, though, and my grandparents adored him too: he was definitely a keeper, as they say.

What was special about it all was that I was now rediscovering Australia through Kris's eyes, and falling in love with my homeland all over again. We went to places together that I'd never seen before. We went to Port Douglas in Queensland and snorkelled on the Great Barrier Reef, chasing turtles and sharks, which is something I'd only dreamed of doing before. Each new restaurant, café or great store we discovered as a couple, we made our own.

*

Before Kris seriously started to look for work in Australia, a strange and wonderful twist of fate completely took us by surprise. When Kris and I had first arrived in Melbourne on the trip, Dad had driven to meet us at the airport, and so, of course, had the paparazzi. Consequently, Kris and I were snapped continuously as we walked through the airport to get to Dad's car, much to Kris's complete astonishment – it's not exactly the ideal scenario when your boyfriend is meeting your father for the first time. But, for once, it turned out to be a blessing in disguise.

The next day, the shots of Kris and me wheeling our trolleys piled with luggage through the airport appeared in several of the national newspapers. It seems that they were spotted by the marketing team at Myer, which is one of the biggest Australian department-store chains. We later discovered that the store had been looking for a tall sportsman with short-cropped hair to model for a new campaign they were running, and Kris had jumped out at them from the gossip pages.

'That's the kind of guy we're looking for,' one of them had remarked, staring down at the shot. 'Who's that guy?'

'Well, he's in a photo with Dannii Minogue,' said another, 'so it shouldn't be too difficult to find out.'

So once they'd tracked Kris down – via some of my Melbourne friends – he was offered a huge modelling contract and has never looked back. Little did we know, when we travelled out to Australia that Christmas with a tentative plan for Kris to try out as a model, that simply getting off the plane would be his audition.

Kris's position at Myer is one of the biggest male modelling jobs in the country, and somehow he'd stepped right into it, which was brilliant. He was with me in Australia *and* with a great job of his own – everything was rosy.

Now, with Kris by my side, I felt I was ready to take on the world.

Chapter 34

A Whole New Girl

With assurances from the producers that the judging panel on *The X Factor* was going to be a much more fun place to be, I stepped back into my role as mentor on the UK's biggest television show in 2009. Was I apprehensive? Yes, but I figured that if I could go in with a fresh attitude, then that was half the battle won. Being the person on the show who seemed to court the most controversy in the past two years had seemed to work in my favour. Everyone was so keen for me to come back for another season, it was hard not to accept.

The only ridiculous and ironic downside, of course, was that Kris was now gainfully employed and working hard in Australia while I was the one who had to head back to London. We'd been together for well over a year. While it had been incredible having him in Oz with me all the time I'd been working on my third season of *Australia's Got Talent*, I was distraught about leaving him there while I was in London. I was going to miss him horribly.

On the first busy day of *The X Factor* auditions in Glasgow, I walked on set, and the first person I saw was Louis Walsh. I was very relieved to see him beaming a smile as he walked towards me.

'I think we should have fun this series, Dannii,' he said. 'I think I got too wrapped up in it all last year.'

'Absolutely!' I agreed.

Everyone was getting tired of all the bitching and backstabbing, it seemed, especially the viewers. With the news full of misery and recession the way it was, people wanted to tune out and have fun when they watched television, and that was what *The X Factor* was supposed to be about – not the behind-the-scenes squabbles of its judging panel. It was meant to be about the contestants, and letting them shine; everyone, including head honcho Simon, wanted to get back to that.

The show's audition process was transformed. This year the contestants had to audition not only in front of the judging panel, but a whole theatre full of people, and having the live audience behind you at those early stages of the competition really lifted everyone's mood from the get-go. I loved having the crowds there with us at the auditions, and I thrived on the extra excitement. I wasn't afraid to speak my mind, and for once I didn't feel there was someone waiting to stick the boot in every time I opened my mouth. It was as if I were filling my lungs with fresh air. To top it all, Kylie agreed to join me as my special guest judge on the 'judges' houses' section of the series, which we filmed in a beautiful resort in Dubai. This really was the cherry on the cake for me, and it brought us full circle from when she'd joined me on *Young Talent Time* to sing 'Sisters Are Doing It For Themselves' twenty-two years before.

As soon as all the audition stages of *The X Factor* were done, and before the live shows started, I hurriedly flew back to Australia. There was a break of a few weeks in-between. While I'd normally have jetted off to Ibiza with my mates for a holiday, I just wanted to get back to Kris and spend as much time with him as I could before coming back to London. While I was there, the time whizzed past. As the day of the flight approached, I kept saying to him, 'I don't want to go. I don't want to leave you.' For the last few days of my stay, it was pretty much all I could think about.

On the day I was due to leave for London, Kris came into the bedroom and sadly helped me pack, then he drove me to the airport, softly kissed me goodbye and told me that he had a work assignment to dash to. I was devastated to leave him for what I knew would be at least three months, but I smiled as valiantly as I could and told him I loved him and I would call him as soon as I landed.

When I arrived in the airport lounge, I bumped into my friend, Shane Warne, the Aussie cricketer, who happened to be on the same flight. Poor Shane, I sat down next to him and gave him such a complete earbashing while we waited for our flight to be called. I went on and on about how miserable I was leaving Kris, and how much I was going to miss him. I'm sure the poor guy couldn't wait to get away from me.

Once on the plane, though, I sat down and a flight attendant came over and asked me if I would like a glass of champagne.

'I think I need one,' I said sadly. 'That would be nice, thank you.'

Then I settled back in my seat and prepared for a whole day of flying.

Eventually, I looked up when I felt someone beside me – must be the glass of champagne, I thought. Instead of the flight attendant, I came face to face with . . . Kris. He was standing there, smiling. I was so shocked, and I screamed so loudly, that Shane jumped out of his seat on the other side of the cabin to come and find out what had happened. I couldn't believe my eyes.

'What . . . what . . . what?'

I couldn't work out what was going on. What was Kris doing on my flight? Didn't he have a work appointment to go to?

It turned out that Kris had been planning this surprise for ages. With the help of Nathan at my management and the airline, in what seemed like some terribly complex and covert operation, he'd not only packed his case and boarded the plane without me knowing but he'd got the seat right next to me too.

'I'm going to be in London for your birthday,' Kris grinned.

I was speechless – and overjoyed.

It didn't stop there, either. Kris had already been secretly planning a surprise birthday party in London with my friend Glenn Horder making all the arrangements. On the actual night, I walked into one of my favourite restaurants for an intimate dinner with Kris, and discovered all my friends waiting there to celebrate with me, as well as Kris's mum and dad, who had travelled down from Manchester – the best boyfriend ever!

2009 was the year to have fun, and that included my look. I fancied doing my own styling for *The X Factor* that year, so while I was in Australia I started gathering clothes from some great Aussie designers. I had to get most of this organised before I returned to London for the live shows. I think I blew my suitcase a kiss as I checked onto the flight departing from Melbourne. I couldn't put a price on all the luxury fabric that was enclosed – best not to think about it, I decided.

My new image included plenty of good old-fashioned glamour, some of it inspired by the beautiful silent-movie actress Louise Brooks, who was famous for her black bobbed hairstyle – though that part happened completely by accident. Towards the end of the previous series of *The X Factor*, I'd gone to a new salon and had a treatment on my hair to seal and nourish the ends, making it look shiny and gorgeous. I was happy with it the first time, so later I went back for a follow-up treatment. However, this time the salon had changed the product and something went horribly wrong, causing my hair to start breaking off all over. Whoops!

I had quite long hair at that point, but it was now coming apart like cotton wool, especially at the ends, so I knew that drastic action was needed. I booked an appointment with my Aussie hairdresser, Fotini Hatzis, as soon as I got back to Melbourne.

'You need to cut it off,' I said to her. 'Really short. Just take it as short as you can go, but keep it in a style.'

'Are you sure?' Fo asked me.

'Yup. Chop it off, doll,' I said. 'I'm ready for it.'

It was a cathartic experience and I was enjoying the change unfolding in front of my eyes. As she chopped away and each piece of hair fell to the floor, I felt like I was wiping away the last year and stepping into the new. After the cut was all finished and blow-dried to perfection, I smiled and felt like a weight had been lifted off my shoulders.

'Let's just hope Kris likes it,' I said.

Cut to *The X Factor* 2009 live shows and my hair and make-up guy in London, Christian Vermaak, decides to make it his mission to turn my hair into a celebrity in its own right, with a new and different twist on a classic style each week. Neither of us realised at first that such a short style could be so versatile, but both of us were in the mood to experiment, so we went completely mad researching different looks. In the end it was a competition between us to see who could come up with the craziest ideas.

'What about this, Christian?' I'd say, holding up a photograph I'd torn from a fashion magazine.

He'd dive into his box of tricks, and then tease, back-brush, curl and attach until he'd come up with something different and utterly fabulous each week – the man's a complete genius.

Then, of course, there were the frocks. All of the couture ones were designed by a couple of great friends of mine, who work out of Melbourne under the designer moniker J'Aton.

I'd been introduced to the J'Aton boys, Jacob Luppino and Anthony Pittorino, a couple of years before, and apart from falling in love with them as people, the way they worked and the dresses they made for me changed all my ideas about clothes, and completely reignited my passion for design and fashion. Working with 'the boys', as I call them, and studying their wonderfully glamorous dresses, I learned so much about precision of design and attention to detail, and gradually I started to get the desire to perhaps design something myself again.

Despite all the fun and glamour of the 2009 *X Factor*, I'd tiptoed in designer platforms right into a near catastrophic situation on the first live show of the series. Danyl Johnson was one of the contestants in Simon's category, the over-25s, and had recently come out in the press as being bisexual, which I imagined these days wouldn't cause as much of a stir as it might have done ten or fifteen years ago – I was wrong. On the very first live show, Danyl, who was a 27-year-old dance and drama teacher from Reading with a fantastic voice but slightly cocky disposition, was performing the song 'And I'm Telling You I'm Not Going', made famous in the musical *Dreamgirls*. The original lyric is sung to a man, but when he was performing the song, Danyl changed the word 'boy' to 'girl'. During camera rehearsals at the studio the day before the show, Nathan, Terry and I joked with him that as he was bisexual, he needn't change the gender slant of the lyric at all. Of course, I didn't think much more about it – in fact, we all laughed about it, including Danyl himself.

However, after he'd performed the song on the live show on Saturday night, I continued the banter from my seat on the panel, suggesting to him again that if we were to believe what we read in the papers, there was no need for him to have changed the gender reference, and, of course, this was live on air. Well, for a moment you could have heard a pin drop in that studio. In the peripheral vision of my left eye, I could see Simon Cowell's head turning to me, in what seemed like scary slow motion, and I'm thinking: 'What? What have I said?' Then Simon asked me to repeat what I'd said, like a naughty schoolgirl, while reprimanding me in front of the entire nation for 'playing games' with poor Danyl.

In a split second, I'd caused a major diplomatic incident: Danyl looked uncomfortable, Simon was pissed off at me, and there was a public outcry about Dannii Minogue 'outing' someone on live prime-time television. It was all over the papers the next day and I was up to my neck in it.

The irony is that all the judges, particularly Simon, make personal comments about the contestants, and cruel ones, too, but mention someone's sexuality and you're suddenly branded 'Satan', and that's what happened to me. The silly thing is that I wasn't implying that there was anything wrong with Danyl being bisexual, I was making a reference to something that Danyl himself had said to the press the previous week, and that he'd joked about the day before. Misguided? Yes, as it turned out. But malicious? Absolutely not.

Of course, straight after the show I spoke to Danyl, apologising and telling him that I'd never meant to hurt him. Danyl, as I suspected, was more upset about the fact that his first live performance had been overshadowed by all the fuss, and he hadn't been bothered by what I'd said in the slightest.

What saddened me most about the whole affair was that some people branded me homophobic. What? Even Perez Hilton's page in an Australian magazine got the wrong end of the stick and said I had 'outed' Danyl – but he was already out. In truth, it was my naivety in thinking that it was OK to talk openly about sexuality that caused the entire furore. It was also quite interesting to me that some people called it a 'slur' on Danyl, which meant that they thought there was something wrong with being gay or bisexual – wasn't that, in itself, homophobic?

Still, the TV complaints commission, Ofcom, had to look into the four thousand or so complaints they received about my off-the-cuff remark. They concluded: 'It was not outside the established nature of the programme for an X Factor judge to make such a comment as Dannii Minogue's, especially in circumstances where the performer had placed information about his sexuality in the public domain.'

I breathed a big sigh of relief.

On the Sunday-night results show, I apologised to Danyl publicly for any offence I'd caused him, and Simon apologised to me for completely overreacting, stating that I was the last person who would ever want intentionally to hurt or cause distress to someone in that way. Eventually, people started to realise that Danyl was openly bisexual and that I hadn't 'outed' him at all. Thankfully, for everyone involved, that was the end of it.

'Well, as usual, you certainly didn't disappoint on the controversy front, honey,' Terry said to me after that first weekend of shows. 'What have you got up your sleeve for next week?'

'Just a pretty frock, and a diamond necklace,' I laughed. 'I think that'll be quite enough, don't you?'

In November 2009, I was invited to be a guest on the TV show *Piers Morgan's Life Stories*, which entails a one-to-one, in-depth, no-holds-barred autobiographical interview with the former *Daily Mirror* editor on national television. It's not something I'd ever considered doing before – baring my soul and talking about my private life in front of a massive television audience – and my initial reaction was to say 'no', because I didn't think I had anything to tell and I thought I would be boring. After a few more declined invitations via my management, I got a very nice personal message from Piers himself telling me that he really wanted me on the show. After thinking about it long and hard, I sheepishly conceded that perhaps I did have a story to tell.

It turned out to be one of the best decisions of my life. I sat there in front of a studio audience and talked completely openly for the first time ever about so many things – about my childhood, my work, my marriage, my sister and even losing my best friend, Laura. Of course, the show is only an hour long, so in the end it felt like we had just scratched the surface, but it was extremely cathartic. It was the catalyst that led me to do exactly what I'm doing now – writing this book. The interview wasn't salacious or sensational, and I wasn't interested in trashing anyone or saying anything I didn't feel comfortable saying. It was simply me talking about me. The show also featured on-screen contributions from some of my nearest and dearest: Kathy Lette, Terry Ronald, my singing teacher Russell Penn, plus Kylie and, of course, my gorgeous man, Kris.

After the show had aired, Piers was kind enough to tell me that in all his years of interviews, it was the best he'd ever done. What meant the most to me though was the completely unexpected reaction from the public. Suddenly, all sorts of people were coming up to me and saying things like, 'Wow! We never knew all those things happened to you.'

And I'd say, 'Well, no one has ever asked me before.'

It was true. I'd spent so long in interviews being asked, 'What's it like to be Kylie's sister?' that there was never any time left for anything else. In fact, after thirty years of being 'famous', I realised that most people didn't know anything about me at all.

But I guess I'm changing that now . . .

Chapter 35

Posh Frocks and Little Bumps

I decided that it was time to set in motion my dreams of designing my own collection of dresses. Ever since I was a kid hearing the sewing machines whirring away in Nain's house and at home, I'd been completely in love with the idea that with a good imagination and some fabric, cotton, and a pair of scissors, the possibilities were endless. I knew what I liked and what I didn't like too, and after styling all the dresses on *The X Factor*, like I had when I was a teenager on *Young Talent Time*, the reaction had been very favourable. A simple wish had now become a passionate urge, so it was time to stop dreaming about it and start doing it.

Tabitha Somerset-Webb is a fantastic handbag and accessory designer, and a long-time friend of mine. We'd met in London after I fell in love with a couple of her handbag designs and tracked her down at her office, which was down the road from me in Battersea. I asked if I could pop in and meet her and see the full collection. Tabitha was sparkly and ballsy from the minute I walked in the room, and I thought she seemed very much like an Aussie girl – full of 'spunk' as we say back home – and I told her so. Ten minutes later, in fact, I was assuring her that the two of us were going to be good friends.

Cut to six years later, when Tabs and I were on one of our weekly power walks along the Thames, which is where we normally catch up on boy talk, work talk and when we might be heading for cocktails next. On this particular night, I casually dropped in the idea of us designing a line of dresses together, keeping a little chuckle in my voice and totally expecting her to say, 'Yeah right, Dan,' and keep walking, but she didn't. When she stopped and turned to face me, I could see that she had a huge smile on her face, and a devilish twinkle in her eye.

'Go on,' she said.

'If I'm ever going to do it, Tabs,' I told her, 'now is definitely the time. I'm not sure if it will work or if it won't work, but if I'm gonna do it, I'd love to do it with you.'

Her beaming grin said it all. Tabs then confessed to me that she had already been researching the idea of branching out into frocks as well as bags and accessories.

'I'd absolutely love to do it,' she said.

As we started to walk again, our pace quickened, both of us letting the idea sink in and considering exactly what a commitment this would be for two people who were as busy as we already were. Tabs and I would be jumping straight into this, and even if everything went brilliantly, it would almost certainly take over our lives completely.

The very next week, I arrived at her place with a bottle of wine and a sketchbook, and the two of us sat down in her front room and started sketching ideas. It wasn't all that easy, to be honest, principally because neither of us can draw, but we knew where we were headed and what we liked. We were both so excited – and probably a little tipsy – that we managed to come up with what would be the basic foundation for our first collection that night: a collection of dresses we called 'Project D'.

The concept we had was a capsule collection of seven beautiful, wearable dresses. The idea was that the seven different dresses would encompass any woman's fashion needs – from the office to a party, cocktails or even a red-carpet event. Our theory was that if Tabs and I could go through our calendars and find a dress in the collection for every appointment or event we had coming up in the next month, then we'd have done our job. There were long dresses, short dresses, dresses with and without sleeves, and they were certainly affordable and definitely practical for people of all different body shapes and varying tastes.

I knew I was overdoing it. *The X Factor*, once it's rolling, is a fairly full-time job: you're working the whole weekend, and by the time you've done all your extra filming, researched and chosen your songs for the week, done any press that needs to be done and attended the camera rehearsals, that's most of the week gone as well. Now here I was trying to cram in the creation and launch of a completely new fashion line with Tabitha in any spare hour I could find. To complicate matters, we'd decided to add a signature fragrance to complement the collection.

There was something else I wasn't quite banking on waiting around the next corner for me while this was happening. In November, I'd noticed that my period was a bit late but put it down to being overtired and stressed at first. Once I was over two weeks late, I decided that I'd better make sure it was only that. Kris and I had already made the decision that it was the right time for us to try for a baby, but, to be honest, even after a year and a half, I was still trying to get my head around the fact that I had a boyfriend at all. With everything that was going on, I don't think I'd really stopped to consider what actively trying for a baby might mean. After all, it was a complete 360-degree turn for somebody who truly thought that she would never get around to having children. The fact of the matter was that my period was late, and I realised I needed to do a pregnancy test fast.

Now, how could I pop to the chemist and pick up a pregnancy test without the whole world finding out about it? I could send my trustworthy assistant, Ayesha, I thought. After all, she'd worked for me for the past year or so and was often called on to run around collecting all manner of strange items, from a mission to find a rubber duck as a gift for Simon Cowell's swanky new private dressing room and bathroom at *The X Factor* studio to being handed a package in a blacked-out car containing a hundred grand's worth of diamonds for me to wear on the show. I could surely trust Ayesha to discreetly pick up a pregnancy test.

The only trouble was, Ayesha wasn't around all day and I couldn't wait. So I called Tabs, whom I trusted completely, and asked her to pick up the test on her way to my apartment. Tabs was clearly excited at the prospect of me being pregnant, and headed to my place with the tester kit right away, almost bouncing through the door in anticipation and thrusting the ominous packet into my hands.

'Right, here goes,' I said, anxiously.

I know that you're supposed to have to wait a few minutes after you've done a pregnancy test to see the results, but I couldn't bear sitting there staring at the bloody thing, so I decided to make Tabs and me a cup of green tea while we waited.

No sooner had I turned my back, though, and headed over to my kitchen, when Tabs said: 'The results are in! Do you want them?'

'WHAT?'

I stopped in my tracks. 'You're having a laugh with me.'

'I swear to God, it's here, Dannii,' Tabs smiled. 'As clear as day.'

By then, of course, I knew what she was going to say: I was pregnant.

I'd known deep down that it was a possibility, but, to be honest, I'd been so focused on getting the fashion line together with Tabs and working on *The X Factor* that it still managed to take me completely by surprise. I was excited, though, but also a little sad, because by this time the 'Daddy' in question was back in Australia, and I'd never pictured that amazing moment happening without him there. So how do I tell him? I decided to send him a private message that said: 'Call me!' And when he did, I broke the wonderful news to a very happy man.

Kris was staying at the apartment of our good friends Jacob and Anthony, the J'Aton boys. When I broke the news to him over the phone, he shouted, 'YES!' and then started jumping all over the guest bedroom like a mad man while trying not to make a sound. He was ecstatic, and although I longed to be there with him to share the moment, it hadn't been possible. It was the story of my life – well, my love life anyway – and we'd just have to make the best of it.

'We can't tell anyone,' I told him before I hung up the phone. 'Not even our friends. Not until it's over three months.'

And though Kris wanted to shout it from the rooftops, he agreed that he wouldn't tell a soul.

After that, I needed to be sure it was what it was, so I called my doctor and went for a blood test, and he confirmed it was true. I was most definitely going to become a mum. Not only that, but the level of the pregnancy hormone hCG in my blood was extremely high. Coupled with the fact that the home-tester-kit results had been almost instantaneous, I started to worry.

'Please tell me it doesn't mean I'm going to have twins, does it?' I whimpered.

'Not necessarily, Dannii,' he smiled. 'But we'll check for that, of course.'

Phew!

The next thing on the agenda was a scan, and, of course I couldn't go to the hospital as normal because I feared that the news would get out before I wanted it to. So, after a few phone calls and a couple of text messages to the obstetrician, I headed to the hospital to have my scan very quietly, at 7.30a.m. on a Sunday – the morning after a live *X Factor* show. It was the only way I could be sure that the hospital would be relatively quiet, and that I wouldn't have to dash into the obstetrics department wearing sunglasses and a headscarf. The scan showed a tiny sign of life – a little flicker of the heart of our baby.

Little did I realise, though, that even at that early hour, the fact that I'd gone for a scan had been discovered. The very next week, when I was hurrying home from a day's filming on *The X Factor* to prepare dinner for my friends, I got an unwelcome call from Nathan at my management company to let me know that the story of my six-week-old pregnancy was about to break.

And that brings us full circle – right back to where you came in.

When I finally got hold of Kris that night, I was in a real state, standing there in my darkened bedroom. Sam and George were in the next room waiting for their veggie lasagne, and were now probably half starved. When I heard Kris's voice, I almost broke down.

'Thank God, I've got hold of you,' I told him, my hands still shaking. 'I've had to make a few decisions today that you need to know about.'

I tearfully explained to Kris that I'd had to admit that I was preg-nant – though well under three months – to my management, my publicist, the Press Complaints Commission and now to a national newspaper – to prevent that same newspaper from announcing our happy secret to the world before we were ready.

Of course, Kris was as horrified as I was, but he lovingly assured me that he'd do whatever I needed him to do. Once I'd hung up the phone, I dried my eyes, took a few deep breaths, stuck on a smile and then breezed back into the lounge to my friends Sam and George.

'Right,' I said, bustling towards the kitchen area and making out it was the chopped onions rendering me all red-eyed. 'Sorry about that boys! Let me get you some food finally, and how about another glass of wine?'

Once I threw myself back into work over the next couple of weeks, I was very pleased to have put out that one fire, but I knew well that with so many people knowing about my early pregnancy now, it would only be a matter of time before another one started blazing. I didn't have to wait long.

I was on a cover shoot for *Glamour* magazine in London. It had been a really fun day and I was so happy with how the pictures were look-ing. Never having shot a *Glamour* cover before, I was quite excited by the prospect, as I've always loved the magazine.

At the end of the day, Nathan and my publicist, Simon, came and found me as the crew were packing up to go home. I could tell by the tone of their voices that something wasn't right, as they were way too smiley and relaxed for my liking. What was going on?

'We need to have a chat to you about something,' Nathan said. 'I wonder if we should go upstairs where it's quiet.'

My heart sank. After a day of gorgeous frocks, glamorous make-up and lovely people, I had a feeling this was going to be bad news.

It turned out that another newspaper had got wind of the fact that I was pregnant, and they, too, were threatening to run the story before my three-month scan. Simon told me that he'd had some calls from other publications letting him know that word was now very much out.

Now I was pissed off. I was still in the very early stages of pregnancy and couldn't believe that I was going to have to go through this again. Even if we did manage to stop the new story, I thought, what's to say that yet another magazine or paper wouldn't be threatening to go to print with the story the very next week?

That evening, Kris and I decided during a phone call that we were going to have to tell our parents and immediate family right away, as the last thing we wanted was them to find out from the front pages. I was so furious. I was due back in Melbourne in a couple of weeks, and we had planned to share the good news with them together.

The next day, Kris went round to Mum and Dad's and broke the news with me on the end of a phone – so at least one of us was there – and they were overjoyed. I could only listen to the cheerful sounds of celebration and Mum and Dad's happy words of congratulation over the phone from halfway across the world, and I felt totally left out. I felt like the wind had been taken out of my sails. Another two or three weeks later and I could have told them and seen my mum and dad's eyes light up for myself. Why did it have to happen like this?

By the time I did get back to Australia, a week before Christmas, instead of feeling like a glowing expectant mother-to-be, I felt anxious and on edge. The doctor in London had told me that the worse thing I could possibly be was stressed, but with my busy X Factor schedule, morning sickness, my self-imposed workload with Tabitha on 'Project D', as well as the strain of trying to keep the press at bay regarding my pregnancy, I didn't see how I could be anything other. Consequently, I started to worry that I might be jeopardising the baby's health, and Kris was beginning to worry about me.

One morning, when Kris and I went to meet a local obstetrician in Melbourne, we got out of the car and I froze as my feet hit the pavement – I remember it so clearly. I could hear a familiar whirring sound – the sound of camera shutters.

'I can hear cameras, Kris,' I said. 'They've followed us here. I know they have.'

Kris looked around and then smiled, reassuringly: 'There's no one here, babe,' he said. 'You're so wound up by all of this press stuff that you're imagining it.'

He was right: I *was* wound up, and being pregnant, emotional and hormonal was adding to it big time. I knew we were constantly being watched from outside Mum and Dad's place and I felt I was being hunted down every time I stepped out the front door. All I wanted was to have my three-month scan in a week's time to find out for sure that our baby was all right before we announced it to the world – you know, ten fingers, ten toes, a beating heart.

As I walked another few steps, I spotted the photographers hiding in the bushes snapping pictures, and walked on. After these pictures appeared in an Aussie newspaper the next morning, with a speculative story about a possible pregnancy, one of the British newspapers, which we'd previously staved off, printed the same pictures with an announce-ment that I was definitely pregnant and that I'd had my twelve-week, nuchal fold scan – which is important to women over thirty-five like me to test for Down's syndrome.

'Hooray!' the world yelled. 'Dannii's pregnant!'

But I hadn't yet had that all-important scan.

After months of expended energy, the resulting Press Complaints Commission ruling came down firmly in our favour, stating that the newspaper reports had been a 'regrettable lapse in editorial judgement' and that 'as a matter of common sense newspapers and magazines should not reveal news of an individual's pregnancy without consent before the 12-week scan'.

I was very happy with the PCC finding, and content to think that it might help prevent another woman going through what I had, but I was also physically and emotionally exhausted.

When I finally did have my three-month scan and we discovered that everything was, indeed, absolutely fine with the baby, we were relieved and overjoyed, and I was ready to start glowing for real. It was great at long last to be able to share the happy news properly with my grandparents, and with Kylie, with Brendan and Bec, with Kris's family and with all our friends on both sides of the pond – in fact, with the whole planet.

'Woo hoo! I'm gonna be a mummy!' I announced on Twitter, simultaneously with a 'Tweet' from Kris: 'Woo hoo! I'm gonna be a daddy!'

Even Kylie got in on the act, posting: 'OMG OMG OMG Perfect!!! So Happy!! A new Minogue!'

We were all ecstatic, and about something that I never thought would happen. I'd never been broody before; I'd never felt there was a clock ticking away inside me – that is, until I met Kris. It was being with him that made me look forward to having a child. Knowing that he was the one and that he would make the most fantastic dad.

Now here we were thinking about baby names and looking at baby clothes, and talking about buying a new house for when he or she was born. It was a whole new world for me and I was starting to enjoy it. I was in my home town with the man I loved and with my family, and there was a hell of a lot of planning to do – and a lot of chocolate to eat. It was time for me to look forward, and I knew there was plenty to look forward to.

As well as the great response I'd got from being on *Piers Morgan's Life Stories*, the 2009 series of *The X Factor* had been an amazing success for me too, despite Danyl-gate.

In November 2009 I was voted 'Ultimate TV Personality' at the *Cosmopolitan* awards in London. I was very proud. Then, following on from that, I was offered a contract to be the new face of Marks & Spencer's fashion along with people like the iconic model Twiggy. On the inside I've always been the same person ever since I was a little girl catching blue-tongued lizards and covered in mud in our back garden in Wantirna. But with M&S being such a British institution, I guess I was now a household name.

One of the most precious moments of the past few months for me was in London in 2010 at the *Elle* style awards. Kylie was presenting the award that night for 'Best TV Star', and she was presenting it to me.

Over the years, I have been asked to present several awards to my sister, and the fact that she was now doing the same for me seemed unreal but so fantastic I couldn't stop smiling.

As I walked slowly up to the stage to raucous cheers and happy faces, and took the award from my sister, I looked into her eyes and I could see how proud she was – and so was I. Kylie looked so radiant and healthy, and with me and my fast-growing bump, we made quite a pair up there together. It was definitely a real 'Cinderella moment'.

Tabitha was with me that night, too. As we were preparing to launch our first 'Project D' collection only a few weeks later, having an acknowledgement from a fashion magazine such as *Elle* was very important to both of us.

As for being pregnant, I guess I felt pretty relaxed about it. Sure, I had little moments of freak-out: it's a baby, for God's sake, and I've never looked after one before, but I'm nowhere near the control freak I thought I might be. I accepted my body was changing and I accepted that my whole life was going to be different at the end of it.

Of course, this mindset has come as something of a surprise to me, because so much is out of my control, and I'm not always good with that. But here I was as relaxed as I could be – and loving it. I go with the flow now.

'Sure, Kris, you pick out some baby names and then just give me a shortlist,' I heard myself say, or: 'Yeah! I'll have another helping of ice cream or chocolate – bring it on!'

Kris said he'd never seen such a quick change in a person, and he told Mum as much at dinner one night, as I tucked into my second bowl of ice cream.

'I could never get Dannii to split a dessert with me in a restaurant,' he complained. 'She wasn't having any of it. Now every time I turn around she's unwrapping a chocolate, or tucking into ice cream, and if we do split a dessert I don't get a look in.'

It's like there's a whole other person in there making decisions for me, but I'm still very organised and I *always* try to stay on top of everything. But I'm calm – really calm. And now I'm looking forward to settling down with Kris, and our new baby. It's that simple.

I feel now that I've drawn a line under so many things, and that I'm starting not just a new chapter but a whole new book, and I think that's how it should be.

I've been incredibly fortunate to have had so many opportunities over the years. Embracing every one with gusto has afforded me some fabulous times along the way. And do you know what? As much as I've had to learn to accept some of the sad, negative and bad things that have happened to me, it's now time to sit back and accept that there are a lot more good things to come. I'm happy with that.

Epilogue
Welcome to the World

On 5 July 2010 at 6.39 p.m., our little boy, Ethan Edward Minogue Smith, came into the world weighing 8lb 3oz. Kris and I were now, officially, Mummy and Daddy, and we were overjoyed! Typically for me, nothing about the birth went according to plan – Ethan was ten days early for a start. I'd really wanted to have a natural home birth. Unfortunately, he wasn't in the correct position for a smooth delivery; so, after twenty hours of excruciating labour, I ended up having him in hospital after all.

When I held him for the first time, though, all the pain melted away. Kris and I looked at Ethan and then at one another, and we couldn't believe that we'd made another whole person together. When your baby is first handed to you, you try to take in every feature – every finger and toe, and every eyelash. I remember thinking: 'Who are you? How did you get here? I can't believe you've been in my tummy all this time and I'm finally getting to meet you.' It was wonderful.

By the time Ethan was born, he had already swum with a dolphin, walked the red carpet, been photographed for magazine covers, sat on the judging panel of two TV talent shows, flown in a private jet and launched a clothing range. I guess pre-school will have a lot to live up to!

When my labour started I was fairly serene – it was everyone else who seemed to get into a flap. As I said, Ethan decided to join us early, so when my waters broke after I'd ambitiously tried to cram myself into a pair of jeans, I called Kris, who was on his way out to the driving range to hit some golf balls. He, in turn, called Mum, who happened to be on her way over to my place anyway. I was quite calm, but I was slightly worried that Kris might drive too fast or miss a red light dashing back to the house.

'Are you OK?' he said, breathlessly, when he arrived.

I think he was more stressed out than I was.

'I'm fine,' I said. 'I'm just glad you're here now.'

My good friend Ben Pauley, was also at the house, visiting from LA, and he and Mum were a hysterical double act during my labour: both running around my kitchen, bumping into one another, saying, 'Right, what do we do? What do we need?'

'We need snacks … rice crackers!' Mum exclaimed decisively. 'And lemons! I NEED LEMONS!'

She had been planning to make a natural energy-boosting drink for me when I was in labour from a recipe that required lemons, and she suddenly panicked when she couldn't lay her hands on any.

'I'll go to the supermarket right now,' Ben announced, charging out of the house and straight past the two fruit-bearing lemon trees on either side of the front door. Later, Kris and I laughed about this so much – there were rice crackers in the kitchen cupboard, too.

By the time I was transferred to hospital the following morning I'd been in pain for quite a long time so the epidural was very welcome. Once I could finally think straight again, I started to worry about all the work tasks that I'd left up in the air. I was meant to be unpacking boxes in our new home; I was supposed to be doing a last check through the manuscript of this book (but my waters broke while I was reading chapter three); and, worst of all, I hadn't even started writing my new column for *Glamour* magazine. It's just the way my brain works. What can I tell you? I can't help it – even when I'm about to give birth! With this in mind, I called Kris over and asked him to call my manager, Melissa, urgently.

'I'll tell her you've gone into labour,' Kris said.

'Well, yes,' I said. 'But can you also tell her that I need her to get me an extension on the delivery of my *Glamour* magazine column? I haven't started it yet.'

Kris's mouth fell open.

'You did *not* just say that,' he said.

Once baby Ethan had made his way into the world, he had a steady stream of admirers coming into the hospital to visit him, and none of them could believe that we'd actually managed to keep his early birth a secret from the media for almost two days. My brother, Brendan, and his wife, Bec, brought their boys, Charlie and James, to meet their brand new cousin and they were wonderful with him, smiling at him and kissing his little head. Brendan, of course, was a very proud uncle too, and I just know that he and Bec are going to be an amazing uncle and auntie team. One of the nicest things to see was Ethan meeting all his grandparents, and, indeed, his great-grandparents for the first time. Mum had been with me throughout the birth, but when she came back in with Dad to visit, she was still taken aback when she saw me holding Ethan in my arms.

'I can't describe the look on your face when I first saw you with your baby,' she later told me. 'I've never seen you smile like that before, and I probably never will again.'

Great-grandma Nain, on the other hand, had some sound advice for me, as always.

'You'll get the hang of it after six,' she assured me.

Right.

Once the news of Ethan's arrival went public, Kris and I were surprised to discover that our baby was the top-trending topic on Twitter, and that everybody seemed to heartily approve of his name, Ethan Edward, and the fact that Kris and I hadn't given him a quirky 'celeb-baby' name. Dad then reminded us of the time that Kylie had taken him out for a coffee with Chris Martin from Coldplay, but Dad really had no idea who he was.

'What's your daughter's name?' He'd asked Chris while they were chatting away happily.

'Apple,' Chris told Dad, who, thinking Chris was joking then said: 'Oh really? And what's her middle name, Strudel?'

Kylie must have been mortified, but Dad couldn't stop laughing when he told us the story again. I'm fairly certain I'll be embarrassing Ethan like that one day.

Kris's mum and dad, Eddie and Elsie, were visiting us for a month, and we couldn't have managed without them. They have both been such fantastic help, especially since I've been back at home, and it's been really wonderful to have them here to bond with little Ethan. They brought with them a Leeds rugby jersey for Ethan with his name and Daddy's number 13 on the back. Kris was over the moon when he saw it; after Ethan has grown out of it, Kris plans to frame and mount it on the wall of his brand new pool room with all his other sports memorabilia.

When Auntie Kylie came to visit – and that particular moniker has really stuck in the Australian media – it was national news. There I was sitting on the couch, breastfeeding in front of the TV, when suddenly I hear: 'Coming up on tonight's six o'clock news, Auntie Kylie comes to visit baby Ethan!'

It was completely surreal and made my head spin a little. Even though there was a constant stream of paparazzi outside the house, I was so immersed in trying to get to grips with being a new mum and taking care of my baby that I'd almost forgotten what big news it was that Kylie was about to meet her new nephew. When she did meet Ethan, it was love at first sight, as the song says. She took him into her arms while I was in the middle of dressing him and hugged him, skin on skin, talking to him all the while. I could see Ethan looking up at her – really intensely concentrating – and because Kylie's voice is so similar to mine I wondered what he must have been thinking.

'You don't smell like my mummy, but you sure sound like her.'

Kylie remarked that Kris had finally brought the tall gene into the Minogue family. She was right: our child is going to be either the tallest ever Minogue or the shortest ever Smith. Kylie also told me how proud she is of me, and having my sister tell me that never gets old.

As for our new home in Melbourne, we're all enjoying that too. Eddie and Elsie are staying with us and there's plenty of space for everyone to do their own thing. Brendan and Bec are close at hand and often come over with the boys. What with Mum, Dad and Kylie dropping by as well, there is a great atmosphere of love and support surrounding me, Kris and little Ethan, shut off from the world and away from everything for a little while.

I wouldn't exactly say it's a quiet house, though. Kris has bought a new 3D TV that looks as big as a cinema with surround sound that makes the house rock. Aside from entertaining lots of welcome visitors, Kris and I can't get through a cup of tea without having to run around and do some errand or other, or feed or change Ethan, or make dinner, or do all those everyday things that every new mum and dad has to do.

It's a whole new world for me. And it's a very happy one.

Acknowledgements

A couple of years ago I was asked if I would consider writing my autobiography. I declined. It scared me because I didn't think that I had a good enough story to tell. Cut forward to November 2009 when I was interviewed by Piers Morgan for his TV show, Life Stories, *where for the first time I was prepared to reveal the sometimes fragile and funny sides of me. There were stories that I told that resonated with family, friends and strangers more than I could have imagined. Talking about my ups and my downs made me feel more comfortable with my past and it was like a huge weight off my shoulders. I'm now happy to draw a proud line under the last thirty-eight years and begin a brand-new chapter with a new ray of sunshine in my life.*

I would like to thank:

My family: Mum, Dad, Kylie and Brendan for always being there with love

Kris for brightening every day and Ethan for opening up our world

My management team: Melissa Le Gear, Mark Klemens and Nathan Smith at Profile Talent Management

My PR team: Simon Jones and Alex Mullen at Hackford Jones PR

My friend, confidant, music maestro and book writing partner: Terry Ronald

My Publishers: Mike Jones and the team at Simon & Schuster

My Literary Agent: Pat Lomax at Bell Lomax Moreton Agency

Eternal thanks to my fans who helped make all this possible. Thank you for taking this amazing and crazy rollercoaster ride with me. I hope you enjoy reading the stories of my dream life that you have been such a huge part of.

Love and kisses
Dannii X

Picture and Cover Credits

Black and white chapter openers

Chap	Description	Credit
1	Danielle: Melbourne, Australia	KDB Artists Pty. Ltd.
2	Danielle: Melbourne, Australia	KDB Artists Pty. Ltd.
3	Dannii: Melbourne, Australia	Johnny Young / YTT
4	Dannii: performing on *Young Talent Time*	Johnny Young / YTT
5	Dannii: Melbourne, Australia	KDB Artists Pty. Ltd.
6	Dannii: 'Love And Kisses' record company press image	KDB Artists Pty. Ltd.
7	Dannii: as character Emma Jackson in *Home & Away*	Channel Seven
8	Dannii: with Lori Lipkies, Sydney, Australia	KDB Artists Pty. Ltd.
9	Dannii: 'Jump To The Beat' USA record company press image	Stephan Lupino © KDB Artists Pty. Ltd.
10	Dannii: record company press image	Andrew MacPherson © KDB Artists Pty. Ltd.
11	Dannii: 'This is It' video shoot, Los Angeles	Steve Rapport © KDB Artists Pty. Ltd.
12	Dannii and Julian McMahon: Wedding, Melbourne, Australia	KDB Artists Pty. Ltd.
13	Dannii: 'Black & White Magazine' photo shoot, Los Angeles	Adam Watson © KDB Artists Pty. Ltd.
14	Dannii: *Playboy* shoot, Nevada Desert	Adam Watson © KDB Artists Pty, Ltd.
15	Dannii: 'All I Wanna Do' video shoot, London	Ken Sharp © KDB Artists Pty. Ltd.
16	Dannii: as character Rizzo in 'Grease – The Arena Spectacular', Australia	Steve Shaw © KDB Artists Pty. Ltd.

Chap	Description	Credit
17	Dannii: 'Everything I Wanted' video shoot, Nevada Desert	Steve Shaw © KDB Artists Pty. Ltd.
18	Dannii and Jacques Villeneuve: Monaco	Gianni Giansanti
19	Dannii: as character Lady Macbeth, Edinburgh Festival	Andrew Hobbs © KDB Artists Pty. Ltd.
20	Dannii: Edinburgh	Andrew Hobbs © KDB Artists Pty. Ltd.
21	Dannii: as character Esmerelda, 'Notre Dame de Paris', London	Andrew Hobbs © KDB Artists Pty. Ltd.
22	Dannii: 'Neon Nights' album cover shoot, London	Matthew Donaldson © KDB Artists Pty. Ltd.
23	Dannii: calendar photo shoot, London	Sandrine Dulmero and Michael Labica / KDB Artists Pty. Ltd.
24	Dannii: 'Terrence Higgins Trust' campaign picture, London	Sean McMenomy © KDB Artists Pty. Ltd.
25	Dannii and Kylie: *Esquire* Magazine photo shoot, London	Steve Shaw © KDB Artists Pty. Ltd.
26	Dannii: record company press image	Sandrine Dulmero and Michael Labica / KDB Artists Pty. Ltd.
27	Dannii: 'The Hits & Beyond' album launch party, London	KDB Artists Pty. Ltd.
28	Dannii and Laura: South Africa	KDB Artists Pty. Ltd.
29	Dannii: *Australia's Got Talent* press shoot, Melbourne, Australia	Channel Seven
30	Dannii: *The X Factor* press shoot, London	Ken McKay © Talkback Thames
31	Dannii: Great Wall of China, China	KDB Artists Pty. Ltd.
32	Dannii and Kris: Sydney, Australia	© Rex Features
33	Dannii: arriving at *The X Factor* auditions, Manchester	© Xposure
34	Dannii: Piers Morgan *Life Stories*, London	Ken McKay © ITV
35	Dannii and Tabitha Somerset-Webb: Project D press shoot, London	KDB Artists Pty. Ltd.
36	Dannii, Ethan Edward and Kris Smith: Melbourne	KDB Artists Pty. Ltd.

Colour plate 1

Page	Description	Credit
1	Danielle	KDB Artists Pty. Ltd.
1	Brendan, Danielle and Kylie	KDB Artists Pty. Ltd.
2	Brendan and Danielle	KDB Artists Pty. Ltd.

Page	Description	Credit
2	Danielle: Christmas Day	KDB Artists Pty. Ltd.
2	Danielle and Kylie: cooking	KDB Artists Pty. Ltd.
3	Danielle: *Young Talent Time* rehearsals	KDB Artists Pty. Ltd.
3	Brendan, Danielle and Kylie	KDB Artists Pty. Ltd.
4	Dannii: *Young Talent Time* concert	Johnny Young / YTT
4	Dannii: last performance on *Young Talent Time*	Johnny Young / YTT
4	Dannii and Vince	Johnny Young / YTT
5	Dannii and Craig McLachlan	Channel Seven
5	Dannii and Gary	KDB Artists Pty. Ltd.
5	Dannii: record company press image	KDB Artists Pty. Ltd.
6	Dannii: New York roof top	KDB Artists Pty. Ltd.
6	Dannii: New York yellow cab	KDB Artists Pty. Ltd.
6	Dannii & Julian: Wedding day	KDB Artists Pty. Ltd.
7	Dannii: orange dress, 1991	Big Pictures
7	Dannii: orange dress, 1995	Big Pictures
7	Dannii: Nevada Desert	Adam Watson © KDB Artists Pty. Ltd.
8	Dannii and Terry Ronald	KDB Artists Pty. Ltd.
8	Dannii: Studio 54 birthday party	KDB Artists Pty. Ltd.
8	Dannii: backstage at Mardi Gras	KDB Artists Pty. Ltd.

Colour plate 2

Page	Description	Credit
1	Dannii: Melbourne Grand Prix	KDB Artists Pty. Ltd.
1	Dannii: on set of *Australia's Got Talent*	David Cook © Channel Seven
1	Dannii: singing 'I Begin To Wonder'	Ken McKay / Rex Features
2	Dannii and Olivia Newton-John	KDB Artists Pty. Ltd.
2	Dannii: record company press image	Ben Hassett © KDB Artists Pty. Ltd.
2	Dannii and Twiggy	Marks & Spencer
3	Dannii and Benjamin Hart	KDB Artists Pty. Ltd.
3	Dannii and Melissa Le Gear	KDB Artsist Pty. Ltd.
3	Dannii and Nathan Smith	KDB Artists Pty. Ltd.
4	Dannii and Kylie: The Atlantis, Dubai	Nathan Smith
4	Dannii and Kylie: Elle Style Awards	© Rex Features
4	Dannii and Kylie: acting on *The Kylie Show*	William Baker © Darenote
5	Dannii, Simon Cowell, Louis Walsh & Sharon Osbourne	Rex Features
5	Dannii, Simon Cowell & Sharon Osbourne	Rex Features
5	Dannii: Louis' rule book	Liam McKenna

Page	Description	Credit
5	Dannii and Cheryl Cole	Nathan Smith
6	Dannii and Kris	Elizabeth Hoff
7	Dannii, Kris, Elsie and Eddie	KDB Artists Pty. Ltd.
7	Dannii and Kris: with dolphin	KDB Artists Pty. Ltd.
7	Dannii and Kris: National TV Awards	© Rex Features
8	Dannii and Kris: Great Barrier Reef	KDB Artists Pty. Ltd.
8	Dannii, Kris and Ethan	Ben Johnson
8	Dannii and Kris: The Australian Open	© Xposure

Cover shoot

Cover photographs © Elisabeth Hoff

Stylist: Angie Smith

Dresses courtesy of Paule Ka (front), Jasper Conran (back), Ralph and Russo (back flap)

All jewellery courtesy of Annoushka

Hair & make-up: Christian Vermaak

Management: Melissa Le Gear & Nathan Smith, Profile Talent Management Pty.Ltd.

Public Relations: Simon Jones & Alex Mullen, Hackford Jones PR.

The publishers have made every effort to contact those holding rights in the material reproduced in this book. Where this has not been possible, the publishers will be glad to hear from those who recognise their material.

Index